WHO'S AFRAID OF
WOMEN'S STUDIES?

WHO'S AFRAID OF WOMEN'S STUDIES?

Feminisms in Everyday Life

Mary F. Rogers and C. D. Garrett

ALTAMIRA
PRESS

A Division of Rowman & Littlefield Publishers, Inc.
Walnut Creek • Lanham • New York • Oxford

ALTAMIRA PRESS
A Division of Rowman & Littlefield Publishers, Inc.
1630 North Main Street, #367
Walnut Creek, CA 94596
www.altamirapress.com

Rowman & Littlefield Publishers, Inc.
An Imprint of the Rowman & Littlefield Publishing Group
4720 Boston Way
Lanham, MD 20706

12 Hid's Copse Road
Cumnor Hill, Oxford OX2 9JJ, England

British Library Cataloguing in Publication Information Available

Library of Congress Cataloging-in-Publication Data

Rogers, Mary F. (Mary Frances), 1944–
Who's afraid of women's studies? : feminisms in everyday life / by Mary F.
Rogers and C. D. Garrett.
    p. cm.
    Includes bibliographical references and index.
    ISBN 0-7591-0173-6 (cloth : alk. paper) — ISBN 0-7591-0174-4 (pbk. : alk. paper)
    1. Women's studies. 2. Feminism. I. Garrett, C. D., 1954– II. Title.

HQ1180 .R64 2002
305.42—dc21   2002001098

Printed in the United States of America

∞™ The paper used in this publication meets the minimum requirements of
American National Standard for Information Sciences—Permanence of Paper
for Printed Library Materials, ANSI/NISO Z39.48-1992.

In memory of Mammo Allen
and Granny Garrett

Contents

Introduction

We began working on this book during the mid-1990s when we sensed that women's studies might be losing some of its momentum, perhaps even some of its spirit and substance. The 1990s challenged women's studies with terms such as "conservative feminism," "postfeminism," and "victim feminism." Often the people drawing on this problematic, if not mean-spirited, vocabulary called themselves feminists. We found ourselves hard pressed to swallow that self-labeling. What, we wondered, had feminism and women's studies come to mean? What, more importantly, *should* they mean as progressive forces in our everyday lives as well as in our institutions?

Along the way some academic feminists seem to have forgotten that feminism comes out of women's experiences, not out of feminist theory books or women's studies textbooks. Feminism came to the academy, not from it. Its first instructors were mostly "seasoned political activists" (Buhle 2000, xx). Rooted in women's experiences and oriented toward practical matters, feminism and women's studies entail advocacy and activism. Both evolve out of these twin commitments, with women's studies having emerged as academic feminists' main strategy for acting on behalf of women on college campuses and beyond. Thus, the relationship of women's studies to the community, women's organizations, and social movements, especially women's movements, differs from traditional town-gown connections.

Women's studies revolves around the voice of the female Other in all her diversity. It represents and brings to the fore the voices of marginalized, excluded, oppressed, and silenced women whose standpoints remain underrepresented throughout society and culture. At the same time women's studies affords women a collective opportunity to see themselves from viewpoints that challenge mainstream culture and offer positive alternatives to it. Women's studies presupposes a skeptical, debunking perspective capable of illuminating women's everyday lives from their own standpoints while casting doubt on the perspectives of the dominant culture. Just as Steven Spielberg's best movies illuminate the world of children by adopting their physical point of view and thus tell a distinctive sort of story, women's studies sloughs off dominant perspectives in favor of women's own perceptions. Women's studies does to masculinity what racial and ethnic studies do to whiteness: An unmarked, presumably universal reality gets seen as the historically contingent, culturally constructed status it actually is. In the process, gender and race (and related hierarchies) get debunked. In these corners of the academy there are no dangerous questions. The real danger is taken-for-granted complicity with oppressive hierarchies.

Yet feminism and women's studies are not of one piece. Varieties of feminism range, for example, from the radical to the liberal and from the cultural to the ecological. "No one stands," then, "within a definition of feminism that would remain uncontested" (Butler 2001, 414). In practical terms, this means that various strands of feminism have influenced women's studies from its beginnings during the 1970s. Feminism and women's studies have a more complicated relationship with one another today, however, than they did twenty or even ten years ago. Above all, *gender studies* has gained ground and is at times seducing women's studies away from its feminist foundations.

Gender studies, as its name implies, considers masculinity as well as femininity, men and boys as well as women and girls. Like women's studies, gender studies is typically transdisciplinary. Yet it is not typically feminist and thus "dilut[es] feminism's visibility" (Bal 2001, 323) in academic life. A quick look at the journal *Sex Roles* (current or old issues) illustrates the nonfeminist nature of gender studies. That same journal might also confirm, though less readily, that gender studies leaves most people more comfortable than women's studies does. After all, gender studies is *inclusive*. At the same time it is less daring. By and large, gender studies offers no frontal assault on the institutions that maintain the *gender hierarchy* that shortchanges girls and women in favor of boys and men. Instead, gender studies mostly illustrates how gender finds expression across various institutional arenas, such as classrooms, offices, bedrooms, athletic fields, and civic associations. In the process, its researchers usually emphasize the scientific character of their methods and findings.

Gender studies is not a more encompassing version of women's studies, then. It is misguided to think of gender studies and women's studies as fundamentally the same, with the latter being just a narrower version of the former. In principle, we might well imagine an equation like the one Leora Auslander (1997) analyzes: Women's + Feminist + Men's + Lesbian and Gay + Queer Studies = Gender Studies. In practice, however, as Auslander herself illustrates, that equation doesn't compute. It doesn't add up in the real world of academic departments and curricular turf battles.

Symptomatically, gender studies largely focuses on gender *differences*. To that extent this field of study duplicates commonsense understandings more often than not. It reinforces people's sense that women and men are *opposite* sexes and that there are *essential* differences between them. Gender studies thus resonates with the cultural and political mainstream. Unlike women's studies, where critique plays a central role, gender studies is often noncritical. Much more than women's studies, it lays claim to scientific—and thus objective—methods and results. To that extent gender studies passes itself off as apolitical and value-free, claims that feminist epistemologists challenge at their roots (see chapter 4). Overtly or not, gender studies also emphasizes that girls and women are not the only ones who have it bad. Gender oppresses boys and men, too. Privilege hurts; it stifles; it warps.

Gender studies has been around longer than women's studies, even though its name is no more than a decade old. Within sociology, anthropology, and social psychology, in particular, gender has been a hot topic for more than twenty years. First introduced in terms of "sex roles," gender has moved to center stage in the curricula of these disciplines and also preoccupies many scholars in these fields. Some do, to be sure, adopt feminist perspectives and values. Most do not. Theirs is, instead, an approach that draws from the traditions of their disciplines and updates them around issues of gender. In a nutshell, gender studies does not challenge patriarchy. Put more mildly, gender studies "does not necessarily hold out the promise it has been assigned" (B. Martin 2001, 356).

Then, too, some scholars and writers who start out as women-centered feminists gradually move away from concerns central to women's studies toward those characteristic of gender studies. Carol Gilligan is one example. In 1982 she challenged the foundations of psychology with *In a Different Voice*, which focused on how girls and women typically approach moral reasoning in ways unrecognized in influential psychological models. Gilligan's early research focused on white, middle-class females, and her findings did not necessarily hold up beyond those racial and class boundaries (see Stack 1994). During the 1980s and 1990s, however, Gilligan and a number of research collaborators conducted a series of more inclusive studies centering primarily on girls and very young women.

By the late 1990s that pattern shifted dramatically. Gilligan was named to an endowed professorship at Harvard where she had been all the while. Her professorship was in gender studies, not women's studies, despite her consistent focus on girls and women over the years. Before long, Gilligan was getting media attention in response to her cry for academic attention to boys. Somewhere along the way Gilligan got gender-balanced religion and moved away from the concerns of women's studies, that is, academic feminism. Gender studies is so often enough nonfeminist that when the University of Southern California was seeking candidates for its Barbra Streisand Professor of Gender Studies (which went to sociologist Judith Stacey), it had to advertise that feminist credentials were among the qualifications for the position.

Susan Bordo has also had a big impact on women's studies, particularly with her 1993 book *Unbearable Weight: Feminism, Western Culture, and the Body*. Perhaps as part of her movement toward cultural studies and a more encompassing role as a public intellectual, Bordo has not written any other book-length works centering on women. In 1998 she published a collection of essays entitled *Twilight Zones: The Hidden Life of Cultural Images from Plato to O.J.* Its range extends from rhetoric at the O. J. Simpson trial to the award-winning movie *Babe* to the food and other memories she and her two sisters have from their growing up together. Perhaps symptomatically, the cover of *Twilight Zones* is scarcely academic. An eerie, negative-like image of O. J. Simpson adorns the top of the cover, with a nearly bare-breasted Pamela Anderson on the bottom. More recently, Bordo has written *The Male Body: A New Look at Men in Public and in Private*. Bordo's volume is not narrowly male-centered, however. For the most part, it focuses on the "career of the male body in popular culture" (Bordo 1999, 147) rather than men's experiences and outlooks. Throughout this collection Bordo's remains a feminist voice. In fact, her stated purposes are those of a liberal feminist. Bordo says, for instance, "For all our differences, so entertaining and lucrative to emphasize nowadays, men and women do *not* come from different planets. One of my goals in writing this book is to demonstrate that" (1999, 35).

Finally, there is journalist Susan Faludi. In 1992 she got a great deal of academic and media attention for *Backlash: The Undeclared War against American Women*. By 1999 Faludi's long-awaited second book made its appearance. Entitled *Stiffed: The Betrayal of the American Man*, Faludi's book represents a move like Gilligan's more than Bordo's. Here we look in greater detail at Faludi's shift of focus, because her work on backlash made her a feminist public intellectual better known than either Gilligan or Bordo.

In *Stiffed* Faludi argues that "ornamental culture"—her stock phrase for an appearance-centered, consumerist culture—has become as much a problem for men as for women. Men need to "liberate" themselves from its omnipresent, objectifying "gaze," yet lack the wherewithal to do so. Their lack of inner resources and self-confidence comes not from the feminists they like to blame for their malaise but from their "absent fathers." These fathers who left their sons bereft include not only real-life parents but also (supposedly) paternal institutions such as corporations, unions, and government that have become harsh, overly demanding, and unappreciative of loyalty and hard work.

Much of Faludi's analysis concerns social class, the changing postindustrial workplace, and the consumer economy driven by ceaseless advertising and excessive, if not mindless, consumption. The men who most concern Faludi—Sylvester Stallone notwithstanding! (Faludi 1999, 362–69, 395–406, 580–93)—occupy the broad middle strata of the American class structure. Although some are shipyard workers and aerospace employees (51–101), most are faceless members of the nonprofessional, white-collar sector of the so-called service economy. For the most part, the men whom Faludi sees as "stiffed" and "betrayed" are not physicians, CEOs, software engineers, venture capitalists, geneticists, or stock analysts. Nor are they men of color. The men who most concern Faludi are the middle-income white men who both subjectively and objectively have lost some cultural, financial, and interpersonal ground over the past several decades.

But Faludi pays little systematic attention to these men's uncertain class positions. Nor does she put much emphasis on the changing occupational structure, the globalization of the world economy, and other major aspects of transnational capitalism. Instead, she focuses heavily on the feelings and perceptions of the many men she interviewed while emphasizing the cultural over the economic circumstances of their post–World War II lives.

Faludi (1999, 7) identifies herself as a feminist and almost entirely avoids the feminist-bashing polemics that we examine in chapter 6. In the end, though, she does leave some room for antifeminist inferences or, at least, misperceptions based on overgeneralizations. Surely, for instance, Faludi could have come up with a less problematic formulation than "Blaming a cabal of men has taken feminism about as far as it can go" (605). To imply that feminism fundamentally has to do with blaming men is misguided, as Faludi's own arguments in *Backlash* powerfully illustrate. Dismissing feminism's "simple and personal adversarial model," Faludi goes on to observe that

> Other paradigms are needed to untangle the invisible skein of stubborn threads that restrains women and other subordinated populations. That's why those populations have a great deal at stake in the liberation of the one population uniquely poised to discover and employ a new paradigm—men. (605)

Thus, Faludi's concluding chapter not only validates but also valorizes the notion of "men's liberation." In the end her stance is noncritical. *Stiffed* offers neither a critique of the institutions—economic, familial, political—that, according to Faludi, trouble the men themselves nor of the consumer culture that gives most of them a "phantom status" (31). Faludi implies time and again that the people she talked with are oppressed *as men*, not as working- and middle-class employees or as citizens in an age of "welfare reform" and "downsizing" or in any major way other than their gender, their "male predicament" (9).

Overall, what seems to be happening is that feminist scholars who had been contributing to women's studies have moved further from that arena than mere gender studies would have taken them. Ultimately, Gilligan, Bordo, and Faludi are supplementing *men's studies* (Carbado 1999; Kimmel 1989). When feminist scholars make such turns, one can scarcely help but wonder what their purposes might be and whose interests they are furthering. But then we might ask the same questions of some women's studies professors and scholars, for their aims and interests strike us as less coherent and more disparate than they used to. Lest we sound as if we are invoking a good-old-days rhetoric, let us reformulate the question at hand: Just how far has women's studies come since the 1970s and early 1980s, when it was struggling for a foothold in academe?

Many measures suggest that women's studies has come a long way. The number of undergraduate major and minor programs, master's programs, and doctoral programs has continued to increase. By now, more than six hundred programs exist on American campuses, and women's studies attracts more students than any other transdisciplinary area of study. In fact, the Department of Education "estimate[s] that 12 percent of all undergraduate students now receive credit for courses in women's studies" (Buhle 2000, xv, xvi). Women's studies also has its own professional association, the National Women's Studies Association established in 1977 with the support of the Ford Foundation (Buhle 2000, xvi). Women's studies journals and other publications are numerous and show no signs of abating. Virtually every week the *Chronicle of Higher Education* includes advertisements for women's studies faculty positions, and the same is also true of the monthly *Women's Review of Books*. Centers for research on women are less uncommon and do garner some support. We think, for instance, of the Center for Research on Women at the University of Memphis and the Center for Research on Women at Wellesley College. On these and other fronts women's studies has surely progressed. The field is much more in evidence than it was fifteen or so years ago, and its acceptance into the academy is much less uncertain than it used to be.

These developments amount to the institutionalization of women's studies. As it builds on the foothold it established during the 1970s, women's studies becomes more and more a fixture on the American campus. As Biddy Martin puts it, "Women's Studies has now settled in" (2001, 353). In the process, it has lost some of its daring as well as much of its critical edge. Introductory women's studies textbooks such as Virginia Sapiro's *Women in American Society* (1994), for instance, survey the history and progress of American women while delineating the remaining impediments to their equality. Yet the overall approach is to survey the situation without incisively dissecting it along strong feminist lines that might offend a sizable number of undergraduate students. Martin concludes that

> Women's Studies scholarship and curriculum have come over time to replicate rather than challenge entrenched wars between the disciplines with the consequence that neither Women's Studies programs nor feminist scholarship are in a particularly good position to take the lead in completing transformations they helped begin. (355)

To some extent, then, women's studies has gone mainstream. At its most tepid it reiterates the liberal feminist values that by now commonly get lip-service support throughout the broad middle of American society.

In our judgment women's studies should continue to focus on women as a dominated sociosexual grouping. Although it rests on diverse bases, our subordination does rest heavily on *gender*—the array of attitudes and behaviors mandated for women or men, respectively, within a given culture. Unlike gender studies, however, women's studies uses feminism to disrupt the "ideology of gender" (Grant 1993, 179). By treating gender as an ideological force, feminists show that what gets taken for granted as feminine or masculine reflects commonplace understandings that generally serve the interests of men to the disadvantage of women. At the same time feminists emphasize the vast efforts continuously undertaken to construct females and males as "opposite" sexes who are "naturally" unequal (cf. Epstein 1988, 16).

From a feminist perspective, then, gender is a fiction written daily in practices and interactions we take for granted. In *Schoolgirl Fictions*, for instance, Valerie Walkerdine (1990) shows how schooling routinely augments that fiction. Barrie Thorne's *Gender Play* achieves the same effect. Thorne (1993, 95) concludes that the different-and-unequal fiction operates "like well worn grooves on a dirt road" that attract traffic because they are familiar and predictable. These and other feminist works show that

> What is remarkable about the gender system . . . is not that it never changes. Rather, it sustains itself by continually redefining who men and women are and what they do, while preserving the fundamental assumption that, whatever the differences are, on balance they imply that men rightly are more powerful. (Ridgeway and Correll 2000, 112)

Gender means that "one *cannot* simply be 'human'" (Bordo 1990, 152). Rather one *must be* a girl or a woman, a tomboy or a crybaby, an airhead or a dumb blond, a chick or a dog. Since gender disallows unadulterated "human beings," the distinctions gathered under its umbrella show up throughout the nooks and crannies of people's lives. In effect, "gender defines existence" (Cordova 1992, 273). It shapes our identities as well as other people's expectations and perceptions of us.

As people of the female sex, we commonly learn a vocabulary of inferiority that structures our consciousness from early childhood onward. Frequently, then, our self-conceptions entail senses of unworthiness intertwined with some acceptance of males' entitlements to greater attention, respect, authority, and material rewards. The vocabulary of gender revolves around "woman" and "man," with "man" serving "as the inclusive term . . . as the kind of human who ought to be dominant" (Minnich 1990, 58). "Man" equates with "human being," and "woman" equates with "Other." While culturally constituting men as fit to rule, that formula sets women up as needing protection (from whom?), guidance (for what?), or other assistance only men offer. A society where such understandings are commonplace and durable has a *patriarchal* structure; its institutions and decision-making processes are male-dominated.

Lyndall MacCowan wrote, "Gender expresses and signals two things: what tasks an individual performs (division of labor) and with whom (what other gender) one has sex" (1992, 318). Gender routinely dictates who does which domestic chores, who has which jobs in the workplace, who plays which sports, who officiates at religious ceremonies, who gets elected to the U.S. Congress, and which parent is more preoccupied with day-to-day nurturance. Over the past several decades we have learned a great deal about such commonplaces of gendered lives. Yet a great deal more awaits discovery. Women's studies is the feminist pathway for discovering more about women, gender, and diversity. As a transdisciplinary field, women's studies is change-oriented as well as woman-centered. These two characteristics crucially distinguish it from gender studies.

In this book we explore six broad topics that hold women's studies together. In women's studies these topics center our thoughts, discussions, courses, research, and activism; they challenge our imaginations and test our resourcefulness; they bring us together in alliances crafted out of frustration and impatience with the status quo. We begin where all women have dense firsthand experiences. We begin with girls' and women's bodies.

Our concern in chapter 1 is with female bodies as a fundamental site of girls' and women's subordination. The chapter opens with a section on the "male gaze" (which many women themselves adopt) as one way women's bodies get culturally miniaturized. We then go on to look at eating problems as another expression of miniaturization. Adopting rhetoric from Richard Sennett and Jonathan Cobb's *The Hidden Injuries of Class*, the chapter also looks at the "hidden injuries of feminine body management." Paramount among such injuries are a "divided self," misspent resources, and a host of discomforts associated with feminine body regimens. Chapter 1 also deals with health, transcendence, and community by drawing lessons from Sandra Butler and Barbara Rosenblum's *Cancer in Two Voices*, which tells how they coped with Barbara's gradual death from cancer, and also from Audre Lorde's *Cancer Journals*. The chapter ends with a discussion of athletics, physical competence, and selfhood.

Chapter 2 focuses on women's anger and desires as grounds for their personal and collective advancement. We argue that anger and desires are what trigger feminist consciousness. Yet anger and desires are problematic in the everyday lives of most women. As the chapter illustrates, some women's anger gets translated into other feelings and experiences, and some women scarcely know the shape—never mind the intensity—of their own desires.

In chapter 3 we return to females' bodies but mostly in indirect fashion as we explore women's sexualities. We focus, in particular, on how a specific variety of heterosexuality has been institutionalized to women's detriment. The institution of heterosexuality commonly muddies women's consciousness. It sets women up not only as targets of sexual harassment at school and work but also as individuals often ill-equipped to react effectively not only to harassment but also to other rituals of subordination and maltreatment.

Chapter 4 looks at feminist critiques of mainstream epistemology and the sciences. It shows how feminist methods problematize the very grounds—"objective" and "scientific"—of gender studies while constructing women's studies on transformative grounds unparalleled in other fields of study. (This is a third characteristic differentiating women's studies from gender studies.) The chapter also explores how feminist methods of acting in and on the world remain much the same across the boundaries dividing everyday life from the political arena, the workplace, and other institutional sites.

Chapter 5 tackles issues associated with women's diversity. It looks at how feminists grapple, sometimes more and sometimes less effectively, with the differences among women—their racial, class, sexual, ethnic, and other differences. This chapter considers social change, personal change, and feminist solidarity in view of the tensions often built up around women's diversity.

Chapter 6 focuses on a sign of the changing times in women's studies. It examines the appearance throughout the 1990s of harsh critiques of the field *written by women who have been a part of it*. This chapter looks at several of these works, including some by Camille Paglia and Elizabeth Fox-Genovese. By and large, their critiques imply that second-wave feminism, which began during the 1960s, has largely achieved its purposes and that women's studies thus need not be as critical as it once was. We disagree, as do many other feminists. Chapter 6 thus raises questions about the focus and direction of women's studies, of tension (or contestation) that define women's studies.

We close with an afterword that explores the question, Who's afraid of women's studies? There we further interpret the critiques surveyed in chapter 6, review the history of this book, and look at a recent "memoir" advocating, in effect, that gender studies displace women's studies. We end by returning to the question of just how far women's studies has come. We believe that the core focus of our chapters continues to map out the field as a lively, transdisciplinary one that enhances our understandings not only of women but also of history, social structure, and culture. We also believe that women's studies needs to continue making us all less comfortable with our privileges (of various sorts) and more concerned about the full and equal rights of those we see as Others.

In the chapters ahead, then, we invite you to join us in grappling with ideas about women's bodies; about our anger and desires; about our sexualities; about methods for changing ourselves and the world; about the wealth of differences among those of us wanting to make common cause with one another; about the backlash against feminists in particular and women in general. These, we believe, are the most important matters feminists address. These are, to repeat, the key sites for thought and debate within women's studies.

Acknowledgments

We deeply appreciate the help and support of Rosalie Robertson and Gloria Mattingly.

1

Bodies

"I feel better when I wear makeup."
"I'm more confident when I'm not carrying extra weight."
"I exercise to stay fit. It doesn't have anything to do with anyone else or what's in style."
"I do it for myself."

Many of us have made claims like these. In this age of feminist awareness and consumer consciousness, women have frequent occasion to account for whatever body regimen we pursue. For many of us, that regimen involves counting calories and grams of fat, taking vitamins, working out, making up our faces, curling or straightening our hair, shaping our fingernails and toenails, waxing various body parts, creaming our skin, glossing our lips, or routinely using any available mirror (or window) to scrutinize our appearance. Marcia Ann Gillespie (1998, 185) argues that "We get sucked in even when we think we're standing pure." Many African American women, she says, "afrocentrize by wearing dreadlocks, twists, cornrows but still there's the desire to have shake-your-head hair that moves and flips and flies." Similarly, Asian American women who have cosmetic surgery deny that they want to look white, yet the look they commonly strive for is a "face with larger eyes and a more prominent nose" (Kaw 1998, 167). Also, the dearth of midlife women with visible gray hair suggests that even those who decry ageism often turn to Clairol to mask a prominent sign of their own aging.

Such racialized and age-graded concerns about appearance are common enough that researchers have developed a "body consciousness scale" based on feminist ideas, including that of female body surveillance. This attitude scale revolves around the cultural assumption

1

that women can control their appearance, "given enough effort" (McKinley and Hyde 1996, 184). In turn, that assumption is common enough that many girls and women *expect* to be unhappy with some aspects of their bodies. As Judith Rodin and others have pointed out, women's dissatisfaction with their appearance amounts to *normative discontent*. To that extent those women who express acceptance of or esteem for their bodies often face disbelief.

Some women do concede that their partners or lovers prefer the look they cultivate through their body regimen; some say they like compliments or looking great in the latest styles; some like to turn heads; and many feel that their "good looks" enhance their work with customers, clients, patients, students, and supervisors. But many other women, especially those attuned to feminism, downplay Other-oriented motives for complying with the codes of feminine attractiveness. They often revert to just-for-me assertions like those at the beginning of the chapter. What "I" speaks such words? How did she come to feel better wearing makeup or to have more confidence when slim?

Feminist selfhood involves awareness of oneself as an agent capable of acting on her own. It entails continual, creative queries about how well one's choices are promoting one's growth and well-being. When we consider our choices about diet, exercise, hair coloring, makeup, toiletries, clothing, and accessories, such queries yield few clear answers. In a consumerist, youth-oriented culture, appearance counts for a lot. For female members, in particular, it weighs heavily as a measure of our acceptability and worth.

As Naomi Scheman emphasizes, dominant groups define and devalue subordinate groups in heavily corporeal terms:

> All the oppressed . . . share in the minds of the privileged a defining connection to the body, whether it is seen primarily as the laboring body, the sexual body, the body insufficiently under the control of the rational will, or some combination of these. The privileged are precisely those who are defined not by the meanings and uses of their bodies for others but by their ability either to control their bodies for their own ends or to seem to exist bodilessly. They are those who have conquered the sexual, dependent, mortal, and messy parts of themselves—in part by projecting all those qualities onto others, whom they thereby earn the right to dominate and, if the occasion arises, to exploit. (1993, 88)

Such domination affects women's movement in public space and safety in domestic space, our control over pregnancy and childbirth, our experiences of menstruation and menopause, our access to organized sports and combat duty, and even our chances of growing old with dignity and self-assurance. When the Boston Women's Health Collective first published *Our Bodies, Ourselves* in 1973, its title underscored women's need to take back control of our bodies from medical professionals, the diet industry, the food conglomerates, and other groupings with no demonstrable commitment to women's well-being—what Joanne Finkelstein (1991, 69) calls the "body industries." Sad to say, twenty years later a new edition of that work was still necessary in American society.

This chapter focuses on our bodies as the ultimate site of our subordination, social regulation, and cultural colonization. It implies how we might reclaim our fleshiness. By seeing how our bodies have been used as cultural currency, we can counteract the body imagery that helps to control us. We can learn to accept the wrinkles and cellulite of our bodies while affirming their strength and their unacknowledged promise.

The Male Gaze and Little Women

Feminist film critics have made much of a cultural phenomenon called the *male gaze*. It is an institutionalized outlook on women's bodies that supposedly reflects the typical interests of heterosexual men. The male gaze is ultimately a controlling one. It controls by assessing. Sometimes it controls by intimidating or belittling. More subtly, it also controls with visual flattery or compliments implying what is *really* worthwhile about a woman.

The male gaze is objectifying. It looks at a female person foremostly as an object capable of stimulating the erotic imagination or pleasing the eye. The male gaze sees not artifice but attractiveness, not a managed appearance but a manageable person. It sees no midlife or old women, no fat women, no women with disabilities. It desexualizes such women, making them invisible *as women*. Ironically, one way women can escape the intrusive male gaze is to violate mainstream culture's codes of sex-object, aesthetic-object femininity. Yet the escape is only partial inasmuch as the same gaze that finds aesthetic or sexual appeal in some women's bodies often finds cause for contempt or ridicule in other women's bodies.

During some cultural periods—the late 1960s or early 1990s, for instance—the male gaze favors "clothes-hanger bodies" (Faludi 1992,

4 / Chapter 1

169) such as the waif-like, fragile-looking bodies of Twiggy or Kate Moss. Those preferences, which tend to hold sway when women, seem to be making social and political gains, idealize the bodies of prepubescent girls as a womanly desideratum. During other cultural periods—the 1870s or 1950s, for instance—the male gaze favored curvier, fuller bodies for women who seemed to be going nowhere that might disturb the male-privileging status quo (Banner 1983).

The male gaze animates mass advertising and popular culture. It is the gaze most often focusing television and movie cameras, the gaze energizing most music videos, the gaze assumed on most magazine covers, and the gaze taken to unabashed extremes in pornography. But that gaze belongs to many more people than fashion photographers, pornographers, filmmakers, mass advertisers, and the MTV crowd. It belongs to many of the men around us and also to many of the women. Like other features of patriarchal culture, the male gaze often structures women's consciousness of ourselves and of other women. Above all, it warns us against being too big.

Louisa May Alcott's *Little Women* could be the title of the script society crafts for women. It calls for a soft-spoken (little voice), sweet-tempered (little passion) woman who will subordinate her hopes and dreams (little ambition) to those of a bigger, better-educated, higher-paid, somewhat older man. (Judy Grahn [1984, 33] sees a difference between heterosexual and homosexual couples along these lines: The latter "who were going together for any length of time were of similar size.") The woman following the heterosexual script typically seeks a man's favor by showing interest in his pastimes, staying slim and firm, looking sexy, generally waiting for him to initiate things, "looking good" when they go out together, and satisfying his sexual expectations without seeming unduly easy or demanding. Broadly, the script calls for females to control their appetites, especially for food and sex, while channeling their desires for success, respectability, and individuality along lines that advantage the men in their lives (see chapters 2 and 3). Here we focus on how culture curtails many women's eating.

Central to many women's body regimens is an internal calorie counter that makes many foods a temptation to "be bad." Food tests such women's willpower; it occasions opportunities to take control; it serves as proof positive of their femininity. In fact, controlling their food consumption often serves as "Western women's principal channel for expression of identity, influence, and will" (Counihan 1989, 368). As Susan Bordo puts it, slenderness is "associat[ed] with autonomy, will, discipline, conquest of desire, enhanced spirituality, purity, and transcendence of the female body" (1993, 68). During historical periods like ours, the fashionable body has few distinctly female traits. Instead, its extreme thinness signals the psychology of subordination whereby women accommodate the male gaze. A "deprivation mentality" informs mainstream femininity (Surrey 1991, 244–45). Overindulging means jeopardizing one's visible femininity and compromising one's sex appeal.

Apparently, for half to three-quarters of American women weight control is a daily concern. A study of Wellesley students showed that nearly two-thirds consider themselves overweight. Yet the average Wellesley student appears to be within five to ten pounds of her ideal weight and eats reasonably (Surrey 1991, 238, 240). One survey found women saying that weight loss made them happier than romance or career success; another shows women reporting greater fear of getting fat than of dying (O'Neil 1993). As Naomi Wolf (1990) and others argue, body standards are a powerful way of making women insecure while diverting attention from projects likelier to advance their interests. And these standards seem to be shaping the experiences of younger and younger girls (Brumberg 1998).

Michelle Fine and Pat McPherson report that the "fetish of body management" is "deeply classed and raced" (1992, 186; also see Lovejoy 2001). More-privileged women are plagued with eating disorders that perplex less-privileged women. Body regimens coded as feminine often reflect the interplay of gender with race and class, then. According to Fine and McPherson, what gets coded as feminine reflects "definitions of (white) womanhood" that marginalize or even erase femininities involving other ways of experiencing one's body.

Findings about anorexia nervosa (self-starvation) and bulimia (binging and purging) also imply connections between relative privilege and extreme body management. Some such women may be hyperconforming to norms of feminine slimness; others may be rebelling by taking those norms to extremes that reveal their cruelty. In any case it is no accident that girls and women exhibit eating problems dramatically more often than boys and men. Our bodies are everyday sites of our subordination and deprivation, with dieting emblematic of what is supposed to preoccupy us. Unless undertaken for occupational reasons, as with dancers, models, and athletes, men who exhibited similar anxieties would be dismissed as self-absorbed or otherwise pathetic.

In her study of women with eating problems, Becky Wangsgaard Thompson includes compulsive eating and extensive dieting as well as anorexia and bulimia. Thompson examines these problems in terms of their possible survival value. Citing findings "that between one-third and two-thirds of women who have eating problems have been abused," she observes that binging can be a numbing experience that costs less than alcohol (at least in the short run). Among the eighteen women she studied, Thompson found that eleven had survived sexual abuse, and most connected that abuse with their eating problems. Some numbed their bodies by eating compulsively; others tried to make themselves smaller by binging and purging or starving themselves in the belief that they had been abused because of their weight. Significantly, Thompson reports that "The particular constellation of eating problems among the women did not vary with race, class, sexuality, or nationality" (Thompson 1992, 550, 551, 554, 555).

Thompson thus challenges, as does Doris Witt (1998), the "culture of thinness model" that associates extreme body management with white femininity in the middle and higher reaches of society. Thompson says that the cultural mandate to be thin did deleteriously affect the women she studied but "is not the primary source of their problems." Rather, their eating problems derive more from painful experiences they squelch by over- or undereating. Theirs are not "appearance-based disorders" as much as "serious responses to injustices" that originate as "solutions to problems" (558, 559).

Thompson may be right. So may Wolf, Fine and McPherson, and others who see eating problems disproportionately cropping up among relatively privileged girls and women. Like many human behaviors, eating problems need not emerge under only one set of life circumstances. Instead, multiple pathways to such problems are probably at work. Some of us may be vulnerable because of relentless striving for "perfection" or an extreme desire to please; others may be trying to dull the pain of abuse or neglect; still others may be avoiding the worst of institutionalized heterosexuality by making themselves conventionally unattractive.

Whatever the reasons for any overeating or undereating we do, whether chronically or periodically, our anxieties about food catalog our stymied desires (see next chapter). With our pleasure in eating widely thwarted or purchased at the cost of ambivalence, other pleasures may also fall by the wayside. If we cannot eat enjoyably, we cannot be freely pleasure-oriented. In the end we may so desire to be desired that we feel undeserving of pleasure except when it is socially approved as part of our femininity, such as the pleasure some of us take in pleasing others.

How we treat food in our everyday lives thus has ramifications beyond our plates and palates. When we unreasonably deny ourselves its pleasures, we participate in our own social control. We become agents of the culture that inferiorizes us by treating our desires and pleasures as secondary and our appetites as unfeminine. As Susan Bordo emphasizes, "thinness is a visual code that speaks to young women about the power of being aloof rather than desirous, cool rather than hot, blase rather than passionate, and self-contained rather than needy" (1997, 128).

As we will see in the next chapter, a "proper" feminine appearance "constructs the woman as desirable, not the woman who desires" (Smith 1990, 175). Constructing the appearance of desirability entails experiencing one's body as an object to "be transformed, an object of work, even of a craft" (186–87). Yet the desirable woman "does not attract [a man]; rather she is or will be found to be, attractive *to* him" (192). His approving gaze, not her efforts, seals feminine success. From parents and peers, magazines and romance fictions, television and movie screens, girls and women hear time and again that their role is to evoke and sustain desire. Embedded in that message is the lesson that our bodies are singularly important. Embedded there, too, is the cultural mandate to fetishize our bodies in order to make ourselves *objects* of desire for male *subjects* (Irigaray 1985 [1974], 114).

Our body language often shows how well we learn the terms of feminine desirability. Typically, it conveys the same messages as our eating behavior. "I'll have just a little, please"—be it attention or food. "Go ahead; I have enough"—be it space or food. The attention and space women claim are, like our food, often less than what we really want. Our bodies tell tales our mouths might never utter. They tell people around us how entitled we feel, how much we aim to please, how privileged or disprivileged we are by race and class as well as by gender and other circumstances, and how careful or careless we mean to be about staying in our "proper" places. Overall, our bodies imply how much we value or reject mainstream femininity, which portrays us as necessary and nice but unworthy of more than second-rate opportunities and rewards. Our bodies thus become semiotic objects whereby we announce the measure of our subordination to the world at large. We enact gustatory, cosmetic, fitness, interactional, and other rituals that constitute a distinctly feminine "dramaturgy of subordination" (Scott 1994). More often than not, our bodies become the means for sending the message, We are only *little* women.

Women's studies professors (and other feminists) are also vulnerable to cultural pressures to present conventionally attractive bodies capable of offsetting the man-hating, old-bag, dyke-bitch stereotypes of committed feminists. They, too, sometimes send the little-women message by staying normatively slender, coloring their hair, wearing makeup, and otherwise feminizing their bodies. This pattern shows up often enough that Bordo sees fit to remind us that "Keeping track of the practical life of our bodies is important to keeping us intellectually honest" (1997, 184). The messages we send somatically, in other words, sometimes diverge from those we send rhetorically.

The Hidden Injuries of Feminine Body Management

Dating and mating studies confirm that heterosexual men assign high, even primary, value to women's physical attractiveness. Women as well as men believe that "good-looking" people are more trustworthy, popular, and happy than less-attractive people. Such findings suggest how the cultural focus on women's bodies gains momentum. Other findings show how that preoccupation can injure girls and women.

For starters, trying hard to meet cultural standards may erode one's "sense of self" by deflecting attention from the "inner sensations and perceptions that are the basis of self-knowledge and healthy self-expression" (Surrey 1991, 244). Put differently, controlling oneself supersedes expressing oneself (245). Sandra Lee Bartky (1990) makes similar points about women's efforts to feed men's egos and tend their wounds. She argues that by trying to adopt the man's point of view in order to empathize, women short-circuit their own moral sense as well as their individuality.

"Loss of self" is too extreme a name for what women usually pay for their corporeal anxieties. More often, they exhibit what Richard Sennett and Jonathan Cobb (1973, 193) call a *divided self*, an alienated state that may serve as a defense of self and an "assertion of sanity." The divided self comprises a "real" me juxtaposed against a socially mandated me called into service by those who dominate me. The "real" part of myself "lies low when performing." The real woman may prove herself not very feminine in the end, for instance, but the performing woman acts self-consciously as a woman—a good wife, a devoted mother, a loyal secretary—is expected to act. Women are not "judgmental dopes" (cf. Garfinkel 1967) easily duped into pursuing projects inimical to our interests. Instead, we commonly experience divided selves. Whatever the measure of our misguided consciousness, it grows out of a massive institutional apparatus and detailed cultural script diverting us from other interests.

As Cobb emphasizes in the afterword to *The Hidden Injuries of Class*,

the hierarchy of social legitimacy in American society has its origin in
. . . calculations of social value. . . . Feeling that you are a legitimate ac-
tor in the world, that is, a person with social rights, comes from feeling that what you do, whether in concert with or opposition to others,
has value. (1973, 265)

Conversely, if one is encouraged to spend substantial time doing what
is culturally denigrated, one's sense of legitimacy and entitlement di-
minishes. Women's body work casts us in that role, even in the context
of an increasingly appearance-oriented culture. Our somatic regimens
can erode our sense of being legitimate agents in the world; they can
deflate our awareness of the rights we do have as well as dim our vision of the rights we still lack. Coupled with the devaluation of the
paid work that most of us do and the lack of public recognition for the
mothering that most of us do, our body work often takes a toll without
delivering the benefits that motivated our efforts in the first place.

All the while, of course, costuming and decorating the body are
forms of self-expression central to most human societies. What makes
self-adornment and other aesthetic self-display gratifying, however, is
their voluntary, ceremonial character. Unfortunately, many women's
body-management efforts have become have-to's emotionally aligned
with other chores. Whatever gratification they provide lies mostly in their
aftermath, namely, in the satisfaction that comes from self-discipline or
from people's positive reactions to our appearance.

Putting a cultural premium on women's physical attractiveness
does hidden injury to many women. Such a premium encourages us to
spend considerable time on activities that inconsistently serve our interests. We devote precious leisure to priming our bodies for inspec-
tion. Our leisure thus becomes something other than strictly "personal
space" (Wearing 1998, 184). These efforts often take money out of our
pockets, too. Whose interests are served by the notion that our undis-
ciplined, unadorned bodies are unattractive? The fashion, fitness,
beauty, and diet industries stimulate demand for their products by promoting such an idea. Less obviously, the men in our lives are also beneficiaries. Their collective capacity to hold sway over us, whether in-
tentionally or not, derives in part from the cultural mandate for women
to hypermanage our bodies. Let's look at how that happens.

Some cultural lore insists that it hurts to become fit and attractive:
No pain, no gain. Who among us has experienced pain-free plucking
or waxing or come across a tempting weight-loss diet? That we un-
dergo deprivation, discomfort, and even pain for the sake of attractive

bodies means we learn to forgo pleasure as a cost of demonstrating femininity. That learning resonates with being taught to put others' priorities and preferences ahead of our own *even if we are left feeling deprived or pained*. Deprivation thus becomes emblematic of femininity.

Were we to experience pleasure visibly and frequently, we might arouse doubts about our femininity. No wonder, then, that the corporate media subject individuals like Hillary Rodham Clinton to critical dissections of their hairstyles and wardrobes. Such coverage reminds us all that femininity is on the line whenever we lay claim to competence, power, and pleasure. The pleasurable prospect of having a voice and making a difference must, in other terms, be bought at likely cost to one's femininity.

Another part of our cultural lore insists that women are entitled to take considerable pride in looking good. Most often that message comes to us in negative, indirect terms, namely, we should be ashamed to "let ourselves go." Yet such letting go could mean opting for pleasure, ease, and an appearance that suits ourselves; it could mean dismissing other people's judgments about the feminine viability of our appearance; it could mean opting out of the contest for aesthetic approval. Interestingly, "letting ourselves go" implies movement that we ourselves authorize. Culturally, we are warned not to tread that ground. Instead, we are promised self-acceptance if we "keep ourselves up." Why, then, are body loathing and body-image distortion far from rare among us? Might not these forms of pain be byproducts of excessive body management?

A third element of our cultural lore has to do with getting and keeping a man. Historically, women's only reliable *chance* of advancing themselves in the class structure was to secure and keep a higher-status husband. Dramatic upward mobility through marriage, however, was and remains uncommon. In fact, its relative rarity is one reason we romanticize it. The vast majority of women, like the vast majority of men, marry someone from the same or an adjacent social class. While women do more often marry "up" than men, neither women nor men typically move far in the class structure when choosing a mate. Thus, women doing body work to attract a mate much higher in the class structure are misdirecting their efforts. Even in a discriminatory labor market women's prospects for substantial upward mobility are brighter if they get the credentials for a better-paying job with opportunities for moving up.

As for keeping one's man, despite some husbands' pattern of leaving their wives for younger and, therefore, presumably more attractive women, many people still believe that how a wife manages her appearance strongly affects her chances of staying married. No evidence supports that belief. Indeed, the absence of evidence points to a cultural myth serving men's interests. The myth reinforces women's sense of having a big stake in staying attractive. It does more than culturally induce narcissism, however. It can inculcate insecurities that might make some wives more pliable.

A final, more slippery element of our cultural lore conflates women's health with their attractiveness. Throughout our culture people assume that the attractive woman is healthy. She is, after all, at a healthy weight; she exercises more or less regularly; she apparently has a lot to smile about, and seldom, if ever, has a cigarette between her lips or fried chicken in hand. Stereotypically, the attractive woman glows with good health. By now, we know, though, that some conventionally attractive women may doubt their essential worth; they may have eating problems; their workouts may be compulsive; their reluctance to show their naked faces or unshaven legs in public may reflect the severe constraints they feel; they may dread "deterioration" as they age. Many conventionally attractive women may move through their lives as divided selves where the "real" self recedes into the shadows of the "performing" self. Such women may or may not be healthy, but as a group they seem disproportionately more likely to face health risks. Their emotional well-being may, in particular, be jeopardized by their pursuit of attractiveness.

Bordo worries about "the ubiquitous and thoroughly *routine* grip that culture has . . . on the female body" and about "how *commonplace* experiences of depreciation, shame, and self-hatred are" (1993, 66). She goes on to observe that

> In this historical era, when the parameters defining women's "place" have indeed been challenged, it is disturbing that we are spending so much of our time and energy obsessed, depressed, and engaging in attempts at anxious transformation (most frequently, reduction) of our bodies. It is hard to escape the recognition . . . that a political battle is being waged over the energies and resources of the female body, a battle in which at least some feminist agendas for women's empowerment are being defeated (or, at a minimum, assaulted by backlash). (66)

Overall, the codes of feminine attractiveness require substantial body work that normalizes irrationality among many women. The subtitle of the feminine script is "female subordination." It teaches us to tolerate, if not welcome, male intrusions into our psychological and physical space; it encourages us to find flattering the attentions of men uninterested in or even opposed to our interests; it sets us up to take for granted that boys and men need athletics more than girls and women; it narrows our chance of feeling the full strength of our bodies and thus intensifies our feelings of physical vulnerability as well as our actual vulnerability to attack and abuse; it encourages sexy good looks but curtails our sexuality; it sets us up to wonder just why we are loved and esteemed, at least during the early stages of heterosexual bonding; it taints our aging by rendering our bodies sites of deterioration. All things considered, we lose by buying into the body regimens our culture presents as pathways to feminine success and satisfaction.

Health, Transcendence, and Community

Judith Butler (1990, 139) says that femininity, like masculinity, is a *corporeal style* involving "a dramatic and contingent construction of meaning." The cultural construction of femininity unfolds in the world of everyday life, though its scripts are mostly written in the worlds of popular culture, mass advertising, politics, religion, science, and therapy. Femininity takes shape around various contingencies, not the least of which are the shape, size, and apparent fitness of our bodies. As we have seen, our bodies must meet certain requirements before we can enter the feminine arena. Even though these are age-graded, they all presuppose relative youthfulness (that is, looking younger than one's age) and a "good" body. Implicitly, femininity also presupposes an able-bodied woman. A body others see as disabled, handicapped, sick, or feeble renders a woman certifiably unfeminine, seen as unable to do what culture mandates for women. Those of us with any stake in mainstream femininity thus have vulnerable identities insofar as our bodies are susceptible to disease and devastation. The more we invest ourselves in those "styles of the flesh" (139) currently defining respectable femininity, the greater are our risks.

Because it is common in our society and radically compromises our bodies as female strongholds, breast cancer woefully illustrates these observations. Each year about 45,000 American women die of breast cancer. Their stories, like those of other women whose bodies turn against them in one way or other, often map out pathways to fulfillment. Such pathways subvert the equation between self-worth and feminine body management.

One story we find inspiring is *Cancer in Two Voices*. This volume interweaves the voices of Sandra Butler and Barbara Rosenblum (1991), who had been partners for six years when Barbara was diagnosed with advanced breast cancer. *Cancer in Two Voices* comes mostly from their journals. The two agree that before her cancer Barbara had been "fluent in the language of [her] body" (131). Unlike many women, Barbara had few food inhibitions. Instead, she found eating a "supremely aesthetic experience" (134). Barbara also enjoyed music and gardening. Cancer taught her that "the agreements and understandings [she] had with [her] body were no longer in effect"; she begins "learning a new language of the body"—"the language of symptoms," not of sensuality (131, 132). Before long, she cannot "remember what it is like to have a normal metabolism, normal energy, normal hair, and a normal body" (79). Her body begins feeling "unfamiliar and alien" (140). Envisioning her readers, Barbara declares, "you cannot imagine how stable and firm and fixed your body looks to me" (138).

Yet Barbara rarely thinks about other people's circumstances. Her focus is living with a "feeling of fullness":

> I mean, very simply, that you feel there is enough inside you, that you feel internally rich and varied, that there are no big empty spaces, no holes that gnaw at the fabric of your being. I am also talking about the size human being you experience yourself to be: large or small; generous and expansive, or tight and pinched and hoarding. (154)

Barbara sees herself as a *neophile*, a lover of new experiences, and announces her intention "to experience everything" (54). Her neophilia "widened and stretched [her world], allowing new interests to develop and transform themselves into other interests" (55). About nine months after her diagnosis she says, "I have cancer but it is not consuming me" (56). Nearly two years later, about two months before her death, Barbara recognizes that she "can be consoled by life" itself (149).

Barbara Rosenblum's and Sandra Butler's journals attest to a femininity that refuses to make the body an emblem of one's womanhood or the center of one's identity. Time and again, their journals show how our bodies and minds and spirits come together in a dynamic wholeness. They tell us that even in the face of extreme and painful changes in our bodies, we can remain full and whole. *Cancer in Two Voices* (which is also available on videotape) shows how we can affirm our bodies as essential, pleasurable parts of ourselves without sabotaging our capacity to love ourselves as our bodies change.

Audre Lorde's *The Cancer Journal* offers similar lessons. As a post-mastectomy, single-breasted woman, Lorde found that fear sometimes "stalk[ed] her like another malignancy." In response, she observed, "I don't feel like being strong, but do I have a choice?" (Lorde 1980, 9, 16, 12, 14). Like most cancer survivors, Lorde faced multiple indignities. One involved a volunteer who visited her in the hospital as part of an American Cancer Society program. The volunteer did offer support and helpful information but also pressed Lorde to begin wearing a prosthesis immediately. To that end she offered this African American woman a "pale pink breast-shaped pad" (42). Ultimately, Lorde decided against it and advocated that postmastectomy women get familiar with their "new" bodies before considering prostheses. Otherwise, Lorde argues, prostheses "are often chosen not from desire but in default" (65).

Hundreds of thousands of North American women have a "battle scar" or two over their heart (Wadler 1992, 166). Yet the organizations set up to assist them often seem as concerned about the scar as the battle. As Sharon Batt (1998) has shown, both the American Cancer Society and the Canadian Cancer Society promote "looking normal" in their programs and books for breast cancer survivors. Even when we face life-threatening diseases, the femininity of our appearance remains an issue.

Although most of us will not get breast cancer, most of us will age to the point of facing fairly dramatic changes in the texture of our skin, the firmness of our muscles, and the color of our hair. We will experience changes in our eyesight, appetite, food preferences, sleeping patterns, hearing, and other bodily experiences. Yet "Change is not loss. Change is change, new circumstances" (Hart 1989, 122). As Sandra Butler put it in her journal,

> My body, too, has changed, grown older, and softened. We have become clearer to each other and to ourselves. . . . We can see through, into each other. We are living in changed and changing bodies—living with full hearts and open minds and great love. (1991, 143)

These and other women with stories like theirs ask us by their triumphs to consider what kind of homage we pay to our bodies. Is it our own hard-won homage to the fleshy part of our selves, or is it a grudging, uneven homage shaped by *Cosmo* and Crystal Light commercials? Our bodies, these women imply, merit reclamation whereby we make them our own on terms meaningful and pleasurable to us. Our reclamation may or may not involve lipstick, styling gel, hair coloring, or a size-ten wardrobe. Whatever it does include, it centers on choices we ourselves make for our own sakes.

Athletics and Selfhood

Title IX of the 1972 Education Amendments makes gender discrimination illegal in educational programs, including athletics. Nearly thirty years after its passage, though, athletic discrimination against female students remains the norm. As Virginia Sapiro notes,

> A 1990 survey of Division I members of the National College Athletic Association (NCAA) showed that women were 50% of the full-time undergraduates but only 31% of the athletes. Women received 30% of the athletic scholarship money, 23% of the operating expenditures, and 17% of the recruiting expenditures. (1994, 146)

Ten years later, little had changed. In the NCAA's Division I (larger colleges and universities) 40 percent of the athletes were women; at Division II (smaller) schools, 37 percent (Suggs 2001).

Like us, you may have had the experience of citing such statistics only to have them dismissed as irrelevant or silly. Too often we still hear that women's sports do not bring in money, raise campus morale, or spark alumni interest the way men's sports do. Such stances ignore the self-fulfilling prophecy built into the statistics. With paltry resources, women's athletics can scarcely compete with men's in the public imagination. Besides, fairness and the law dictate equity.

Why the disinclination to sign girls up for competitive sports? Why the resistance to muscular, physically competent female athletes? Might some people resist females' athletics because it benefits girls and women? The Institute for Athletics and Education reports, for instance, that females "who participate in sports are three times more likely to graduate from high school, 80 percent less likely to have an unwanted pregnancy and 92 percent less likely to use drugs" (Wallace 1995, A9). Might athletics help to liberate women?

During the nineteenth century many feminists thought so. They fought for less restrictive clothing for women, better diets, and greater opportunities for physical exertion and athletic participation. Despite the prohibition of exercise (except dancing) among fashionable American women at the time, "some colleges and women's seminaries began to add physical exercise to their curricula by the 1820s" (Banner 1983, 54,

90). All the while a major obstacle to women's athletics "was the belief that strenuous activity produced muscular bodies and destroyed the rounded curves that were the day's desiderata." Thus American "women's commitment to exercise [was] limited in the post–Civil War Years." During the latter part of the century they "took up croquet, archery, and tennis in turn. But while participating in each, they wore their regular, confining clothing, including tightlaced corsets" (140, 141).

During the twentieth century, debates about women's physical strength and athletic participation continued. By now, we know that sports "are clearly about gender" (Gorn and Oriard 1995). Indeed, American sports culture both expresses and promotes sexism (Nelson 1994). Sports are a major means of "constructing a masculine identity, a legitimated outlet for violence and aggression, and an avenue for upward mobility" (Lorber 1993, 571). Especially when they move beyond highly feminized sports, such as gymnastics, ice dancing, and figure skating, girls and women enter a deeply masculine arena. Their athleticism challenges male domination (Sabo and Messner 1993, 16). It jeopardizes sports as "a key cultural location for male dominance, a site where traditional patriarchal values are upheld and transformed in response to changes in the broader society" (Cahn 1994, 278).

Sports and sports coverage are organized so as to undercut that jeopardy by feminizing female athletes' strength and stamina. Judith Lorber observes, for example, that

> Gymnastic equipment is geared to slim, wiry, prepubescent girls and not to mature women; conversely, men's gymnastic equipment is tailored for muscular, mature men, not slim, wiry prepubescent boys. Boys could compete with girls, but are not allowed to; women gymnasts are left out entirely. Girl gymnasts are just that—little girls who will be disqualified as soon as they grow up. (1993, 571)

Gymnastics thus "illustrates the private and public contradictions of women's athleticism," and "bodybuilding shares with gymnastics many of the same tensions around the control and emancipation of the gendered body" (Cahn 1994, 276). Figure skating exhibits similar patterns. For example, at "the 1992 Winter Olympics, men figure skaters were required to complete three triple jumps in their required program; women figure skaters were forbidden to do more than *one*" (Lorber 1993, 572).

Sports *are* about gender. If sports commonly valorize physically skillful and powerful men and justify male competition and violence, what do they valorize and justify for women? To the extent that "power and eroticism meet most conspicuously in the athletic body" (Gorn and Oriard 1995), we can infer the predominant patterns for female athletes, at least those who achieve fame and material success. Mainstream standards depict the sexy woman as soft, relatively small, and responsive to male sexual dominance. Only pornographic imagery makes much room for strong, aggressive women as sexual players in male fantasies. Thus, celebrated female athletes—such as Kristi Yamaguchi, Tara Lapinski—tend not to violate the imagery associated with mainstream femininity.

Media coverage of female athletes speaks to their contradictory status as women and as athletes. Media imagery revolves around their "feminine beauty and grace (so they are not really athletes) or their thin, small, wiry androgynous bodies (so they are not really women)" (Lorber 1993, 573). Sapiro (1994, 226) cites research showing that television cameras often "zoom in on body parts" during broadcasts of women's sports. Moreover, during broadcasts of men's sports the cameras often give "regular attention . . . to women in the stands who serve as comical targets or objects of sexual innuendo. . . . So popular is this practice that the term 'honey shot' was coined back in the 1970s to describe it" (Cohen 1993, 175). Even as sports fans, women face sexual objectification.

Lorber (1993) cites further data from *Sports Illustrated*. Less than 10 percent of its "editorial and pictorial coverage . . . is about girls and women." In 1989, less than 40 percent of its pictures of females showed athletes. Overall, women appeared more often as models than as athletes in the "highest-circulation sports magazine in the country" (Sapiro 1994, 225). Even when female athletes do get photographed, the shot that gets printed usually has an "erotic quality" (Hargreaves 1994, 164). Lorber concludes, "Sports . . . construct men's bodies to be powerful; women's bodies to be sexual" (1993, 573). She goes on to cite Catharine MacKinnon's reasoning as to why.

According to MacKinnon (1987, 122), physical strength and self-possession fly in the face of women's supposed vulnerability to physical domination (including rape). Women's physical competence—their physical prowess, stamina, strength, and control—makes male dominance a practical uncertainty. It can open people's eyes to the social construction of male dominance, to its contingent character, and its foundation in arbitrary rules and conventions. The two of us know, for instance, a woman who has been practicing the martial arts for more than fifteen years. Despite her small stature her ways of walking, sitting, and gesturing send unmistakable messages about her physical strength and self-assurance. Her muscles are visible, though not bulging; her movements are sure, though not aggressive; her stance is confident and straightforward, though not intrusive.

What if most women's bodies gave off such messages of competence and confidence? We suppose that the world would become a lot less gendered. Our bodies *are* the sites of our subordination as much as our consciousness is. But then we speak in dualities when we mean to emphasize the wholeness that athletics and fitness inculcate. Feeling whole—undivided, unfragmented—means transcending gender by overcoming the divided self. For female athletes, it also means defeating the cultural divide between femininity and "musculinity" (Hargreaves 1994).

Jennifer Hargreaves says that "Since bodily skill, strength and muscularity have symbolically been the source of empowerment of men, feminists should look to sports in their struggle for greater autonomy" (1994, 173). (This brings us to the topics of autonomy, agency, and empowerment taken up in the next chapter.) Having talked with "hundreds of women who participate in sports," Hargreaves reports that "most of them talk about a sense of well-being and enrichment that comes to their lives as a result" (289). We would expect nothing less, but not all women experience such gratifying outcomes. Susan K. Cahn reminds us that even though "many women do indeed experience sport as a form of physical liberation, the all-consuming concern with fitness and thinness forms a distinct countercurrent to that goal" (1994, 274). Struggling against that countercurrent, it seems to us, is part and parcel of being a North American feminist today.

In our everyday lives, then, we need to resist the *anorexic logic* that sets "mind over body, thin over fat, white over black, masculine over feminine, individual over community" (Heywood 1996, xii). Such resistance entails less emphasis on "achievement" and more emphasis on well-being and social justice. It also entails overcoming bodily "timidity, uncertainty, and hesitancy. Typically, we lack an entire trust in our bodies to carry us to our aims" (Young 1990, 146). We need to build up that trust. Marital arts training is one way. Less obvious, more accessible methods revolve around mindfulness of our bodies and their terrific power to send alternative messages. Practice screaming, for instance, to ensure that you are not one of the women "unable to yell even in attack situations" (Searles and Berger 1987, 65). Or practice holding your ground on sidewalks and in aisles rather than stepping aside when other people, especially bigger men, remain directly in your path in violation of pedestrian conventions. Let us see our bodies as "maps of power and identity" (Haraway 1990, 222) and insist on being creative cartographers of our own bodies.

2

Anger, Agency, and Desires

The vocabulary of gender says little about our agency. Thus, we need to name ourselves and other women as initiators, resisters, creators, healers, instigators, activists, and rebels. After all, many of us have stopped "act[ing] circumspectly and humor[ing] the men in power or join[ing] them only to imitate them." Instead, we are "carrying out the patient work of spreading feminist ideas among the great mass of women [so that] they will [not] be eternally swindled" (Castro 1990, 10).

In this chapter we affirm women's agency and challenge the cultural constraints on women's desires; we take women's anger seriously and recognize it as a source of strength and power. We envision a world where women's talents, "tough" emotions, and desires get more than token recognition. Feminism insists on a world where women's agency, emotions, and desires get taken into enough account to widen our opportunities and enhance our rewards. This chapter implicitly asks what women cannot do, what we cannot feel, and what we cannot desire. Its answer is: nothing of any value to ourselves, humankind, or the planet.

Intimacy and Agency

In the social and behavioral sciences, as in American middle-class culture, "agency" commonly translates into "autonomy." Shaped particularly by developmental psychologists, autonomy connotes "maturity" and "self-actualization" and is a hallmark of middle-class individuality. Many feminists find this concept problematic. Sarah Lucia Hoagland, for example, regards autonomy as a "noxious concept . . . [that] encourages us to believe that connecting and engaging with others limits us . . . and undermines our sense of self" (1988, 144–45). The concept implies that "Relationships are something you *have* when you are not working or living your life, at night or on weekends." The autonomous person is the unencumbered individual of classical liberalism. Autonomy anchors a worldview where individuals count for everything while relationships are little more than "a detraction from or a means to one's self-enhancement" (Kaplan 1991, 208). Autonomy is no more and no less than individualism writ large.

Sharon Doherty offers as fine a feminist critique of modern individualism as we have ever come across:

> Individualism as a dominant cultural force remains compatible with inequality and self-centered actions. To live without consideration of social context, power relations, and ties to other people requires that a person be in error, even if sincere (a problem of theory or perspective); or aware of human connections, power, and social context but willing to use others to pursue his or her individual goals (a problem of strategy).
>
> Those who benefit from individualism—be they sincere but wrong or aware but exploitative—in practice either directly oppose the well-being of others or manage to place others in their service without recognizing (or admitting) it. Placing others in one's service without acknowledging it is a central element of institutionalized patriarchy. (2000, 350)

Doherty concludes that individualism (or what higher-status people like to call "autonomy") is a "deeply patriarchal perspective."

Individualism's appeal is widespread. Not surprisingly, it is linked with social class as well as gender. The higher people stand in the class structure, the more autonomous they seem. Such individuals do relatively unsupervised work allowing for initiative and creativity. They face a plethora of daily choices capable of certifying their sound judgment, and they move about with relative ease and confidence. They seldom look alone, if only because they look complete in and of themselves. However satisfying, their relationships seem not to stand at the center of their daily lives. Instead, bonds with other people seem like accessories to the costume tailored for their careers and pastimes. In Richard Sennett and Jonathan Cobb's (1973) terms, autonomous individuals have "developed insides" giving them an aura of being in command and able to fend for themselves.

The autonomous person is masculine as well as affluent. He is one or another version of the Marlboro Man. He is Bill Gates or Ted Turner,

Clint Eastwood or Jack Nicholson, Chris Rock or Tiger Woods. The autonomous man is patently capable of getting what he wants—sex, celebrity, votes, promotions, deals, profits. Michelle Fine and Pat Macpherson (1992, 182, 183) observe that class-privileged women, like their male counterparts, build their identities on a "sense of self as exception," where achievement sets one apart from the group. If they marry and mother, however, these women exhibit less autonomy than their mates even while enjoying greater autonomy than most other women and many other men.

We agree with feminists like Doherty who critique the concept of autonomy (or individualism) along these lines. Pro-feminist men such as Allan G. Johnson also emphasize the pitfalls of individualism.

> From an individualistic perspective, if you aren't consciously or openly prejudiced or harmful, then you aren't part of the problem. . . . If your feelings and thoughts and outward behavior are good, then *you* are good, and that's all that matters.
> Unfortunately, that isn't all that matters. There's more, because patterns of oppression and privilege are rooted in systems that we all participate in and make happen. (2001, 90)

Yet the concept of autonomy does include some valuable features of human existence that women are often denied. The concept of agency also includes these features without the gender and class biases associated with "autonomy."

"Agency" implies a person's resourcefulness, individuality, and impact in the world. Agency means being a subject, not a mere object of the pressures and constraints people put on us. Unlike "autonomy," it means recognizing the interdependence of self and other, individuality and community, biography and history. Agency means making a difference against the odds and seeing how culture enables as well as constrains us. Making room for female agency in feminist thinking means all of this plus problematizing the concept of victim. "Victim" centers attention on the power of society, while "agent" centers attention on the power of individuals. Agentic terms affirm our impact on people and situations.

Lately, agency has come under postmodernist attack, much as autonomy has come under feminist scrutiny (Harding 1991; Bordo 1990). *Postmodernism* is a perspective that emphasizes how unstable, ambiguous, and indeterminate our realities tend to be. It may be no coincidence that skepticism about agency emerges precisely when women as well as men of color "all over the world are beginning to find a historical voice and to assert their subjectivity" (Young 1990, 13). It may be no coincidence either that such a stance emerges when more and more women are showing that one can be an effective accountant, nurse practitioner, or manager while enjoying parenting, friendships, civic involvements, and other meaningful bonds with people. Increasing numbers of women are thus showing us the practical meaning of "agency." At the same time they are demonstrating that fulfilling relationships can go hand in hand with personal "autonomy."

Yet women are often denigrated for our "immersion in caring and open need for connection" (Jordan 1991, 289). Popular culture and everyday interactions not only imply that our relationships compromise our other achievements but also that stable, satisfying relationships are no real achievement at all. For the autonomous person sketched by developmental psychologists, relationships just emerge and develop. Such a person gives little priority to relationships and therefore has little practical idea of what they require to remain viable and satisfying. On average, women are likelier than men to see successful relationships as the achievements they *in deed* are. *Androcentrism*—male-centered stances—thus comes to the fore when we face scorn for trying to make our relationships good.

In fact, some of our relationships do not merit such devotion. Sometimes we "care for people who are not worthy of [our] care and who do not care for us in return" (Schweickart 1993, 188). Mainstream culture encourages us to accept such second-rate returns. For example, it inculcates a look-the-other-way, stand-by-your-man mentality that involves us in our own emotional shortchanging. Such lopsidedness means that the "activity that was supposed to be the means of realizing [our] humanity becomes the means through which [we] are reduced to the status of things" (188), serving as means to someone else's autonomy. The distinctly *feminine* agent is thus a cultural paradox. She is "a disappearing subject, the subject who does not assert herself, who is absent from her own actions" (Smith 1990, 191).

So, our relational commitments can sometimes make us "complicit with unjust conditions" (Schweickart 1993, 189). Even though we ourselves "accrue no value by being nice" (Hart 1989, 80) and can hardly expect to promote social change that way, we routinely enact the "niceties" expected of us by friend and foe alike. Being "nice," however, is more than an enactment of cultural dictates. Its moral reach covers empathy, compassion, patience, tolerance, kindness, and magnanimity. It encompasses many worthy dispositions in short supply today. Thus, being "nice" should be a source of pride. Instead, it feeds into a "double bind" where seeking our rights and our "share of social power and moral authority" seems to collide with our "ethical ideal of [our]selves as caring beings" (Schweickart 1993, 189). We are held back, it seems, by the very caring we often find meaningful, by our "sense of self and of morality [that] revolve around issues of responsibility for, care of, and inclusion of other people" (Miller 1991b, 25).

Yet we can be both "nice" and agentic. We are capable of learning to be both caring and assertive, both empathetic and independent, both loving and insistent on our rights, both committed to relationships and committed to self-actualization. Moving toward a both/and stance requires seeing that autonomy is more than a cultural value reserved for the straight white male minority and the comfortably affluent. Such movement starts from Evelyn Fox Keller's (1985, 99) notion of "dynamic autonomy" (Keller 1997, 152), whereby autonomy translates into agency as a moral and political value linked as much with social justice as with personal integrity. This broader conception of autonomy is what we call *liberationist agency*. Feminism promotes such agency by serving "as an instrument of struggle against dominant groups and a tool for the empowerment of the dominated" (Hartsock 1996, 257).

What of agency and intimacy? We assume that agency promotes genuine mutuality. A woman clear about her own values can better negotiate her close bonds with other people and is thus likelier to make sustainable commitments. Agency is crucial. Without it intimacy gets compromised. Our desires are often a cartography of such compromises, as we will see. Agency unleashes our desires, promoting exhilaration and equanimity as well as grounds for full mutuality.

In our view, then, autonomy must mean daring agency—agency unafraid of its power, proud of its potential, insistent on its expression. Agency belongs to women who know their heritage, mostly from the stories and rituals passed to them by mothers, grandmothers, crones, and mentors; women who celebrate their worth and demand its recognition at home and in public; women attuned to the rhythms of their bodies, the poetry of their hearts, and the hum and buzz of nature's cycles and culture's calendars. In Karlene Faith's terms, the agentic woman is

a renegade from the disciplinary practices that would mold her as a gendered being. She is the defiant woman who rejects authority which would subjugate her and render her docile. She is the offensive woman who acts in her own interests. She is the unmanageable woman who claims her own body. . . . She is the woman who cannot be silenced. (1993, 1)

Such an agentic woman enjoys "a self who is terrified neither of solitude nor of gatherings, a self who is both elemental and related, who has a sense of herself making choices within a context created by community." She is both "separate and connected." In Hoagland's terms (1988, 145) this sort of woman has discovered "the self in community."

Angry Agents

From early childhood we learn the art of dealing with our own and others' emotions. For most girls, the emotional curriculum provides few lessons and little homework on anger and other "tough" emotions. Instead, being nice gives normative coherence to girls' emotional upbringing, just as sticking up for oneself serves the same function in boys' parallel curriculum. The feminine curriculum promotes care taking as a strategy of protecting oneself from others' rejection and scorn; the masculine one promotes autonomy as a strategy of defending oneself against others' demands and intrusions.

Social class, sexual identity, race, ethnicity, and much else also shape the emotional curricula in use among Americans today. On those maps, though, anger usually follows a gendered axis that leaves females less free to express that emotion and more prone to experience it as an ugly feeling. We can scarcely overemphasize the pressure to be nice that most girls face. Invoking the feminist theologian Mary Daly, Hoagland (1988, 82, 83) talks about feminine "niceness" in terms of the "virtues of subservience." Historically, the virtues expected of women—generosity, compassion, modesty, patience—cut them off, as we have implied, from effective competition with men, from fulfillment beyond home and hearth, from emotional honesty, from development as full-fledged, multifaceted human beings. To be good meant to count less, to come in second, to identify with subordination, to hide one's achievements, and to forgo some achievements altogether for the sake of femininity. For girls and women, goodness too often consists of "self-diminishing acts" (Krieger 1996, 127).

Hoagland says that conduct applauded *only* for women usually "channel[s] women's energy and attention away from [themselves] and their own projects" (1988, 83). Who among us has not misspent energy in the service of misguided virtue? We have built up other people's egos at the expense of our own; we have cleaned up their messes while neglecting our own; we have offered our shoulders for their tears when we already ached from our own burdens. For many of us our bonds with other women routinely involve reciprocal, satisfying sharing; with men and children, though, reciprocity often eludes us. In our culture men's needs outweigh ours in legitimacy and urgency, and children largely rely on us for physical and emotional sustenance. Thus, many women's "stark realization" that they are often supposed to set aside their own feelings for the sake of their children and husbands sometimes triggers anger. In a study of postpartum depression, for instance, more than half the women whom Verta Taylor interviewed were angry, hostile, or resentful "toward their husbands or partners for failing to share child care and household responsibilities" (1996, 52).

Like their unpaid (and often unrecognized) work in the home, women's paid work often evokes anger. Sexual harassment alone is common enough to account for considerable anger among women employees. Then, too, women often have jobs requiring expressions of femininity that underscore their social subordination. For example, in much of the tourist industry feminine displays often amount to job requirements, and in the *pink-collar ghetto* inhabited by women office workers "their sexuality and femininity are core defining features" of their roles as virtual wives, mistresses, and mothers (Dunne 1997, 162).

In *The Managed Heart* Arlie Hochschild (1983) shows how women usually work in occupations where inhibiting their "tough" emotions goes hand in hand with displays of feminine niceties. In the sex-segregated workplace one-third of female employees work in settings where most other workers are also women (Reskin and Padavic 1994, 52–53). In these occupations, have-a-nice-day posturing is a commonplace norm, and visibly getting angry on the job is anathema. Employers often provide what Erving Goffman (1959) called "back regions" where workers can let off steam, employees' lounges or lunchrooms being the most common forms. But as films like *Norma Rae* dramatize, back regions are often incapable of holding all the emotional runoff from employees' transactions with customers, students, patients, clients, and supervisors. Often such spaces, at one and the same time essential and insufficient, add further insult to standing injury. Especially injurious to women, as Hochschild and others have documented, is the alienation that grows out of the daily battle to inhibit one's "nasty" side.

Anger is also likely when these same women go home to their second job as wife and/or mother. As Beverly Skeggs found among white, working-class women in England, "The desire to be valued and to demonstrate respectability and responsibility predispose [them] to voluntary and unpaid caring" (1997, 72). As a result, mothering fundamentally structures "most women's lives . . . and shapes their relations to all other institutions" (Thompson 1999, 230). Regardless of their husbands' employment status and earnings, then, wives do the vast majority of household work and mothers do most of the childcare. As a student in one of our classes put it, "Only dads—not moms—can babysit their own kids."

Thus, at the end of the workday many of us rejoin our kids expecting nothing less of ourselves than giving them "quality time"; many of us rejoin husbands expecting little more of them than that they tell us about their day and not complain about leftovers for supper. Under these demanding circumstances our tolerance of emotional inequity may grow, and with it grows our tendency to inhibit the expression of our anger. Jean Baker Miller (1991a, 185) lays bare a poignant paradox: Under commonplace conditions women realistically hesitate to disrupt their central relationship with displays of anger and other "unfeminine" behavior, yet negotiating one's way in an unequal relationship "continually generates anger."

Taught no demeanor as relentlessly as that of "being nice" and typically living in circumstances that inhibit expressions of anger, females often adopt a self-effacing ethic that promotes diverse inequities, including emotional unevenness. Commonly we learn to be effusive and solicitous at the expense of insisting on our rights and protecting our priorities. Few of us want to be emotional bullies or robots, yet many of us habitually lean toward the opposite extremes. The virtues of subservience involve biting one's tongue, swallowing one's pride, and eating one's words—all metaphors aptly suited to the diet-prone, food-conscious beings our culture would have us become.

Our emotional biographies are writ large with the virtues of subservience. Woven into these virtues is an entitlement to "anger *in the interest of someone else*" (Miller 1991a, 184). Most of us have ourselves been or have known a mother whose child was mistreated by a teacher or a classmate. Her anger usually gets straightforwardly expressed. We are capable, too, of venting our anger when our partners have endured unfair treatment or when our parents on a low fixed income are denied adequate social services. Our anger can also find effective expression on behalf of people personally unknown to us. Culturally, our anger is not as great a turnoff when it is on behalf of refugees, political prisoners, or people with AIDS or Alzheimer's. Even so, our on-behalf-of anger is best expressed with a maternal demeanor, not that of a pissed-off person refusing to tolerate more of the same.

When we are angry because our own rights or priorities have been undermined, women face less emotional latitude. Commonly cast as mediators, nurturers, or emotional cheerleaders, women shake a lot of people off center by expressing anger in no uncertain terms. Sadly, we often also shake ourselves off center that way. Prone to feel guilt or shame about angry feelings toward others, we inhibit our anger more often than civility dictates. Emotions are rarely pure, but women's anger gets so tangled up with other feelings and with moral judgments that it often finds only partial or indirect expression. Too often we hold our anger back where it festers and eventually becomes an outburst signaling loss of control and suspension of two-way communication. Significantly, those "who say they keep their emotions to themselves report feeling angry more frequently than others" (Mirowsky and Ross 1995, 459–60). Emotionally controlled women are less in touch with their feelings than common stereotypes suggest.

Hoagland says that "being in and out of control are agendas of the fathers" (1988, 186). Patriarchal priorities mandate that men mostly control other people, if only women and children, but that women mostly control themselves and whatever children, if any, are their charges. Those same priorities mandate that men be deemed "out of control" mostly when they violate the male pecking order, but that women be deemed "out of control" whenever they challenge the feminine mandate, "Men and children first and foremost." Lesbians, child-free women, careerist women, pleasure-indulging women, fat women, never-married women, proud crones: All are widely seen as out of control, that is, selfish, self-centered, self-indulgent women who are not very nice.

More often than not, such cultural constructions make us fearful of or anxious about our anger, eager to dispose of it quickly and get back to the project of being nice. As Nett Hart reminds us, though, "Fear cannot stop the thing feared; it can only stop us" (1989, 96). Dodge it as we might, our anger finds expression despite all the constraints on it.

In the end the only women vaguely authorized to express anger in our society are its unfeminine or defeminized ones. Impoverished women are so entitled, for example. Picture one of them on the evening news deriding "welfare reform" in a tirade punctuated by a sound editor's discreet beeps. Her femininity already sorely compromised, such a woman is unlikely to elicit snide responses about how "strident," "opinionated," or "loudmouthed" she is. People expect no better from an unfeminine woman!

Often they also expect no "better" from a feminist woman. People expect her to be adept at expressing her anger and skillful at channeling it in self-serving directions. As long as they leave room for feminist women's humanness—their human lapses and inconsistencies—such expectations make sense. Generally, feminists consider self-knowledge a "task of our freedom" (Hart 1989, 54). Agency demands no less of us, especially agency aimed at social transformation as well as self-satisfaction. Chapter 4 on feminist methods explores these notions.

Here we anticipate them with a cursory look at how our cognitions and emotions, our thoughts and feelings, our minds and hearts work together in practical defiance of the dualisms that pit these realities against one another. By now, feminist and other scholars know that throughout our waking moments we remain feeling as well as thinking creatures. Crossing the threshold into a laboratory or turning on the computer to do statistical analyses in no way means abandoning our feelings. We may suspend or bracket them (in the phenomenological sense), that is, we may put them more or less out of play. We cannot, however, render ourselves wholly unfeeling. To suppose we would even want to do so is to entertain a strange notion about human desires.

Put differently, understanding our agency necessitates understanding our feelings as well as our thoughts. To be an agent means to experience a self-in-community while directing one's feelings and thoughts toward ends one finds meaningful and satisfying. If one chokes on her anger, unable to put it to her own good uses, her agency gets thwarted whenever her anger comes into play. To the extent that we cannot use our anger as agents, a lot of our time in this patriarchal world will be spent as "victims," that is, as "passive objects of injustice" (Hoagland 1988, 49).

Feminist consciousness undercuts that eventuality. It grasps anger's transformative potential (Lorde 1984); it emphasizes the "generative unrest" (Salvaggio 1999, 117) that anger breeds. Feminist ethicists, in particular, emphasize that "being outraged" and "being moved to act" are as much a part of moral maturity as caring is (Little 1995, 127). For feminists, anger is thus "the beginning of fighting back" (Hoagland 1988, 188). It originates transformational actions, which are commonly within reach once we see that "What we choose is what we've decided to try to create" (92). Once we see our choices as commitments to action, opportunities for transformative undertakings seem plentiful.

Fighting Back

By rendering anger an occasion for fighting back, feminism raises two crucial questions. First, against whom do we fight back? In the face of heterosexism, misogyny, racism, or other tentacles of elitist ideology one fights back by dealing with the flesh-and-blood promulgators of elitism—coworkers who refuse to take one seriously, mass advertisers who portray women as technological idiots, household members who fail to do their fair share of the domestic work, public officeholders uncommitted or opposed to women's rights, and everyone else whose actions or failures to act spark our anger. Most of the time, we fight back by targeting the people right in front of us whose behavior is unacceptable because it is presumptuous, intrusive, intimidating, belittling, or preemptive. We fight back by responding to those who have not yet "gotten it." Time and again, we remind them that we are not "trying to get a better deal with men" and are not "interested in replacing men with women without thoroughgoing changes in the social system itself" (Penelope 1992, xiv, 15).

Second, how do we fight back? For the most part, agents of transformation see that "anger is political" (Hoagland 1988, 179) in the very same feminist sense that "the personal is political." To wit, anger raises issues of power—who has it, the tactics of its deployment, the ends it serves. On average, the less power people have, the more anger they experience and the more they feel the need to inhibit its expression. Low-power people cannot take for granted other people's expressions of respect, let alone compliance with their wishes. Thus, our anger often traces the limits of our power. It tells us where our sense of agency falters, where we feel vulnerable or manipulatable, where we tend to avoid confrontation, where we need to hone our skills.

While we do need to know the limits of our power, we also need to know its full reach. First, we face the challenge of grasping all the kinds of power we do have. The most touted is *power over*, the power to command or order other human beings and expect their conformity to our dictates. Parents, supervisors, law enforcement personnel, teachers, and caseworkers routinely use this kind of power. So do many husbands. Friends, partners, teammates, and our fellow citizens less often use power over. Instead, they consider our feelings and preferences just as they expect us to consider theirs. Such *power with*, or power sharing, involves reciprocal influence that is balanced over time. Equality entails power with (cf. Starhawk 1990; also, Allen 1999, 125–29).

Power from within involves "centering and remaining steady in our environment" while experiencing something "akin to the sense of mastery" (Hoagland 1988, 118; Starhawk 1990, 10). Power from within "is creative; . . . it is an affecting and transforming power, but not a controlling power" (Hoagland 1988, 118). Its language "is action, which speaks in the body and to all the senses in ways that can never be completely conveyed in words" (Starhawk 1990, 15). Power from within concerns the plenitude of our being and becoming. Seen from the outside, it is the individual's *power* to, or her transformative potential with respect to self-in-community, other people, and her environment. Power to is a measure of how much we are capable of shaping the social contract, both close to home and in the centers of power over where policy is set and laws are passed.

What we often overlook is that the more power from within and power to we gain, the more gratifying is our participation in power with. We then have more "power" to share, more transformative possibilities whereby to inspire, energize, comfort, and evoke hope in those with whom we work, make homes, shape community, share leisure, and otherwise live out our days. While abjuring power over, then, we need to cultivate the other varieties of power that help us "see the world as a pattern of relationships" (Starhawk 1990, 15) shaped mostly by the labors and lapses of people like us going about our ordinary lives.

Another challenge we must face in order to know and expand our "power" is honesty. As Adrienne Rich observes in her essay "Women and Honor: Some Notes on Lying," truthfulness "means a heightened complexity" (1980, 193). Consider the dense complexities usually hidden from view in patriarchal societies:

> Wives are not supposed to give away the secret of male dependence . . . ; secretaries are not supposed to tell about male incompetence or the incoherence they make presentable; lesbian women are not supposed to "flaunt" their sexualities . . . ; mistresses are not supposed to tell about the contradictions inside heterosexuality, monogamy, and the promises of marriage; women with disabilities are not supposed to expose the social obsessions with attractiveness and illusions of lifelong independence and health; prostitutes are not supposed to tell about the contradictions of intimacy and sexuality; daughters are not to speak of incest; and maids or domestics are not supposed to talk about the contradictions of the world of paid work and family life under advanced capitalism. (Fine and Gordon 1992, 19–20)

Our silences, our pretenses, our dodges, our white lies and our dirty ones—all so understandable—maintain men's image as autonomous beings basically different from our inferiorized selves. Our dishonesty bolsters the very circumstances that evoke our anger but proscribe its expression.

Finally, we face the challenge of ceasing our own oppressive actions if we want to expand our power, particularly our *power to* liberate ourselves. Our oppression derives from our own oppressive practices as well as those of other people. Every time we make an elitist remark or engage in elitist behavior, we help to strengthen hierarchy in American life. Our own elitism may seem to have nothing at all to do with gender or women's rights, but the various tentacles of elitist ideology complement and reinforce one another. Out of them grows the *matrix of domination* (Collins 1991), whereby not only a person's gender but also such circumstances as her color, age, religion, sexual orientation, social class, and degree of ablebodiedness either privilege or disprivilege her in social hierarchies. Since society's systems of domination intersect with one another (Collins 1998), we must weave the banner of women's rights so that it reflects women's social, cultural, and physical diversity. To make *common* cause with one another we must recognize the *diverse* circumstances that elitists have used to divide and oppress us.

For virtually all of us, such recognition means seeing that on average some groupings of women endure pain and hardship greater than our own while also seeing the full sweep of our privilege within the matrix of domination. Those of us who are heterosexual, for example, need to acknowledge the social ease, psychological comforts, legal rights, and other benefits this routinely confers, albeit at woeful costs to many women; those of us who are white need to probe the institutionalized, taken-for-granted ramifications of our skin color and try to grasp white-skin privilege as keenly as we ask men of all colors to grasp their gender privilege. Audre Lorde says, "To acknowledge privilege is the first step in making it available for wider use" (1991, 265). Such acknowledgment leads toward insisting that the same civilities, opportunities, and rewards be fully available to people not entirely like ourselves.

Considered as benefits and entitlements extending beyond a person's or a group's basic human rights, *privilege* entails more than a proportionate share of opportunities and resources. Women are underprivileged. As a group, we face fewer opportunities and command fewer resources than men with the same abilities, skills, and relevant experiences. Yet we are not all equally underprivileged. Many women are also underprivileged by virtue of their class position—their limited schooling, their unenviable jobs, their paltry pay. Some are also underprivileged by virtue of their physical challenges, their "advanced" age, or their religious beliefs. Many women thus hold membership in multiple *minority groups* in the sociological sense—groups disproportionately deprived of power, status, and material resources in society regardless of their numerical size.

Lorde insists, "Each of us is blessed in some particular way, whether we recognize our blessings or not." Each of us enjoys some measure of privilege—each of us who is literate, for instance. Lorde goes on to say that "each of us, somewhere in our lives, must clear a space within that blessing where she can call upon whatever resources are available to her in the name of something that must be done." Lorde had the imagination to see and the guts to say that our own measure of privilege empowers us to do something. Such awareness promotes a sense of efficacy. In the end we can put our anger to use in the service of agency. We can use it to fight back less in the on-behalf-of fashion and more in the power-with way. Such progress can be ours if we have the courage of our desires.

Desire and Agency

For many people, "desire" connotes passion, sexuality, and related experiences of no small relevance to feminism. During the 1970s feminists such as Shulamith Firestone and Ti-Grace Atkinson insisted that "love" serves the "political function . . . [of] persuad[ing] the oppressed one to accept her or his oppression" (Castro 1990, 83). More recently (Jonasdottir 1994), such standpoints have begun resurfacing. Sure enough, "But I love him" is the closing line of many women's sad tales about their male partners' neglect or cruelty. "Love" serves many men who would otherwise go without the low-paid housekeeper and childcare worker whom they call "the Mrs." More pointedly, love is often the social-psychological parallel of the economic dependence many women experience in marriage. Both states induce tolerance of unacceptable behaviors and situations. Gradually, that tolerance can make a bad situation seem more or less acceptable—more acceptable than its practical alternatives, though less acceptable than one's dreams, romance novels, soap operas, and fantasies.

Love, wrote Zora Neale Hurston, is "de very prong all us black women gits hung on. Dis love! Dat's just whut's got us uh pullin' and uh haulin' and sweatin' and doin' from can't see in de mornin' till can't see at night" (Hurston 1978, 41). Ironically enough, the love she means is not unlike the kind promulgated by Madison Avenue and popular films, music, television programs, and fiction. It defies rationality, yet few parents, teachers, religious leaders, or others inveigh against it. One is supposed to "fall" into it, be swept off her feet, walk on air, or float on cloud nine. In that exuberant state one is to choose a long-term, even lifelong, partner and begin planning a life together. Often, the planning centers on a fan-fare engagement and a gala wedding involving bridal registries, showers, flowers, jewelry, gowns, and other formal wear all in concert with photographers, printers, hairstylists, travel agents, caterers, and musicians as well as family and friends, plus some officiating presence. The huge, joyous challenge of making a home together takes a back seat to preparations for what many women consider the biggest day of their lives. In our society 96 percent of those women adopt their husbands' last name, a custom emblematic of the dramatic changes such women embrace on their way down the aisle. They center attention on that festive day because their lives are changing much more than their grooms' are.

Desire *is* played out on the stage where bride and groom join hands, but the desires bringing them together are far from equivalent. Her family, peers, teachers, and counselors have joined together with the promoters of popular culture to whittle her desires down. They are unfeminine until their *main* focus is marriage to a man and mothering one or more children. The underside of the cultural scripts repeatedly handed to women imply that in patriarchal society few informed, thinking women would freely choose marriage and motherhood as they are currently institutionalized. Instead, women have to be conned into institutionalized marriage and motherhood. A woman has to become madly, head-over-heels in love; she has to be steered away from lucrative or even good-paying occupations, discriminated against in the employment and child-support systems, and denied reliable access to medical insurance and childcare services through her own job or earnings. She has to be taught that without a man at her side she is incomplete, and without marriage and motherhood she can find no lasting fulfillment. Her desires and life chances thus narrowed, a woman is primed not to rebel against domestic inequities. Feminism promotes such rebellion. Feminists often see the practical, egalitarian wisdom of keeping love in its self-actualizing place in one's life. Vivian Gornick says of Simone de Beauvoir, for instance, that "it stood her in infinitely better stead to hold work rather than love as a first value. It made her a better human being" (1999, 72). Perhaps, too, it made de Beauvoir's 1949 feminist classic *The Second Sex* all the stronger.

That a culture so thoroughly channels females' desires suggests that those desires have nothing less than revolutionary potential. Nett Hart implies as much:

> Separation from desire makes us subservient, socially pragmatic. Separation from desire separates us from the whole of life and creates loyalties to particular regimes of socialization, makes survival seem scarce and protection necessary. We have been socialized against desire. . . . We have been socialized against desire so that we renounce our authority over our lives. (1989, 21)

In a related vein, Ann DuCille observes that for former slaves, both real-life and fictional, "freedom meant the right to love 'big'"; it meant "entitlement to desire" (1993, 5). Thus, in multiple respects "desire is . . . at stake in the feminist politics of pursuing alternative definitions of female subjectivity," with "desire" meaning nothing less than "women's desire to become" or our "desire for recognition" (Braidotti 1993, 6; Benjamin 1988, 126). Rosa Braidotti gets to the roots of desire when she describes it as "the propelling and compelling force that is attracted to self-affirmation" (2001, 400). Braidotti emphasizes that desire seeks change, not preservation; it "is a deep yearning for transformation or a process of affirmation." Desire thus moves toward superseding self-abnegation, overcoming subordination, and transforming suffering into joy, pleasure, or contentment.

We need to reclaim our desires and, with them, our bodies. As Dorothy Smith shows, these two reclamation projects are intertwined. Smith notes that the airbrushed images mapped onto women's bodies in mass advertising and popular culture "organize the gap that generates 'desire'" (1990, 190). Smith shows how desire takes shape around the gap between what is and what might better satisfy us. Desire thus grows out of absence. In fact, whatever evokes the experience of absence tends over time to evoke desire. Much of our socialization and many of our daily experiences revolve around such evocations. During girlhood we learn what we are not but should be, and desire begins taking shape around not being sufficiently slim, not being "naturally" pretty, or not being paired off with a boy. In our daily lives we hear diets touted, romantic love heralded, and aging scorned in the mass media and in everyday talk. Cumulatively, such messages structure the gaps that create desire. To one extent or other they focus our identities on what we are not and give status-quo shape to our motives. In these ways identity becomes "a normative ideal rather than a descriptive feature of experience" (Butler 1990, 16). To that extent identity work is in order. Negative identities promote not women's liberation but our continuing subordination.

Judith Butler considers identity a set of practices making us "culturally intelligible subjects" (1990, 145). Typically, identity is "*a regulated process of repetition*" whereby we engage in the normative practices that make us observable (or intelligible) as feminine women. Significantly, agency then concerns the "possibility of a variation on that repetition." With respect to identity work, agency might best revolve around possible variations on the gaps evoking desire. The regulated repetitions undergirding most femininities include, for example, expressions of body loathing based on gaps between how our body looks and how it should look. The more we focus on those gaps, the more we feed our desire for the elusive body beautiful.

We can focus our awareness elsewhere by carving out our own gaps and insisting on our own meanings. We might, for instance, take up bodybuilding during midlife, not in pursuit of the lean, mean body but as an "aesthetic discipline" (Frueh 1999), adding pleasure to our everyday lives. Feminist agency impels such creativity. It promotes honesty. Feminist agency entails choosing "to act by what we know rather than what we are told." It means "choos[ing] truth over obedience" (Hart 1989, 22).

Such autonomy can advance self-in-community while deflecting others' power over. We can choose power with and power to built on recognizing that countless

> women have struggled to assert their self-worth, dignity, and capacity for independent action. They have worked to preserve a sense of themselves as individual people with their own feelings, values, identities, capacities, and goals, often in contexts in which conventional values would have them disappear into derivative relational identities such as daughter, wife, or mother. These struggles are naturally interpreted as women's quests for greater autonomy. Thus it is somewhat paradoxical that prominent feminist theorists reject the idea of autonomy—and rather reassuring that others see a need to reconstruct the concept. (Govier 1993, 104)

We can indeed reconstruct that concept, as we have begun to do in this chapter. We can "celebrate [our] empathy and fluidity . . . as a psychic refusal to separate from others; [we] can . . . see in it the seeds of a new and more productive ethics" (Michie 1992, 60). As agents, we can also see that relationships, far from impeding development, actually promote it. Our attractions can thus "reveal developmental motivations" (Burch 1993, 144). Let us shape gaps that evoke desires not for what is absent but for what can become more—more justice, intimacy, truth, creativity, dialogue; more gardens and more feasts. Let us seek "not so much an identity as a social location within feminist blueprints for social change" (McDermott 1998, 409). As female agents, "We invent ourselves and our world . . . in the realm of the not yet real/realized. We move toward pleasure, bring into play new modes" (Hart 1989, 14). In that movement we enact variations on the regulated repetitions once holding us back, and we narrow the gap between what we are and what we can become. Agency thus serves desire, and pleasure displaces anger.

3

Sexuality

Girls' and women's connections with men typically shape their daily experiences, short-term prospects, and long-term outcomes. At least potentially, those connections involve men's sexual dominance. In the home, workplace, church or synagogue, gym, civic organization, union, and other corners of the social world, men commonly, though often implicitly, take sexual charge. Our culture licenses them to be sexually aggressive and dominant while also mandating that they protect us, at least as fathers and husbands. Only other men can provide protection from male predators by virtue of that same license to be aggressive not only in sexual conquests but also in defense of one's turf. Needless to say, not all men follow these cultural scripts (cf. Christian 1994; Kimmel and Mosmiller 1992).

The overwhelming majority of men are, though, entitled to do so, and to varying degrees they act accordingly. Linda LeMoncheck (1997, 160) generalizes that in societies like ours women are encouraged to depend *"on men* for protection *from men."* Thus, male dominance derives support both from men's sexual intimidation of women and their protection of women from such intimidation. Their power over us always involves in principle, if not in practice, their capacity to sexually embarrass, intimidate, or overpower us. In our society most women cannot readily turn the tables on men. If we inappropriately ask about their sexual comings and goings, they generally react with something other than embarrassment or anxiety. If we lean too close to a male classmate or coworker, if we touch him inappropriately, if we compliment him on his buff body or tight buns, he may take offense or grin with pleasure or wonder what is going on, but he is unlikely to feel intimidated or vulnerable *even if we happen to be bigger or more aggressive.*

Sociologist R. W. Connell has dissected how this global dominance of heterosexual men undercuts women's sexual security. For women, that dominance mandates

> the display of sociability rather than technical competence, fragility in mating scenes, compliance with men's desire for titillation and ego-stroking in office relationships, acceptance of marriage and childcare as a response to labour-market discrimination against women. At the mass level these are organized around themes of sexual receptivity in relation to younger women and motherhood in relation to older women. (1987, 187)

This "emphasized femininity" revolves "around compliance with this subordination and is oriented to accommodating the interests and desires of men" (183).

All the while, most women are drawn to a close relationship with a man. In fact, as Sandra Lee Bartky (1990, 9) reminds us, many women—especially those in tight financial straits with overburdened daily lives—desire the sort of heterosexual relationship discussed in this chapter. These circumstances make all the more pressing the need to interrogate heterosexuality. For the sake of our safety, security, and satisfaction, we need to ask what a heterosexual identity means for a contemporary woman, how it takes the typical shapes it does, and how it can coexist honorably with a feminist identity.

Because heterosexuals (like members of other dominant groups) largely define themselves by those who strike them as "different," in this chapter we also look at the experiences of women who are not heterosexual. We need to ask what gains and losses their sexual identities entail and then look at the parallel figures for heterosexual women. We may find that some of the sexual costs of being women are fairly constant, whether one is lesbian, bisexual, asexual, heterosexual, or in between where ambiguity prevails. In any case we need to know about one another—"how we survive, what we comprise, how we emerge, what we lose of our selves, our successes." We need, too, to understand that "each of us participates in heteropatriarchal culture to varying degrees" (Penelope 1992, 37). That insight invites attention to heteropatriarchy and to the institution of heterosexuality. As we turn to these matters, we expect to say nothing definitive. Rather we explore the social constructs capable of providing a framework for thinking critically and creatively about our sexualities. Our primary interest, then, is neither "findings" nor "generalizations" but an open-ended exploration.

Heterosexuality 101

Heteropatriarchy refers to a social hierarchy overseen by high-status heterosexual men that entitles men to dominate women as well as nonheterosexual and other lower-status men. Within every social class, racial/ethnic group, age group, and mixed-sex organization in our society, heteropatriarchy prevails. It undercuts women's power and status but does so in distinct ways for various groupings of women. Women of color, for instance, often report an emotional and political alignment with men of color that white women are less likely to claim with their male counterparts (cf. Combahee River Collective 1998; Stack 1994, 297). Lower-income women are unable to live as independently of men, in attitude or in practice, as higher-income women, and most heterosexual women can wend their way through heteropatriarchal structures in ways that lesbian and bisexual women often find impossible. Whatever the distinctive challenges any group of women faces in heteropatriarchal society, their experiences take shape as much from the institution of heterosexuality as from the weight of patriarchy.

Until recently heterosexuality went mostly unnoticed. It was "just there"—a predictable, universal, taken-for-granted feature of the social scaffolding. In the past, for instance, courses on human sexuality narrowly centered on heterosexuals' sexual development, fantasies, activities, and dysfunctions. Even more often than today, textbooks included only a few pages or a separate chapter on homosexuality. Even today, though, just about "every published study about sexual functioning and menopause [still] assumes that women's sexuality is intercourse-based and heterosexual" (Cole and Rothblum 1991, 184). More generally, most of what is reported about dating, coupling, marriage, and family is at least as much about the institution of heterosexuality. Because of *heterosexism*—the assumption that heterosexuality is the "normal" sexual orientation—scholars and commentators commonly assume that what they observe about heterosexuals points to "natural" patterns. By now, though, some scholars treat heterosexuality as a social institution—a socially constructed, not a naturally ordained, array of social actions. Thanks mostly to feminist theorists and queer theorists (who theorize from nonheterosexual perspectives), heterosexuality now gets interrogated (Katz 1995).

Most people balk when they first come across the idea that heterosexuality is a social institution not unlike religion, education, or government. It strikes them as a radical notion that may be strategic for some purposes but is ultimately untenable. Yet a look around the planet or through history shows that heterosexuals' behavior is culturally contingent. In some societies rape is virtually unthinkable. In some societies premarital sex is proscribed, while in others it is prescribed or at least expected. In some societies heterosexuality entails public kissing and petting; in some societies it involves men visibly dominating "their" women in public, whether they are daughters or wives; in some societies it emphasizes reproductive sex between wives and husbands and sex for pleasure between husbands and mistresses; in some societies fathers sexually initiate their (supposedly) heterosexual sons by taking them to a brothel.

An *institution* is a distinctive set of social actions widely taken for granted as meaningful and functional within some social system. Institutions channel people's choices. They dim our awareness of alternatives by making their dictates seem necessary and natural; their grooves become our daily routines. Institutions point to what we take for granted together as the familiar contours of our world. Increasingly, feminists recognize the "need to problematize notions of heterosexuality as a single, uniform sexual identity." More and more, they interrogate heterosexuality as a social institution normalizing men's dominance of women (Hoagland 1988, 7). Heterosexual women commonly *learn* to seek someone well qualified to dominate them. Typically, they look for someone "older, more highly educated, taller, more 'worldly,' more highly paid" (Minnich 1990, 58). Nothing intrinsic to heterosexual bonding necessitates that pattern. Feminists show how such arbitrary, contingent elements of heterosexuality benefit men as a group to the disadvantage of women as a group.

Treating heterosexuality as an institution, feminists come up against the "fiction of heterosexual coherence" (Hennessy 1993, 25) pervading our culture. Heterosexuality is not only deeply taken for granted but also feels logically and emotionally coherent to most people. It coheres with other institutions such as the family, religion, and government in ways that make it seem natural, not socially constructed. Less recognized is how heterosexuality coheres with the economy. Julien S. Murphy says heterosexuality might better be called

> heteroeconomics, for it pertains to the language of barter, exchange, bargain, auction, buy and sell. . . . Heterosexuality is the economy of exchange in which a gender-based power structure continually reinstates itself through the appropriation of the devalued party in a duo-gendered system. (cited in Hoagland 1988, 29)

"Heteroeconomics" applies to the economy at large, especially insofar as pay gaps between the sexes intensify the pressures on women to couple with higher-earning men. Moreover, the workplace reflects the structure of the male-headed household. A certain transinstitutional coherence thus lends massive, quiet support to the institution of heterosexuality. That support is pervasive enough to make heterosexuality compulsory for all practical purposes in our society.

Compulsory heterosexuality is the taken-for-granted, widely enforced norm that people must be heterosexual. Adrienne Rich (1980) emphasizes the absence of readily recognizable, accessible alternatives to the institution of heterosexuality. Compulsory heterosexuality involves, in other terms, monolithic institutional forces against which lesbians, bisexuals, gay men, and other sexual minorities develop their sexual identities. The compulsory character of heterosexuality is central to understanding how *thoroughly necessary and meaningful* sexual minorities find their "abnormal" identities. Indeed, their "abnormality" is better read as "nonconformist sexualities" (Wilkinson and Kitzinger 1996, 375). As Amber Hollibaugh puts it, "All of us have worked very hard to be queer, to be lesbian, to be out—in spite of all the cultural stop signs." Similarly, Joan Nestle says, "They can't ever scare us out of the way we live. They can't judge us out of the way we love. They can't ridicule us out of it, because it is not a masquerade" (cited in Castro 1992, 455, 461).

Other evidence of heterosexuality's institutionalized nature derives from sexual socialization. If heterosexuality emerged as a matter of natural course in people's lives, little would be necessary to ensure its adoption. Yet a great deal of cultural work goes into inculcating and reinforcing people's heterosexual identities along institutionalized lines. From querying toddlers about their "boyfriends" or "girlfriends" to encouraging cross-sex coupling through school-sponsored dances and other gatherings, from virtually prohibiting realistic media portrayals of sexual minorities to defining medically nonheterosexual identities as other than healthy and normal, from this institutional prong to that, from this cultural value to that, people face relentless messages about how intolerable homoerotic feelings, needs, and activities are. Those jabs and shoves move most people into the grooves of heterosexuality, but their movement in that direction is far from "natural," indeed, far from complete. Freud, the Victorian patriarch whose thinking still shapes much discourse about sexuality, saw that

> exclusive heterosexuality [is] the socially restricted result of an original, roving sexual instinct. His normal heterosexuality is by no means

natural. It's the limited product of a difficult developmental process. (Katz 1995, 73)

Linda Christian-Smith (1990), for instance, describes how using teen romance fiction in high schools draws female adolescents into the institution of heterosexuality. Her study of teen comics yielded Valerie Walkerdine similar findings. Walkerdine says that "although hetero-sexuality is not an overt *issue*, the other features of femininity are so produced in the pages of the comics as to render 'getting a man' the 'natural' solution" (1990, 97). More recently, Barrie Thorne describes

> the transition to adolescence . . . as a period of entry into the institu-tion of heterosexuality: While this transition brings new constraints and vulnerabilities for boys as well as girls, girls are particularly dis-advantaged. Disturbing national statistics paint an overall picture of adolescence as "the fall" for girls: compared with boys of the same age, and with themselves at earlier ages, girls who are twelve, thir-teen, and fourteen have higher rates of depression, lower self-esteem, more negative images of their own bodies, and declining academic performance in areas like math and science. (1993, 155)

Not coincidentally, preadolescence and adolescence are when most girls' heterosexuality is being shaped with increasing specificity and subordination. Thorne emphasizes that "girls are more pervasively sexualized than boys." For many of them,

> appearance and relationships with boys begin to take primacy over other activities. In middle school or junior high the status of girls with other girls begins to be shaped by their popularity with boys; same-gender relations among boys are less affected by relationships with the other gender. In short, the social position of girls increasingly de-rives from their romantic relationships with boys, but not vice versa. (Thorne 1993, 155)

These patterns derive from the apparent rewards and discernible pressures constituting "heterosexual bribery" (Penelope 1992, 40). Such bribery revolves around "the dangerous fantasy that if you are good enough, pretty enough, sweet enough, quiet enough, teach the children to behave, hate the right people, and marry the right man, then you will be allowed to co-exist with patriarchy in relative peace" (Lorde 1984, 119). In any case our socialization as females widely inculcates beliefs such as these, namely, that straight white middle-class feminin-ity is in our best interest. All the while, one wonders why such a worthy club requires such intensely positive publicity to get us to accept a lifetime membership.

Heterosexual privilege is, to be sure, a reality. Heterosexuality's legal guarantees, social acceptability, moral hegemony, and economic benefits as well as the psychological ease it allows are substantial rewards for getting and staying on heterosexual course. As one of twenty-one heterosexual feminists who discuss their sexuality and politics in *Heterosexuality: A Feminism & Psychology Reader*, Halla Beloff speaks to heterosexuality's taken-for-granted payoffs. Above all, she says, being heterosexual "means being 'ordinary'" and thus able to "enter into most cultural narratives, that is, novels, films, fine art, on the basis of simple and satisfying identification." It also means, albeit with the help of "a significant degree of luck," one has the option of making one's sexual partnership and motherhood the bases of "a family home." Beloff acknowledges that "Others can have that, but the cement seems harder when a nexus has formal recognition all around." She concludes that "a heterosexual position brings one 'inside'" (Beloff 1993, 39). Mary Crawford cites another benefit: "Being taken for a standard-issue heterosexual bestows a credibility that can be used to subvert heterosexism" (1993, 44). When sexual minorities rail against those prejudices, many heterosexuals presume they are only grinding an axe to advance their own interests.

Yet the "insider" position that heterosexual women enjoy as dominant-group members gets compromised by the subordination their heterosexuality entails. That generic complaint shows up in many of the narratives in *Heterosexuality*. Caroline Ramazanoglu observes that "For many heterosexual women, sex is not particularly satisfying or pleasurable" (1993, 59). Indeed, as Nicola Gavey (1993) has shown, it is often unwanted or even coerced. No less a figure than African American feminist bell hooks concedes, "Often I felt compelled to engage in sexual intercourse when I did not want to" (1994, 111). Hers are words many women might utter during moments of sexual honesty.

Yet "as institution, identity, practice and experience, heterosexuality is not merely sexual" (Jackson 1995, 18). Women's heterosexuality can mean not only "spending considerable time in the company of men" but also "spend[ing] an inordinate amount of time keeping our feelings to ourselves, holding our opinions—especially our feminist opinions—privately" (Lips and Freedman 1993, 56). Tamsin Wilton says her heterosexuality entails "a continual struggle to assert [her] autonomy, get [her] needs met and have [her] subjective experience recognized" (1993, 273). Alison M. Thomas says a heterosexual woman "pays for her 'normality' by jeopardizing her autonomy and her right to a separate identity" (1993, 84). More generally, says Nira Yuval-Davis, "heterosexual women—according to all feminist analyses and especially radical feminist separatist ones—enter unequal partnerships in which sexist norms and power relations prevail" (1993, 52). Rosalind Gill and Rebecca Walker, young and white as well as heterosexual and feminist, say they "live inside contradictions" wherein they feel "so hungry, so needy, [and] want so much *more*." Yet being heterosexual need not mean "identifying with heterosexual culture" (Reinharz 1993, 66). That said, we are equipped to begin untangling the tensions in female heterosexuality, especially feminist women's heterosexuality, which Ramazanoglu sees as "politically sensitive, personally painful and insufficiently studied" (1993, 59). Put differently, heterosexual women's "femininity is at best shaky and partial: the result of a struggle in which heterosexuality is achieved as a solution to a set of conflicts and contradictions in familial and other social relations" (Walkerdine 1990, 88).

Nevertheless some straight women do manage to establish satisfying, relatively egalitarian heterosexual relationships. Such achievements require deviating to some degree from institutional dictates, however (Schwartz 1994). Equality pulls heterosexual couples away from the institution of heterosexuality and its patriarchal dictates, opening up the tantalizing gap between social institutions and lived experiences. As Rich (1976) showed with reference to motherhood, an institution is one thing and specific people's experiences of it are another. Thus, criticizing the institution of heterosexuality implies nothing about specific individuals' experiences. As Amber Hollibaugh and Cherrie Moraga (1992, 244) state, echoing Shulamit Reinharz, "There *is* heterosexuality outside of heterosexism." A minority of people can act within *and* against an institution so that the divide between collective patterns and personal experiences widens to their satisfaction. Just as democracy commonly requires good citizens to dissent and protest, participation in other social institutions often requires stepping out of line so as to make the institution accommodate one's hard-won self.

Stepping out of heterosexual line, even while remaining within the institution's boundaries, involves poignant challenges. Part of the difficulty is that heterosexuality is tightly bound with, if not defined by, state-authorized marriage and mom-dad parenthood. Susie Orbach says, for example, "Heterosexuality has been especially focused for me since becoming a parent" (1993, 48). We all know that both marriage and parenthood typically entail gross inequalities and that one parent is largely left to do the best she can if the other parent up and leaves. No straight woman's sexual orientation necessitates her participation in legal marriage, but if she wants a child, the pressures on her to marry are considerable. We understand those pressures, yet we wonder why heterosexual women of privilege and good sense enter into marriage and prospective motherhood with no prenuptial agreement about how she and her partner will divide the financial and other responsibilities for raising their child(ren). Pressured to marry, of course, they are also pressured to act irrationally (as we have seen) even as they make one of life's most consequential choices. Ultimately and always, however, in societies like ours the *decision* to marry is just that. That circumstance needs constantly to be shored up in our minds. Heterosexuality no more necessitates marriage than it necessitates reproduction, adoption, foster parenting, or any other standing responsibilities for bringing up children.

In any event "'heterosexual' and 'lesbian' are not symmetrical; the consequences of accepting them are different, as are the consequences of letting them go." These two cultural labels "are *not* opposite ends of the same continuum. Because 'lesbian' is an intrinsically politicized identity, and heterosexuality is not, the two terms are not commensurate." Sue Wilkinson and Celia Kitzinger (1993, 8) go on to conclude that "what is needed is not the depoliticization of lesbianism . . . but the politicization of the category 'heterosexual.'" Such politicization could start from the recognition that one is "responsible for being heterosexual—it's not like the colour of your eyes," as Anna Wilson (quoted by Wilkinson and Kitzinger 1993, 19) states.

Reinharz likes to "envision a heterosexuality that does not originate in the male standpoint and that does not transform women into sexual objects." She concludes, "We cannot dismiss heterosexual women as having 'false consciousness.' And yet it would be good for us also to empower women to understand their lesbian potential" (1993, 66). Such a stance allows for the egalitarian, satisfying sexual partnerships some heterosexual women manage to achieve while also undercutting the homophobia that makes many heterosexual women unaware of all their sexual and parenting options. Julia Penelope says that "a majority of women simply do not conceive of themselves as having choices about whom they are supposed to love, because lesbianism and celibacy . . . are seldom visible as options at the time that most women must choose how they are going to live" (1993, 264). What might happen for women in general "if lesbians were visible in an ordinary, casual, taken-for-granted way" (Paula Jennings, quoted in Wilkinson and Kitzinger 1993, 23)? It may be that "heterosexuality would not occur to women as a viable way of living!" (Penelope 1993, 264).

Put differently, women would begin insisting on another heterosexuality. Those who chose a heterosexual course would demand a different institution for themselves—one less tied to traditional femininity and masculinity, one more oriented toward passionate friendship, one more amenable to the distinctive propensities each individual brings to and develops within a heterosexual partnership. For now, though, we must do our utmost to honor every woman's dignity by seeing that she "has to live a life where she is and according to her own sense of political and personal belief" (Robinson 1993, 81). Each of us is negotiating a course where purity is a pipedream and absolutes have no practical meaning. Privilege and bribery intertwine as heterosexual women make their way through patriarchal society, and all of us participate in one way or other in their privileging and bribing.

Our Sexual Selves

Eve Kosofsky Sedgwick (1990) and Judith Butler (1990), among others, emphasize how multifaceted and dynamic our sexual identities are. They involve much more than the gender of the people who attract us, including rich, even wild, fantasies and diverse preferences that may or may not seem consistent with one another and that often shift across our lifetimes. We each tend to prefer certain sexual actions over others; more or less tenderness and roughness in our sexual encounters and greater or lesser frequency; some measure of exhibitionism or voyeurism or both; more or less sadomasochistic pleasure; monogamous, less than monogamous, or nonmonogamous sexual relationships. Or we may abjure sexual relationships for the time being, favoring anonymous sex or strictly casual or recreational sex with "no strings attached." We lean toward one-with-one or group sex, more or less private or public sex, and so forth. That all these facets of our sexual identities get erased by whether our sexual partners are members of the other sex or the same sex or both is absurd. Yet social efficiency and political utility promote such narrowing.

In part, that narrowness takes hold in connection with gender dualism. The sexes have been culturally constructed as "opposites" with femininity and masculinity following suit. Instead of thinking of "neighboring" sexes (and "next-door neighbors at that"), we see females and males through lenses of difference and dualism (Schuman and Olufs 1995, 108). In "The Traffic in Women: Notes on the 'Political Economy' of Sex," Gayle Rubin (1975) bemoaned opposite-sex rhetoric. Protesting the "suppression of natural similarities," Rubin emphasized how women must repress "the local definition of 'masculine' traits"; men, "the local definition of 'feminine' traits" (quoted in Katz 1995, 133). Such repression represents the high price of becoming feminine or masculine. It also creates a "need" to draw the Other toward oneself as an expression of what one has repressed.

Butler argues that heterosexualizing desire necessitates "oppositions between 'feminine' and 'masculine'" that in turn make some "gender identities" seem like "developmental failures or logical impossibilities" (1990, 17). The tomboy who carries her I-can-do ways into adulthood is one such gender identity. Another is the sissy who, as a heterosexual man, is "conceptually homeless" (Hunter 1993, 158). The "persistence and proliferation" of such identities attest to gender's diverse real-life shapes. Insofar as they become targets of harsh stereotypes, such identities also attest to how domination presupposes "an ideology of difference and superiority" (158, 161). Whether the domination involves people of one sex subordinating those of another sex or people with one sexual orientation subordinating those with another sexual orientation, that ideology prevails. "Opposite" is its central term.

So that "opposite" can exert its ideological force, sex and gender as well as sexual orientation come in forced-choice pairs—female/male, feminine/masculine, gay/straight. The hermaphrodite, the androgyne, and the bisexual serve less as third realities and more as misfits, psychological anomalies, or developmental slipups. Once dualism sets in, "opposite" captures consciousness enough to close down awareness of the dramatic diversity lying beneath ambitious labels such as "woman" or "heterosexual." The work of "opposite" proceeds by making "woman" a derivative of "man," an inferior variation of "man," or an absence of "man" or by making "heterosexual" an unmarked, privileged status whose inferior variation is "lesbian" or whose absence makes for "queerness." Diversity, versatility, multiplicity, variations, and gradations get washed away as "opposite" overrides people's lived identities.

The cultural construction of such opposites as feminine/masculine occurs in myriad ways. "Sexual dysfunction nomenclature," for example, revolves around

> the construction of an autonomous, performance-oriented male sexuality which can be used as a means of dominating women. Female sexuality, of necessity, is the reverse of this: receptive, dependent,

feeling-oriented, and presented as problematic when it does not conform to a male ideal of sexual practice. Heterosexual intercourse is at
the centre of this system and sexual "dysfunctions" have been largely
defined in terms of the extent to which they impede it or its comple-
tion in orgasm. (Boyle 1993, 215)

Note that the nomenclature presupposes not only a dominant (that is,
masculine) male and a subordinate (that is, feminine) female but also a
heterosexual couple. In this scheme, assertive, desire-driven, heterosexual women are sexually dysfunctional, as are nonheterosexual people.

Our interest lies in grasping the lived ins and outs of sexual orientations. We see sexual identities as expressions of people's needs to
connect, to love, to create, to explore, to express, to enjoy intense pleasures, and sometimes even to transcend. Even though sexual orientation is one of the circumstances that "divide women [and] also unite
some women with men" (Hartsock 1990, 158), we need not let sexual
orientation dim our awareness of what we have in common as women.
Here we look at the similarities our sexual identities leave intact as well
as the dissimilarities they introduce.

In societies like ours, sexual identity affects virtually all aspects of
our lives. Routinely, our sexual identities affect how and where we
worship, how secure our child-custody rights are, how we manage our
appearances, how we view our paid work, how we respond to men's
sexual interest, how likely we are to use long-term contraception, and
even such things as our experiences with physicians (Stevens 1996).
Different as homophobic formulations make them out to be, though,
lesbian, heterosexual, bisexual, and other sexual identities among
women all take shape "within the structure of the institution of heterosexuality" (Meese 1992, 16). That circumstance means elite men have
more influence than anyone else over how women with this or that sexual identity are seen and what they are or are not entitled to do. In their
roles as advertising executives, songwriters, film and television direc-
tors, religious leaders, policymakers, medical researchers, social scientists, journalists, psychologists, novelists, and purveyors of pornography such men put the stamp of their fantasies on the public's images of
women as sexual beings of one sort or other.

Non-elite as well as elite men generally see us as "all alike" when
it comes to sexual violence or harassment. Rapists and sexual harassers
generally make no allowances for this or that sexual identity. Our bodies are theirs to control, and public space ultimately belongs to them.
Thus does the nineteenth-century doctrine of separate spheres—home

and hearth for women (private), business and politics for men (public)—continue asserting itself.

Another commonality women share regardless of their sexual identities is motherhood. Most women in every major sexual category have daughters and sons and thus face the challenge of balancing their own needs, including their sexual ones, with the needs of their children. Yet most people still assume mothers are heterosexual. In the process they reinforce the stereotype that sexual identity has some necessary connection with maternity. As many as 70 percent of American lesbians may be mothers (Grahn 1984, 141; also see Dunne 2000). Although that estimate seems high to us, it nonetheless points to a common circumstance rarely entering the popular imagination. Significantly, while lesbian motherhood gets radically marginalized, lesbian sexual imagery gets appropriated in publications like *Playboy*. Heterosexual mothers face a reverse erasure. Whereas lesbian motherhood often gets marginalized because of the homophobic reduction of lesbians to sexual creatures, heterosexual mothers often find their sexuality marginalized because of the patriarchal definition of them as sexless nurturers. Thus, when Demi Moore appeared nude and pregnant on the cover of *Vanity Fair*, the ensuing brouhaha was predictable.

Even though our sexual identities have been culturally constructed to ensure chasms and gaps among us where there need not be any, women's sexual identities *are* a source of significant diversity among us. For one thing, lesbians and bisexual women characteristically endure what Nancy Fraser (1998, 141) calls *injustices of recognition*. Routinely they are misrecognized as heterosexual or as stereotyped deviants on the sexual landscape. In effect, their misrecognition denies sexual-minority women "parity of participation in social life" (144).

For another thing, "lesbian existence is connected . . . in certain ways with female agency" (Hoagland 1988, 6), or female resourcefulness and independence. (On agency, revisit chapter 2.) While some lesbians do enjoy the benefits and incur the costs of heterosexual marriage, most currently live outside those boundaries (cf. Bradford and Ryan 1991, 150). Typically their lives "point toward an alternative to institutionalized relationships of domination" (Burch 1993, 119), as Gillian Dunne (1997) powerfully shows. Above all, they demonstrate the attainability of an equal partnership between two agents as an alternative to the one full partner and one junior partner institutionalized in heterosexual marriage. Needless to say, not all lesbian partnerships are equal any more than all heterosexual marriages are unequal. The odds do favor lesbians, however, partly because their sociosexual situation casts them more consistently as agents than do the situations typical among heterosexual women, especially those who are married or cohabiting.

In part, lesbians' heightened agency comes from having "grow[n] up into an identity that's unmentionable in any positive or helpful context" (Penelope 1992, 35). Moreover, gay women usually exercise more circumspection over their love lives than straight women can readily imagine. Whether or not to hold hands at the movies, whether or not to hint or say that one's "friend" is one's partner, whether or not to ask for a king-sized bed at the hotel, whether or not, whether or not. . . . Taken for grantedness is a rare achievement for lesbians facing public hostility in our society, a circumstance partly accounting for the appeal of neighborhoods heavily populated by lesbians and gay men. Heterosexual women, especially feminist ones, sometimes overtly reject the dictates of hegemonic heterosexuality and pay a great price for their sexual or marital deviance. As a general principle, one finds that the more one departs from the approved forms of heterosexuality, the more likely one is to experience contempt, rejection, or even violence.

Other differences between gay and straight women concern the emotional character of their long-term partnerships. Among lesbian couples it seems more likely that "body size, menopause, [and] emotional fragility are . . . waiting to be incorporated into daily moments of intimacy" (Nestle 1991, 181). The circumstances that sometimes become problems in heterosexual partnerships are likelier to occasion tenderness in lesbian partnerships. On average, for example, lesbians may experience menopause more positively. Among other things, menopausal lesbians find sex "as good as or better than ever" (Cole and Rothblum 1991, 193).

Also unlike heterosexual women, lesbians constitute the only sizable grouping in our society "whose lives are focused on women" (Penelope 1992, 80). Many nonhomosexual women are hard pressed to understand the everyday ramifications of not caring one iota how men *as men* see you, of not finding their attentions worth as much as the attentions of women, of not seeing the world and oneself through men's eyes. Needless to say, lesbians working with male supervisors or studying with male professors or loving their fathers and brothers take those people's judgments more or less into account *but not because they are men.*

Because of lesbians' women-centered lives, many people—themselves included sometimes—valorize them as vanguard feminists. As Susan Gubar notes:

The lesbian in contemporary representations may emerge as a paradigmatic female, a prototypical feminist, or a queer, but she frequently signals possibilities about women's humanity beyond the impoverished probabilities established by many heterosexual scripts. (2000, 67)

Such a stance can render the lesbian

a disrupter of heterosexuality, a presence standing outside the conventions of patriarchy, a hole in the fabric of gender dualism. She cannot be contained within these institutions; she exposes their gaps and contradictions; she signifies a radical absence. Her desire functions as excess within the heterosexual economy. (Zimmerman 1992, 4)

Bonnie Zimmerman goes on to note, "This is heady and romantic stuff." No sizable grouping of human beings comprises only heroic models for the rest of us. Also, to the extent that lesbians are seen as "unique[ly] position[ed] to deconstruct heterosexuality, patriarchy, [and] gender," their cultural commonality with other sociosexual groupings gets obscured. Heterosexual feminists, some bisexuals of both sexes, and some gay men also "stand in opposition to dominant structures" (7), and who is to say which group's opposition is the most consequential? Recognizing which individuals are substantially oppositional and which are status-quo supporters is the more important challenge, which, when met, allows for building strong social-justice alliances while respecting the stunning diversity within a grouping such as "lesbians" or "feminists."

Sometimes, though, one does want to assess a group's oppositional potential. One way of doing that is to show how its members' typical commitments challenge dominant structures. Among lesbians two such groupings are women identifying themselves as butches and femmes—"lesbian-specific genders, two of potentially many ways to be both a lesbian and a woman" (MacCowan 1992, 322; also see Crawley 2001). Butches' visible departures from straight femininity range from their styles of dress and body languages to their sexual tastes and interpersonal styles. Femmes, by contrast, fashion feminine appearances for themselves, but their feminine "look" is not meant to attract men. Femmes thus reject the fundamental purpose of "feminine" body regimens. Uninterested in attracting men or male attention but appearing "normally" feminine to many people, femmes routinely issue "the most powerful challenge to the hegemony of heterosexuality" (Roof 1991, 250). Femmes and butches are often "dumbfounded by heterosexual structures" to the point that whatever "role playing" they do "occurs with humor and a sly awareness of the meaning behind such patterns." They reveal "the utterly constructed status of the so-called heterosexual original. Thus, gay is to straight *not* as copy is to original, but . . . as copy is to copy" (Butler 1990, 31).

In other words, some heterosexual women play roles not unlike those some lesbians shape for themselves. Some negotiate their way in the world as a "steel magnolia," a woman (from *any* region) whose appearance and interpersonal style exude mainstream femininity. On the surface steel magnolias seem to accommodate men. Typically soft spoken and solicitous, steel magnolias exhibit enormous inner strength and visible assertiveness when circumstances demand it, especially when their loved ones are in pain or in need. *Steel Magnolias* dissects the contradictions and satisfactions of this mode of heterosexual femininity. Vivien Leigh played a steel magnolia in *Gone with the Wind*; more recently, Mary-Louise Parker played one in *Boys on the Side*. Such steel magnolias exhibit a femininity as deceptive as that of femmes, albeit serving different social functions.

Whatever role or interpersonal style one favors, heteropatriarchy makes femininity a challenge most women feel, at least during some periods of their lives, whether they are bisexual, heterosexual, gay, or otherwise sexually identified. Whatever their sexual identities, women largely adapt emphasized femininity to their values and situations. Thus, when we look around us for a flesh-and-blood example of *the* feminine woman, we find diverse variations on who she is *supposed* to be. We find people's historically and biographically specific ways of expressing themselves while more or less addressing cultural expectations.

Those who fail to see that heterosexual women develop practical variations of emphasized femininity fail to see that roles never literally determine people's behavior. Instead, we can identify roles because we see real people exhibiting more or less typical responses to whatever is more or less socially mandated in their routine social situations. Similarly, those who see butches and femmes as man-like and ultra-feminine, respectively, imply that certain attitudes and behaviors are properly monopolized by men or women. Such people treat (gender) roles as other than cultural—and thus arbitrary—constructions. Further, they tend not to see their own role playing, let alone its parallels to other people's role playing.

Whether or not butches and femmes constitute a lesbian vanguard, they do, like other lesbians, show that "women can survive without men, do not need to put up with men" (Hoagland 1988, 6). In and of itself their sexual orientation challenges the core assumptions of heteropatriarchy. So does female bisexuality. It commonly challenges not only "heterosexual supremacy" and "male supremacy" (Katz 1995, 153), but also the very idea of a gay/straight dichotomy. Neither bisexual women nor lesbians are a homogeneous grouping "shar[ing] the same desires, fantasies, and inclinations, nor . . . the same history" (Burch 1993, 36). Yet both sexual identities burst open the cultural space where feminine fulfillment is supposed to flow from masculine domination in the institution of heterosexuality. Is it not strange, they implicitly ask, that one never hears of "masculine fulfillment"? As the following section indicates, when discourses about love and sexuality and pleasure are cast in masculine terms, there is no need to say what the discourse itself quietly shouts.

Not Necessarily So

Elizabeth Kamarck Minnich suggests that "*all* talk of sex concerns the issue of power over women's bodies" (1990, 126). In connection with sex education and health clinics in public schools Michelle Fine has documented that circumstance. She identified four sexual discourses "articulated by various 'authorities'" whose ideas express "unacknowledged social ambivalence about heterosexuality" (1992b, 48). The first discourse is *sexuality as violence*, which predominates in mass-media attention to rape, wife battering, and the heterosexual abuse of children. This discourse speaks to American women's common sexual situation:

> a woman's relation to her sexuality is profoundly mediated by the [sex/gender] hierarchy in a way that breaks through any neat divisions between women constructed in terms of class or race, however influential these *also* are. Consider that sexual abuse and violence and harassment of all sorts affect all women, as threat all the time, as actuality with stunning frequency. (60)

Fine (1992b, 33) says sexuality as violence, which is the "most conservative" discourse about human sexuality, is often used to stymie sex education in the schools in favor of home-based versions. All the while, though, this discourse, like the other three, comprises some valid points. As Nicola Gavey observes, "To say that women often engage in unwanted sex with men is paradoxically both to state the obvious and to speak the unspeakable" (1993, 93). Women often face "heterosexual coercion." As one of Gavey's research participants illustrates, "part of [the] difficulty in having the language to say no was related to her fear that it may have no effect." Given that fear, the woman "instead of risking being raped, . . . did not say no; therefore not signalling her nonconsent prevented whatever followed from being construed as rape" (103). Such dense realities find the light of day, however obliquely and partially, in discourses centered on sexuality as violence. To the extent, though, that heterosexuality is the focus of most sex-education courses in our public schools, this discourse denies gay, lesbian, and bisexual students grounds for exploring their own stances toward and experiences of violent sexuality.

Moreover, sexuality-as-violence discourse often gives too much attention to the heterosexual stranger and too little to the heterosexual partner, family member, date, or coworker. In 1994, the U.S. Justice Department's Bureau of Justice Statistics summarized data on the rape of girls and teenage women in the District of Columbia as well as those eleven states that report rape victims' ages. About 50 percent of reported rapes in 1992 involved females under eighteen years of age even though they are "only 25 percent of the female population" in those jurisdictions (Reinharz 1994, A12). Significantly, "the younger the victim the more likely the attacker is a relative or acquaintance," with "one in five rape victims under age 12 . . . raped by her father." Such data usually get reported with no attention to the institutions of heterosexuality and the patriarchal family. Instead, sexualized violence routinely gets sensationalized in tandem with the most influential of the four sexual discourses, sexuality as victimization.

Sexuality as victimization is the discourse that predominates in the public schools where adolescent women are addressed "primarily as the potential victim of male sexuality" and thus "represent no subject in [their] own right." These women learn "to fear and defend against desire, and in this context there is little possibility of their developing a critique of gender or sexual arrangements" (32). Like other discourses casting women as victims, this one "may actually disable young women in their negotiations as sexual subjects" (48). It mutes their sense of agency, of options, of prospective pleasures; it undercuts their chances for sexually satisfying lives. It is bad enough for a discourse popular in our public schools to hold out the role of victim to female students. It is worse to deprive them of means for naming and exploring their desires. Fine reminds us that if sex education were designed primarily to prevent victimization but not to prevent exploration of desire, wouldn't there be more discussions of both the pleasures and the relatively fewer risks of disease or pregnancy associated with lesbian relationships and protected sexual intercourse or of the risk-free pleasures of masturbation and fantasy? Public education's concern for the female victim is revealed as deceptively thin when real victims are discredited and when nonvictimizing pleasures are silenced. (1992b, 48)

Sexuality as individual morality, though a traditional discourse, does "introduce explicit notions of sexual subjectivity for women" (Fine 1992b, 35). It thus allows for a measure of choice and the prospect of agency. To the extent, however, that it measures moral goodness by current codes of sexual propriety, this third discourse also holds women back. Characteristically, it casts them in the roles of the sexual watchdog or seductress—ambiguous moral grounds, to put it mildly. This discourse reflects the pervasive good girl/bad girl dichotomy, sometimes also called the madonna/whore dualism, that draws narrow sexual boundaries around women. These boundaries, which revolve around age and marital status, hem women into a heterosexual world where men generally initiate and largely control sexual encounters.

A *discourse of desire* is what the public schools seem insistent on keeping from young people. As "the site for identifying, civilizing, and containing that which is considered uncontrollable" (Fine 1992b, 33), public schools try to regulate, not illuminate, sexuality. Thus, a discourse of desire "remains a whisper" there. All the while this fourth discourse is essential to liberating women from the excesses of patriarchy and heterosexuality:

A genuine discourse of desire would invite adolescents to explore what feels good and bad, desirable and undesirable, grounded in experiences, needs and limits. Such a discourse would release females from a position of receptivity, enable an analysis of the dialectics of victimization and pleasure, and would pose female adolescents as subjects of sexuality, initiators as well as negotiators. (35–36)

Women of all ages could benefit from the diffusion of such a discourse. By now, "sexuality can be understood as a continuum of desire which is informed by socialization processes and sexual politics" (Faith 1993, 211). Too few women explore their sexual longings from that perspective, however. Modern history has "pathologize[d] [our] passion in favour of nurturance" and made "romance, not sex, . . . the key to

[our] sexuality" (Walkerdine 1990, 73, 98–99). Often, too, modernity has offered women a parasexuality based on glamour and visual allure rather than a sexuality based on desire and physical pleasure. Parasexuality "is sexuality that is deployed but contained, carefully channeled rather than fully discharged" (Bailey 1990, 148).

Even among feminists, sexual desire is far from unproblematic. *Third-wave feminists*, younger feminists making their presence felt after the wave of activism and legal reforms from the 1960s until about 1990, address that matter (Kaminer 1995). While some of their work strikes us as unduly critical of second-wave feminism—for example, Rene Denfeld's *The New Victorians* (1995) (see chapter 6)—their attention to women's sexual desires, agency, gratification, and autonomy is a step forward.

All the while, heterosexuality remains "the foundation of the social structure of male dominance" (Schacht and Atchison 1993, 121), and homosexuality and bisexuality are proscribed. Our desires are routinely problematic, then, whatever our sexual identity. Put differently, we cannot interrogate our sexual desires, let alone make them distinctly our own, without stepping outside male-centered—that is, institutionalized—heterosexuality. We also need to step beyond the heterocentrist (and monosexual) world so as to consider lesbian and bisexual desires that may inform our own sexuality. Sandra Lee Bartky implies that feminist theory promotes such movement, if only by showing that "male supremacy is perpetuated not only openly, through male domination of the major societal institutions, but more covertly, *through the manipulation of desire*" (1990, 50, emphasis added).

However manipulated our desires may be, they nevertheless demand at least a modicum of respect. As Shane Phelan insists, "The possibility that I am neurotic or unaware of my oppression or in other ways defective should not be allowed to function as a reason to ignore or denigrate my self-understandings and desires" (1989, 155–56). Phelan's is the voice of agency. Another such voice belongs to Judith Butler who argues for rendering identity, "in whatever form, permanently problematic" (1990, 128).

Feminism and Flux

Feminism has a great deal to do with identities. It challenges patriarchal mandates to identify ourselves largely in connection with men and children; it shifts the labels we put on ourselves, other people, and our bonds with one another; it asks who we are as human beings who happen to be women. At both the personal and the collective levels feminism also focuses on change. It demands greater opportunities for women to develop and express themselves; it pushes for economic, legal, religious, educational, and other changes capable of enhancing women's prospects; it advocates selfhood in community wherein growth emanates from the unpredictability of sharing and coordinating. Thus, feminism is suited to tackle identity as a problematic phenomenon. It is especially equipped to illuminate identity as a process, not a steady state. From feminist perspectives, identity is an ongoing outcome.

Feminists tend to see identity as a perpetual project, a dynamic opportunity, a lifelong venture. From this perspective identity is less something we have and more something we do. Instead of an emphasis on *being* mothers, the emphasis shifts to mothering; instead of an emphasis on *being* a citizen or an employee, the emphasis shifts to civic activities or working. Such shifts underscore identity as a series of performances whereby one lays claim to this or that attitude, value, or trait *for the time being.* Identity is thus contingent. Yet in everyday life it is often treated as a fairly fixed part of our being. In Butler's (1990) terms, people's identities often become a means of self-regulation and social control. They then measure our compliance with expectations rather than describe the regularities in our behavior over time. In the extreme, identities can feed off totalizing tendencies.

Totalizing conceptions delineate membership in a group using extremely few characteristics. Such conceptions promote either/or thinking; they are lowest-common-denominator stances that erase intragroup diversity in favor of a rough-hewn sameness; they often treat "the body as a predictor of who the person will be" (Gagne and Tewksbury 1998, 99); they are the seeds of stereotypes and the grounds of social control. Totalizing often narrows a group's members to one role, membership, or status, leaving little room for seeing them as anything more. Such conceptions are commonplace with reference to women in general, heterosexual women, and lesbians. They also surface with reference to butches and femmes. To regard butch and femme as identities is reasonable and meaningful; to totalize them as identities is, however, heterosexist stereotyping.

Seeing butch and femme as spin offs from the heterosexual world is at best naive. These identities "resignif[y] . . . hegemonic categories" (Butler 1990, 123). Clearly, "the butch-femme erotic system [does] not consistently follow the gender divisions of the dominant society."

Butches, for instance, are "associated with the giving of sexual pleasure, a service usually assumed to be 'feminine.'" In contrast, "the fem[me], although the more reactive partner, demand[s] and receive[s] sexual pleasure and in this sense might be considered the more self-concerned or even more 'selfish' partner" (Kennedy and Davis 1992, 73). One might, then, regard a butch as "a lesbian who finds herself attracted to and complemented by a lesbian more feminine than she, whether this butch be very or only slightly more masculine than feminine" (LaPorte 1992, 211). Again, however, mainstream notions of femininity and masculinity creep in. In the real world femininities and masculinities proliferate. The same is true of butch and femme. Often, though, people "don't ask butch-femme women who they are; [they] tell them" (Nestle 1992, 140). In that telling one hears a totalizing voice, dictating what or how one must be to be "one of those." Like other totalizing postures, this one fails to see that "the participants in butch and femme are often interchangeable, or actually much more similar than their Saturday-night garb indicates" (Grahn 1984, 155).

Such totalizing predictably targets lesbians in general. Most stereotypes leave no room whatsoever for the heterosexual experiences most of them appear to have had. For example, one-third to over half of lesbians have been heterosexually married (Bradford and Ryan 1991, 150; Sang 1991, 207). More generally, a number of women change their sexual identity at midlife or, at least, change the sexual identity they claim and are comfortable with (Charbonneau and Lander 1991). Philip Blumstein and Pepper Schwartz's (1983) study of American couples drove home the message now clear to many feminists, both gay and straight: our sexual identities, like our religious and political and other identities, exhibit both continuities and discontinuities; they are processes responsive to our changing world and our changing slants on the world.

As people who have often emigrated from heterosexual to homosexual locations on the social map, lesbians have a lot to tell us about the dynamics whereby sexual identities flow within channels that are far from rigid and narrow. They also reveal a lot about how "Each sexuality has to work itself out in its own language" and how "sex is always . . . about freedom and control" (Nestle 1992, 263). Finally, lesbians speak to the hazards of totalizing identities. To the extent that their sexuality comprises "a leave-taking of heterosexuality, a self-naming that contests the compulsory meanings of heterosexuality's *women* and *men*," they face the challenge of "keep[ing] the name of lesbian from becoming an equally compulsory category" as those it contests (Butler 1990, 127). How, in general, can we keep our definitions of this or that identity from becoming prejudgments about how actual individuals must make their choices and live their lives in order to claim that identity? Above all, we have to keep reminding ourselves that identity is a project, not a product, of selfhood.

Rubin offers some helpful preliminary principles:

> Individuals should be allowed to navigate their own trails through the possibilities, complexities, and difficulties of life. . . . Each strategy and each set of categories has its capabilities, accomplishments, and drawbacks. *None is perfect*, and *none works for everyone all the time.* (1992, 477, emphasis added)

From Judith Roof (1991, 250) comes the insight that a sexuality does not in and of itself equal an identity. From Butler comes the notion that "sexuality is to some degree always closeted, especially to the one who would express it through acts of self-disclosure" (1991, 25). Butler points to the substantially hidden character of sexuality. Precious as the freedom is that heterosexuals enjoy to publicize their affection, in the end our sexual knowledge of most people is shot through with holes.

Diana Fuss says a sexual identity is "less a matter of final discovery than perpetual reinvention" (1991, 6–7). Such a position bursts the "comforting myths of heroines and unfractured/unimpeachable identities"; it forces acknowledgment of the diversity bubbling beneath the "unified and heroic self-image" many people try to craft for themselves (Lewis 1992, 19, 20). It reminds us that identities are "always and necessarily riddled with contradictions and denials" (25). Lynda Hart sees identities as "prosthetic devices," which are "in a conflicted relationship with sexuality and its practices" (1998, 2).

Thus, no women's or other movement can forge political strength out of a totalizing identity. While "it is difficult to mobilise, analyse and agitate without falling back on the sense of a shared and uncontradictory identity" (Lewis 1992, 20), it is far from impossible. Phelan concludes that

> If we are to be free, we must learn to embrace paradox and confusion; in short we must embrace politics. Identity politics must be based, not only on identity, but on an appreciation for politics as the art of living together. Politics that ignore our identities . . . is useless; but non-negotiable identities will enslave us whether they are imposed from within or without. (1989, 170)

Besides, our "categories invariably leak. . . . We use them, and they use us." On those bases Rubin advises, "Instead of fighting for immaculate classifications and impenetrable boundaries, let us strive to maintain a community that understands diversity as a gift, sees anomalies as precious, and treats all basic principles with a hefty dose of skepticism" (1992, 477–78). Feminism demands no less. A feminist, after all, "does not presume to know anything else about a person on knowing that person's sex" (National Lesbian and Gay Survey 1992, 143). Unwilling to give totalizing significance to a person's gender, feminists are similarly bent on denying such significance to any other facet of an individual's social identity.

4

Feminist Methods

This chapter explores feminist methods of learning as well as feminist methods of collective action and personal growth. As we will see, feminists tend to experience life's web of connections in ways that make it impossible to separate learning from teaching, collective action from personal growth, and knowing from changing. Such attunement to connections derives from women's social positioning.

Drawing on Georg Simmel, Karl Mannheim, and other male forerunners, Patricia Hill Collins (1986) wrote a classic second-wave essay about how women's social positions affect our consciousness. Her work illustrates that feminists can appropriate established ideas and reshape them for our own purposes. Collins's essay, which centers on the "outsider within," also illustrates that few, if any, of us are wholly outsiders. Instead, we are more or less marginalized—more or less distant from the positions, formal and informal—where authority and clout are vested and respect is readily available. Overall, Collins reawakened interest in marginality as a source of creativity and insight. She portrayed institutional margins as sites of distinctive opportunities as well as obvious disadvantages. Although she does question "the continued efficacy of marginality as a space of radical openness," Collins (1998, 129) remains alert to its positive possibilities.

By focusing on outsiders-within Collins avoids romanticizing outsiders. Her position is like Diana Fuss's: "Any misplaced nostalgia for or romanticization of the outside as a privileged site of radicality immediately gives us away, for in order to idealize the outside we must already be, to some degree, comfortably entrenched on the inside" (1991, 5). Says Fuss: "Every outside is also an alongside." Each of us is privileged and disprivileged, then.

Put differently, our location on the social map is multidimensional. It grows out of our gender, sexual orientation, social class, ethnicity, race, age, and degree of ablebodiedness. Very few of us face consistent advantaging or disadvantaging along those axes. Instead we have "multiple and self-contradictory identities and social locations," and these knotted realities account for the "ways of knowing that feminisms have tended to favor" (Harding 1991, 103). Our complex positionings can provide nondualistic knowledge capable of subverting patriarchal hierarchies. Like Eli Clare, many of us become "activist[s] of multiple loyalties" (1999, 60).

Cognitive Deviance

Often feminist methods revolve around notions of subversion, transgression, and other challenges to the status quo. Susan Leigh Star (cited in Reinharz 1992, 241), for instance, emphasizes "strategic heresy." As Shulamit Reinharz notes, such heresy

> coincides with Catherine MacKinnon's "rational skepticism of handed-down doctrine," Marge DeVault's "strategic imprecision," Elisabeth Schuessler Fiorenza's "hermeneutics of suspicion," Judith Fetterley's "resistant reading," Celia Kitzinger's "resisting the discipline," and my own discussion of "feminist distrust." (1992, 242)

Reinharz goes on to say that the common ingredient among these stances is "deliberate cognitive deviance." Feminists methodically step out of cognitive line. In Helena Michie's (1992, 7) terms such deviance involves "defamiliarization"; in Peter L. Berger's (1963) terms it involves "debunking"; in Dorothy Smith's (1999, 43) terms it revolves around the "concealed standpoint . . . that is taken for granted" as part of institutionalized systems of dominance. Cognitive deviance requires suspending such taken-for-granted understandings so as to look at what underlies them, what holds them in place, whose interests they serve, and whose advantages and whose disadvantages they rationalize or even "naturalize."

Feminist methods thus revolve around what Sandra Harding (1991, 109) calls "traitorous identities." For the sake of transformation one takes up the work of betraying social structure. Sometimes a "communion of resistance" (Raymond 1987, 165), growing out of shared discontent and feminist solidarity, fuels such betrayal.

Another circumstance motivating betrayal of the status quo has to do with many employed women's experiences. During the work week many cross a divide that feeds their consciousness of social discontinuities. They face

> a daily chasm to be crossed, on the one side of which is this special . . . activity of thought, research, teaching, and administration, and on the other the world of localized activities oriented toward particular others, keeping things clean, managing somehow the house and household and the children—a world in which the particularities of persons in their full organic immediacy (feeding, cleaning up the vomit, changing the diapers) are inescapable. (Smith 1990, 20)

Smith's observations apply to females employed in information processing and other office-based enterprises. Because their paid work sharply diverges from their unpaid work in the home, they experience a disparity few men routinely face. These women daily taste the world's multiplicity—from its organic to its bureaucratic features, from its bodily exigencies to its cognitive demands, from its pragmatics to its theoretics. Commonly, their consciousness gets bifurcated (20). As a result, these women build up keener senses of diversity and paradox than do most white-collar men. Men's experiences involve fewer disjunctures as they move from home to workplace and back again.

Many blue-collar women, especially women of color, face fewer discontinuities but keener paradoxes as they move from home to workplace. In 1990, the "top occupations" for African American women included cook, janitor, and maid (7.8 percent of the African American female labor force); among Latina Americans, janitor, sewing machine operator, nurse's *aide*, and maid are heavily represented (11.5 percent of that labor force). Among Asian American and white American women the only comparable occupation was food serving (about 2.5 percent of each of those labor-force segments) (Reskin and Padavic 1994, 58–59). These occupations duplicate in the workplace what most women do in their homes.

Domestic workers, in particular, experience intense duplication. While their paid work and unpaid work involve the same activities, they involve few of the same meanings. As Mary Romero (1992) and others (Glenn 1986; Rafkin 1998; Rollins 1985) have shown, domestic workers face emotional and social paradoxes that few white-collar women routinely experience. Domestic workers often struggle against becoming "one of the family" and thus (more) exploitable; they continually have to protect the terms of their work agreements, lest they face increasing workloads over time; they have to negotiate an emotional terrain between familiarity and distance so as not to be cast in roles such as confidante, surrogate mom, or ingrate. Often their workplace struggles involve "the experience of *displaced mothering* or more generally, *displaced caretaking*" (Parrenas 2000, 576) that amounts, like their work in their own homes, to unremunerated nurturance of others. Imagine, for example, the real-life job of "helper for at least a few hours each day" to a unemployed ex-lawyer in the Boston area who now works in the home as a wife and mother of three, volunteers in the community, and "tries to schedule some heavy-duty exercise for herself at least once a day" (Blais 1998, 49). The prospective collision of their employers' material privilege and multiple options with their own material struggle and multiple constraints raises the specter of intensely mixed or negative feelings among these workers.

Women engaged in the social construction of knowledge—artists, researchers, journalists, pollsters, academicians—also face distinctive work-related paradoxes. The challenges to their consciousness lie mostly within the workplace rather than between work and home. Above all, these cultural workers "are bound in very real ways to the concept of culture upheld by those institutions" employing them. To some degree they necessarily "trade in the dominant currency." For many of these women, "What [they] in theory reject, [they] often unwittingly find [them]selves reconstituting in [their] own practice." Angelika Bammer goes on to say, for example, that feminist academics' "professional investment in the institutions of bourgeois culture is in tension with [their] political opposition to those same structures" (1991, 253).

Kathryn Pyne Addelson and Elizabeth Potter address the same circumstance:

> How are we to go about the business of dismantling the masters' houses while we are trying to get computers for the offices we have set up inside them? This dilemma faces all those who work for social change by boring from within institutions. To dismantle from within requires not only to locate ourselves within institutions but also to wield their forms of power and authority *for our purposes*. (1991, 271, emphasis added)

Addelson and Potter point to the incongruities of working "inside the system" one wants to change. Their observations point to the intense sense of *alternative* purpose one must cultivate in order to have any realistic hope of changing things "by boring from within" the system. To sustain that deviant sense, establishing a community of like-minded agents within the same institution is essential. Women's studies often serves that purpose for feminist agents in "higher" education.

Living in a neighborhood beyond the boundaries of bourgeois-life ways can also bolster one's sense of purpose, in part by providing a social chasm to cross between workplace and neighborhood that feeds one's sense of social multiplicities and thus of social alternatives. These and other social grounds are probably necessary for keeping sight of one's goals while laboring for change inside misbegotten institutions. Audre Lorde pointed to our standing need for social support: We "must constantly encourage ourselves and each other to attempt the heretical actions that our dreams imply" (1984, 38).

Learning, Teaching, Knowing

Wendy Luttrell summarizes the many claims "made about how women construct and value knowledge in ways that are relational, oriented more toward sustaining connection than achieving autonomy, and governed by interests to attend to others' needs" (1993, 506). No matter how much these claims hold up or not, the fact remains that "gender, power, knowledge, and the sense of self are closely intertwined" (Minnich 1990, 173). To know the ins and outs of one of these aspects of a person is to know, on average, a great deal about the other aspects. That gender is tangled up with power, knowledge, and a sense of self is thus a first principle of most *feminist epistemologies*, or women-centered theories of learning and knowing.

Another orienting principle is that communities build up around their members' efforts to "construct and share" knowledge (Scheman 1993, 203). If women *as women* are similarly (though not identically) situated in their families, at work, in school, at church or temple, and in public space, those commonalities give them practical knowledge in common that can render them a kind of community despite the differences among them. Women's cultural kindredness derives not only from how we are institutionally situated for similar outcomes but also from what we know as wives, secretaries, students, shoppers, or mothers. What is noteworthy with women is that our cultural kinship has often gone unremarked, probably because of our more manifest—though no more significant—cultural diversity.

A final orienting principle concerns "whose views we care about and why" (Scheman 1993, 29). We care not about the views of those who would keep us back or hold us down. We need not defend our goals or practices to those uninterested in or opposed to our progress in the world. We do, though, need awareness of the biases in our own as well as others' viewpoints. We need to ask ourselves continuously whose judgmental voices we are hearing, whose standards are at work, and whose interests are taking priority. With this and the other two orienting principles in mind, we are ready to explore further how women develop critical consciousness. As we turn to that project, let's be clear about the meaning of "higher education." Like Karlene Faith:

> By higher education [we] refer not only (and not necessarily) to college and/or university study, but to political education and consciousness-raising which expand one's understanding of social choices and lead to skills required to sustain one's equilibrium as well as livelihood. (1993, 318)

Feminist learning, teaching, and knowing overlap dramatically. Learning is often collaborative, a venture in teaching one another; knowing often entails learning the limits of one's knowing; teaching is learning in conjunction with others who translate insights from the terms of one life into the terms of another. Feminists are attuned to the social dimensions of learning, teaching, and knowing; they are in touch with how sharing shapes these undertakings.

Feminists also see connections between their methods of doing these things and their methods of research, advocacy, personal growth, family making, and much else. Their work rests on "an interactive relation between theory and practice, thinking and doing" (Morris 1997, 479). Theory thus serves as one kind of feminist practice—a *political* one, at that (Ebert 1996, 18; Hartsock 1998a, 1). As Nancy Hartsock states, "What is to count as truth, methods for obtaining it, criteria for evaluation . . . are profoundly influenced by extant power relations" (1998b, 406). Epistemological issues are thus political issues as well.

Feminists not only theorize about such issues but also grapple with them in practices such as teaching, community activism, research, and writing. Reinharz characterizes feminist research, for instance, in terms broadly applicable to feminist methods of doing other things. She says it "involves an ongoing criticism of nonfeminist scholarship"; it is often transdisciplinary; it "aims to create social change"; it "strives to represent human diversity"; it often "involves the researcher as a person" who aims to "develop special relations with the people studied" (1992, 240). All these characteristics, albeit in translated forms, apply to feminist methods of learning, advocating, and so forth. In our diverse roles, we maintain a critical consciousness of nonfeminists' claims about us; we refuse to respect established boundaries between disciplines such as anthropology and psychology or between roles like mother and citizen; we work hard to include all groupings of women within our purview; we reject the narrowness institutionally mandated for "students," "teachers," and "scholars," and acknowledge that our whole selves are implicated in all our roles; we try to be more to and with our collaborators and coparticipants than is commonly required or expected. Holism is a password into our cognitive community.

What, how, and why we learn also distinguishes feminists. For starters, we recognize that

> Accountability begins with tracing relations of privilege and penalty. It cannot proceed until we examine our complicity. Only then can we ask questions about how we are understanding differences and for what purposes. (Razack 1998, 170)

Thus, we ask how the "silence ghetto" that female students commonly inhabit in coeducational classrooms perpetuates females' restricted opportunities to participate in classroom discussions. What we study, then, is often gender itself. Also, feminist learning and teaching and knowing focus on women's experiences, outcomes, and prospects. Like multiculturalists, feminists largely agree that "an equal education for all women of all groups, as for the men of unprivileged groups, cannot be the same as the education that has been developed in a culture that is based on our exclusion" (Minnich 1990, 109). Thus, women's studies often serves as a primary method of developing critical consciousness together.

As a transdisciplinary, women-centered, feminist undertaking, women's studies counteracts our historical invisibility. As Elizabeth Minnich points out, "invisibility itself teaches something. It is not just an absence. Students who never hear of a woman philosopher have trouble believing in such a creature" (1990, 78). That situation only slightly improves when several of "us" show up on a course syllabus as "oddities in the dominant tradition, . . . always *a kind of human*, a kind of writer or whatever, and never the thing-itself" (79). To have courses centered on women's scientific, artistic, civic, and familial contributions, on our politics, our spirituality, and all else of interest to us is, therefore, essential to our education as human beings entitled to know our past history, current circumstances, and future prospects.

Many people would deny us that opportunity. Commonly they make three objections to women's studies—and to Chicana/o studies, African American studies, gay and lesbian studies, American Indian studies, and other curricula centered on historically excluded groups. First, opponents claim such curricula are separatist and divisive. What they fail to mention is that we have long had straight white elite men's studies. Commonly, we are required to study that minority's literature, history, philosophy, music, and politics—or apparently so—for our instructors often fail to mention a thinker's homosexuality. Moreover, "higher" education ensures some separatism by virtue of what women and men major in and how most fields of study have taken androcentric shape. Such separatism goes unrecognized, however, not only because it is strongly institutionalized but also because men are its main beneficiaries.

Second, as we will see in chapter 6, opponents of women's studies often deny its rigor. Peter Shaw, then a member of the advisory board overseeing the National Endowment for the Humanities, is illustrative. He unashamedly argues that "second-rate traditionalist scholarship is ultimately more valuable to the country than first-rate feminist works" (Burd 1994, A25). Shaw implies that "feminist scholarship" is an oxymoron. He seems blind to how "excellence" often gets conflated with "exclusivity"—so much so that "Calls for a new inclusiveness on any grounds, particularly when . . . couched in terms of equity, are heard as threatening to excellence-itself" (Minnich 1990, 98). About such foolishness Minnich says:

> We are not asking them to "lower" their standards when we suggest that an exclusive tradition needs, at the very least, augmenting. We are asking them not to apply particular standards as if they were universal, and to *take the time to learn something about new materials* before they rush to judge them by old, inappropriate standards. (99, emphasis added)

Minnich points to a widespread circumstance probably accounting for a lot of the resistance to women's studies. Many scholars intensely involved in their traditional work resent and resist spending time familiarizing themselves with feminist literary criticism, art history, social theory, musicology, and so forth.

Finally, opponents deride women's studies as politicizing the curriculum by espousing values. Such opponents seem unaware of the values they promote when teaching courses on the Bill of Rights, the Revolutionary War, human development, marketing research, or pedagogy. Publicly funded education rests on deeply entrenched values centering on literacy, rationality, upward social mobility, and democracy. At the classroom level the naiveté of opponents' criticism is more apparent:

> The feminist teacher who is calling into question accepted beliefs and attitudes about gender no more imposes her own meaning and culture upon the classroom than does the traditional teacher who wants students to accept authority and the status quo. (Weiler 1988, 136–37)

In women's studies classrooms, more is usually at issue than gender and women's experiences. Women's studies foregrounds those values "unacknowledged" in most curricula, namely, "empathy, nurturance, and sensitivity that support personal growth and development" (Luttrell 1993, 539). Feminists explore such values as practical options in the workplace and other institutional arenas beyond the "private" sphere. Overall, we aim to override "past prejudices and beliefs that derived from and justified the assignment of physical and daily maintenance work to lower-caste people." In the process we discover that

> we need to know much more about all that truly makes life possible and human, from mothering, to community-building, to surviving with imagination and dignity intact in deprivation and poverty, to working with our hands with art and integrity. (Minnich 1990, 118)

All the while, we remain cognizant that rigid, hierarchical roles in the classroom are inimical to making a community together. Thus, "teacher" and "student" gain in fluidity. For feminists, equality prevails as an insistent ideal. Yet feminist communities often eschew equality as sameness. The equality capable of yielding common ground makes of diversity not "exclusive categories" but different "types, modalities, styles of existence around which the particular experiences of particular women vary. We can discover as much about our experience by saying 'It is not like that for me' in response to another woman's expression as by saying 'Yes, I feel that too'" (Young 1990, 17).

As Smith states, "for any set of actual events, there is always more than one version that can be treated as what has happened, even within a . . . cultural community" (1990, 24). The multiplicity of women's voices, even when they are telling "different" versions of the same story, energizes feminist communities.

Women's studies commonly grapples with diversity by giving care and compassion as much priority as rights and justice. Fairly often, "We indulge our compassion, give it room to expand and make its demands upon us. Always it will lead us to an internal truth; always it will lead us toward greater connectedness" (Hart 1989, 112). In feminist communities and women's studies classrooms, compassionate involvements can temper "facts" and institutionalized "knowledge" with "a recognition of the value of [our] own voices" (Weiler 1988, 149). Compassion also helps us simultaneously see both "sameness" and "differences" among us.

Besides what and how we share with one another, why we share unites us. We share so as "to begin to change who and how we are in the world" (Minnich 1990, 80). We join hands in "the constant process of identity definition and development" (79). We share to empower ourselves as agents wanting not only to take charge of our own lives but also to transform the world we make and share in common. Our methods are meant, then, to move ourselves and the world forward.

Feminist Maxims

Before turning to feminist strategies of making knowledge, let us consider some of the practical knowledge feminists garner from pursuing all manner of changes in themselves, their homes, their communities, and their societies. The lessons they learn promote survival and enhance agency.

First, *pay close attention to names*. The labels people attach to themselves, other people, and their experiences are consequential and rarely neutral. Consider *"date* rape" or "fore*play*." Also consider "surrogate mother" to name "the woman whose egg and/or womb is involved . . . , while the man who donated but did not implant sperm is called a 'father'" (Minnich 1990, 125). Think about "nature." Jane Flax observes, "More and more the natural ceases to exist as the opposite of the cultural or social. Nature becomes the object and product of human action; it loses its independent existence" (1990, 50). How about the "common good"? It begins "unravel[ing] once the diverse needs and entitlements of those placed outside the 'deserving' community are revealed" (Fine 1992a, 113).

Some labels are inherently suspicious, especially those pointing to "deficiency" or "difference." About girls' "math deficiencies," for instance, Valerie Walkerdine notes that "constantly and continually, girls have to be proved to fail or to be inferior at mathematics, despite the extreme ambiguity of the evidence" (1990, 61, 62). She says that were girls found to perform the same as or equivalent to boys, "a constant threat to sexual difference and to the existence of 'man' as supreme and omnipotent mathematician" would surface. Walkerdine thus indicates how commonplace labels function as terms of difference. "Femininity" and "masculinity" are two such names. One pinpoints deficiency and difference; the other, plenitude and typicality.

Such names are far from symmetrical. Minnich (1990, 70, 71) says they are not even dualistic or oppositional; rather they constitute a "hierarchical monism." "Male" and "female" are "related to each other as inclusive term to subkind, as norm to deviant, as ideal to inferior, as thing-itself to Other." To that extent paired labels invite scrutiny. Often they are the terms of social inequalities "justified" on the basis of supposed group differences.

Similarly in need of scrutiny are singular terms. Where paired terms point to supposed differences *between* groups, singular terms often imply uniformity or sameness *within* groups. "Femininity" is suspicious in its very singularity. Don't most Americans take Oprah Winfrey to be a feminine individual? Don't most also take Sharon Stone to be one? "Femininity" refers not to a single style of being, but to those traits and behaviors deemed necessary or appropriate for females of a given age, social class, race, ethnicity, degree of ablebodiedness, and so forth. Femininities are much in evidence, but the pluralized name strikes many people as contrived. Its singular form, like "woman" or "mother," has monolithic cultural force, which dims awareness of women's diversity and thus of the culturally contingent character of femininity. The singular name stifles awareness of alternatives, then.

Second, *be wary of facts*. In no way can they speak for themselves. We should bristle whenever we hear self-serving usages such as "The fact of the matter is . . ." or "As the facts show. . . ." The facts show things only at the interpretive behest of the person invoking them. *In fact*, facts are constructions. They are real, to be sure, but they are neither self-generating nor self-evident. As Smith states, "The actual events are not facts. It is the use of proper procedure for categorizing events which transforms them into facts" (1990, 27).

Third, *question objectivity*. Claims to objectivity are often used to "forc[e] unanimity" (Minnich 1990, 158) or preclude discussion. Such claims, particularly alongside charges about the "subjectivity" of those who see things another way, often involve intellectual bullying. Reconsider the claims about girls lagging behind boys in mathematical achievement. Such claims seem to rest on objective (2 + 2 = 4, does it not?) measures of individuals' abilities to solve mathematical problems. Yet the claim to objectivity can only be mild-mannered in the end, and even then it is suspect. Word problems in mathematics are often stated in biased narratives where boys on average feel more at home. Those same test-takers have on average gotten more encouragement and attention from their math teachers and have as a result not only greater average aptitude, but also greater confidence. Also, boys are likelier to anticipate working in fields where mathematics is central. Then, too, one must bear in mind that the girl–boy difference in the math arena rests only on group averages that fail to show up in all societies. So whatever objectivity is at work is at best limited.

"Objectivity" is a philosophic, scientific, and legal ideal, not an attainable absolute capable of sealing this or that account as the only defensible, tenable, or valid one. Those who appeal to the objectivity of their findings or judgments see themselves as occupying no "specific place at all." The "objective position" functions as a "nonplace" where "one gets to take the specifics of one's real place as irrelevant. It used to be God's place; now it is the scientist's" (Scheman 1993, 161). All the while, the objective position remains a position of domination.

Fourth, *look for lived experiences*. Too often in this world filled with documents, notes, databases, files, records, and texts of all sorts, we treat *represented* persons as direct stand-ins for flesh-and-blood people living their lives unmediated by texts. We forget that "There is an actual subject prior to the subject constituted in the text" (Smith 1990, 5). The images circulated by mass advertisers, fashion magazines, popular movies and television programs, advice columnists, and other makers of texts often take hold of consciousness with a grip as strong as that of lived realities. When we watch, read, listen, and otherwise engage with texts, we should continually look for evidence of people's lived experiences—evidence of the embodied actualities of their lives. Some critical consciousness is usually a good idea, if only reminders that airbrushed pictures or media mothers stand at a far remove from the lived experiences of people like you, us, or even the women involved in the representations.

Fifth, *question credentials*. Often degrees, licenses, certifications, awards, and other credentials get stretched way beyond the arenas where they presumably have merit and meaning. Celebrity endorsements of consumer products and political candidates are classic examples. Equally commonplace but less noticeable are recommendations, judgments, and other pronouncements by "experts" gesticulating about matters unrelated to or way beyond their professional ken. The "halo effect" of expertise is, to say the least, considerable. When a professor lambastes the president or argues against gay, lesbian, and bisexual rights in an opinion piece for the local newspaper, few people see that her professorial status is largely irrelevant if her field is engineering or marketing. Her Ph.D. does not, in other words, make her *opinions* on those matters more valid or credible than other readers' *opinions*. Yet in our society all kinds of "epistemic authority" are handed over to people whose lived experiences would seem not to have equipped them to offer practical advice, let alone wisdom or profundity. Naomi Scheman observes, for example, that

> modern epistemic authority has attached to those who did minimal physical labor, who neither bore nor reared their own children, grew or cooked their own food, built or maintained their own homes, produced or cleaned their own clothing, nor nursed the illnesses or eased the deaths of those close to them. (1993, 196)

Of such authority we should, at the very least, be suspicious.

Finally, *reformulate*. Reword the assertions held out to you; reorient the questions others pose and the facts they present. Instead of accepting as adequate a question about how prostitution and pornography affect the perceptions and treatment of women in our society, ask "What effect does society's perception of women have on prostitution and pornography?" (Arrington 1987, 173). Notice formulations such as "one-half to two-thirds of women who live with a man will be beaten." They skew the picture by saying only indirectly what needs saying forthrightly, namely, what a high percentage of men living with women physically abuse them (Hoagland 1988, 18).

All these feminist maxims "demystify . . . power and hierarchy" (Minnich 1990, 180–81). They keep us alert to how dominant people maintain their grip on an unfair share of authority, clout, respect, and status. These maxims cultivate *critical consciousness*, that is, consciousness attuned to the socially constructed injustices that keep many human beings from enjoying their rights and advancing their interests on an even playing field.

Passionate Scholarship

Feminists who make knowledge often pursue "passionate scholarship." Their work "is inspired neither by a desire to dominate, to control, to possess certainty, nor by external rewards"; it involves individuals "pursuing their own questions" (Minnich 1990, 163). Passionate scholarship presupposes a pressing interest in what one studies. It builds bridges between theory and practice, findings and applications, classrooms and research sites.

Beyond their proclivity for passionate scholarship, feminist makers of knowledge share some other dispositions. First, they typically launch their work from their own experiences, and they acknowledge that circumstance. (See Naples with Clark [1996] for a particularly powerful example.) Second, they focus on people's lived experiences and everyday lives more than other researchers. Third, they aim to illuminate and enhance women's (and other oppressed groups') positions and challenge groups with excessive power over that oppress other people, especially women. When they build up knowledge, then, feminists include their whole, biographically unique selves in conscious ways, and they attune themselves to the wholeness of others. Such investigators know that "Personal evidence *is* evidence" (Behar 1994, B2). Inclined to write in the first-person singular and plural (cf. Behar 1994), feminists do their utmost to keep themselves and other *actual* people at the center of their attention. They avoid falsifying people's experiences by using a vocabulary, voice, and level of abstraction that minimize the gap between the text and its subject matter. Further, feminists reject the cognitive imperialism that divides "researchers" from "subjects."

Feminists use methods that "are both rooted in the mainstream disciplines and represent a protest against them." They use their "power to name or rename" while "eschewing standardization in format" (Reinharz 1992, 22). Their interests in lived experiences and holistic portrayals not only sensitize them to social multiplicities but also dispose them toward using "multiple methods in a single study," which is called *triangulation* (197). Feminist researchers are often drawn to some version of what Sherene Razack calls the "methodology of storytelling" (1998, 42).

Feminist investigators often focus on "how a given version is authorized as that version which can be treated by others as what has happened" (Smith 1990, 24–25). Whose story gets heard as "true"? That query leads to feminist critiques of nonfeminist studies, often with dramatic results. Michelle Fine and Susan Merle Gordon (1992, 6) found, for instance, that prestigious journals in psychology are singularly disinclined to publish studies about how social class, gender, sexual orientation, race, or "disability" shape people's experiences. Moreover, they found that in 1980 about 70 percent of the studies in those journals had been done in laboratories; by 1985, that had risen to almost 80 percent. For the same two years, three-quarters and four-fifths, respectively, of the social-psychological studies had "used" students as subjects (10–11). Thus, generalizations about how *people* act under given circumstances or how their attitudes change or what motivates them rest heavily on findings about white, middle-class people whose race and class are usually not taken into systematic account. Such biases mean that some groups' experiences get virtually no attention. Worse yet, privileged groups' experiences serve as a gauge for other groups.

Actually, the problems run even deeper. Most nonfeminist research in the social and behavioral sciences only slightly concerns *anyone's* lived experiences. Rather, the predominant concern is with their quantifiable responses to mild shocks, multipage questionnaires, formal interviews, or small-group experiments. What cannot be measured in anticipation of statistical manipulation and mathematical modeling gets discounted as unimportant or unamenable to "rigorous" investigation. Feminist researchers face prodigious challenges as they counteract such biases about what is "scientific."

Yet it is easy to "exaggerate the extent to which, in its narrowest, most easily caricatured sense, [the scientific method] dominates approaches to research" (Randall 1994, 13). Without feminist or related training, many people overestimate just how "scientific" the social sciences are. What, for instance, is scientific about studies of the aforementioned type where no control is exercised over consequential variables such as race and sexual orientation *and* where they are not taken into systematic account? When such studies conclude with generalizations about human behavior, human needs, human motivation, and human development, nothing remotely scientific has eventuated. Quite the opposite: The extrapolations required for generalizing about "people" on the basis of introductory psychology students' responses in a small-group experiment overwhelm the best of scientific imaginations. Worse yet, "faulty generalization leads to circular reasoning in which the *sources* of standards, justifications, interpretations reappear as *examples* of that which is best, most easily justified, most richly interpreted by those standards" (Minnich 1990, 84). Thereby the white, middle-class folks serving as the main source of systematic psychological data later reemerge in psychologists' models as exemplars of autonomy, self-esteem, and the ability to defer gratification.

Rigor concerns not one's method(s) per se but the care one takes to pay proper respects to that method's limitations. Were such care routinely taken and were study after study completed of a given topic of inquiry, rigorous findings would surely result. Typically, however, such care is the exception rather than the rule.

Consider a method of research that quantitative researchers have largely discredited over the past several generations. The *case study* is an intensive rather than extensive method that requires looking in great detail from many angles at one instance of a phenomenon. The topic of inquiry might be becoming a single teenage mother, experiencing menopause, coming out to one's family and friends as a lesbian, or completing an apprenticeship in one of the trades. Together, the researcher and the person(s) whose experiences focus her work construct a coherent account that is as comprehensive and as true to the individual's lived experiences as possible. Not surprisingly, well-done case studies require a lot of time, emotional energy, and painstaking effort. That didn't keep "Female sociologists in Chicago connected with Jane Addams and Hull House [from] carr[ying] out many case studies at the turn of the century" (Reinharz 1992, 166). Mary Abby van Keek was prominent among them; her specialty was studies of women in the trades. More recently, Jane Mansbridge (1986, 165) did a case study of how the Equal Rights Amendment was defeated.

Because it favors depth over breadth and a microscopic over a telescopic stance, a case study usually produces dense, rich findings. Conceivably, a dozen or so carefully executed case studies of the same phenomenon could yield valid, reliable findings capable of advancing whatever "science" is under way. Unfortunately, funding such research—unfashionable as it is in the world of high-stakes grants—is difficult. Moreover, the time required for first-rate case studies often exceeds the time allotted for gaining tenure in a faculty position.

Case studies and other methods attractive to feminist investigators nevertheless seem to be gaining credibility. Thanks in large measure to feminists' efforts, more people now appreciate that "science" gets invoked with reference to many scientifically dubious practices and that its practitioners can never be wholly disinterested. "In practice," as Denise Frechet emphasizes, "scientists are always making choices— and denying the interests, passions, and unconscious motives involved in those choices" (1991, 213).

By contrast, feminist researchers often take pride in letting their passions find meaningful expression in their work. They strive to tap into their diverse motives enough to discipline them for the sake of valid insights into the lived experiences inspiring their work. Such investigators refuse to act as cognitive imperialists or elitists. Indeed they routinely scrutinize their work for signs of being "reductionist, totalizing, inadequately nuanced, valorizing of gender difference, unconsciously racist, and elitist" (Bordo 1990, 135). Determined to promote social justice, feminist researchers are bent on disclosing realities that nonfeminist scholars have ignored or misstudied. Their work takes a characteristic—and methodologically important—form:

> We may not rewrite the other's world or impose upon it a conceptual framework that extracts from it what fits with ours. Their realities, their varieties of experience, must be an unconditional datum. (Smith 1990, 25)

Finally, when they theorize, feminists not only critically dissect theory-as-usual (Sprague 1997), but also incline toward bridging the theory/practice divide by continually asking, "Does this social theory move people to struggle?" (Collins 1998, 243). By now, then, feminists have a significant "history of producing and rearticulating struggle concepts," such as "sexual politics" and "sexual harassment" (Ebert 1996, 252).

The Personal Remains Political

Feminists' efforts to transform society and culture and their efforts to promote their own and other women's growth and development are inseparable. As they challenge the status quo, feminists are aware that they advance their own development as individuals in community. At the same time they recognize that efforts to change oneself often require challenging the social and cultural limits one faces as a lesbian of color, a working-class single mother, an office worker or engineer, or a teenager seeking an abortion. To grow and expand, to test the limits of our power to and power with, to feel the full sweep of our energies and imaginations often requires pushing against the boundaries meant to define who we are and where we should stay put. The more substantial the growth we seek, the more we have to resist other people's expectations and demands. The more we want to grow, the more we also have to grapple with the norms, values, and attitudes manifested in mass advertising, school curricula, and weekly worship services. To grow as a feminist—that is, to grow as a proud, strong woman in community—means to grow as a social change agent, then.

The method for progressing along both fronts—the cultural and the personal, the macro and the micro, the social and the psychological—requires a "pragmatic eclecticism" that "turn[s] us all into tinkerers, handy-people, picking up tools to solve problems, discarding them as we see fit" (Hanssen 2001, 85). Methods of transformation broadly fall into two overlapping categories shaped by individual women's circumstances and style. Each method is highly flexible and fluid: bell hooks calls the first method "talking back"; Gloria Steinem calls the other method "outrageous acts." Talking back, a fairly continual enterprise in the lives of feminists, is a style of interacting. By contrast, outrageous acts comprise distinct projects aimed at promoting transformation. Such acts may or may not be daily undertakings.

As hooks (1989) delineates it, *talking back* means "interacting as an equal with a person in authority." The other person may be a supervisor, coach, or professor of either sex. In a patriarchal society the other person can be just about any man regardless of how the lines of formal authority position him. Talking back means talking *with* that authority figure. It means refusing to be a passive recipient of that person's monologue; it means rejecting the habit of being a "good listener" who almost never gets her full turn to talk; it means jumping out of the "silence ghetto," where many women bite their tongues or bide their time. Talking back can range from "daring to disagree" to just "having an opinion" that gets registered in one fashion or other.

As hooks observes, black women's "struggle has not been to emerge from silence into speech but to change the nature and direction of our speech, to make a speech that compels listeners, one that is heard" (1989, 6). In varying degrees most women face the challenge of making themselves heard, at least in certain types of situations. Talking back in order to meet that challenge means forswearing "talk that [is] in itself a silence"; it means setting aside "right speech" in favor of truthful talk; it means abandoning "talk which identifies us as uncommitted, as lacking in critical consciousness, which signifies a condition of oppression and exploitation" (7, 8, 9). We are reminded by hooks that our speech, like our bodies, can be emblematic of our complicity with patriarchal practices. It can promote our silencing or discrediting rather than extend our voices so that people seriously listen to us.

Talking back belongs to a repertoire of transformative practices whereby "Oppressed people resist by identifying themselves as subjects, by defining their reality, shaping their new identity, naming their history, telling their story" (hooks 1989, 43). Talking back means not finding but *making* one's voice. It means treating language as "a place of struggle" where "we create the oppositional discourse, the liberatory voice" (28, 29) capable of serving self and community by promoting dialogue, "the sharing of speech and recognition" (6). Because a "liberatory voice will necessarily confront, disturb, demand that listeners even alter ways of hearing and being" (16), people often assume that such a voice presupposes confidence and courage. To some extent claiming one's voice does require those characteristics, but for the most part talking back *develops* confidence and courage. Just as importantly, the more we talk back, the more we find that some people like and accept us even after finding out that we have strong convictions and firm values. The more we talk back, the more we see that transformational activities advance our personhood in unanticipated, fulfilling ways. Such activities, hooks concludes, "can be healing, can protect us from dehumanization and despair" (8). They make "new life and new growth possible" (9).

"Women and men need to know what is on the other side of the pain experienced in politicization." We need to know how our lives become "fuller and richer as we change and grow politically" (hooks 1989, 26). Too often the corporate media focus on the downside of resistance to domination, favoring negative portrayals of women who refuse to stay in their institutionally assigned, culturally mandated positions. Commonly portrayed as "strident" and "opinionated," such women are seldom seen hugging their children, laughing with their partners, or having coffee with friends. We can counteract those portrayals by looking at the passionate, engaged women around us. By and large the energetic and energizing, the inspired and inspiring women in our midst are the very women hooks describes as "talking back." They show us how exhilarating as well as exhausting such efforts can be. Usually, they also show us that talking back is anchored in a community where they find sustenance, encouragement, and good humor. There they find a safe place where they

> can draw breath, rest from persecution or harassment, bear witness, lick [their] wounds, feel compassion and love around [them]. . . . Safety in this sense implies a place to gather our forces, a place to move from, not a destination. (Rich 1986, 206)

What women gain from their communities is, however, only one side of the story of talking back and resisting domination. By "improving" themselves, hooks says, they are "heightening the freedom and well-being of [their] community" (see Chua 1994, 27). Strengthening themselves, they strengthen their communities; strengthening their communities, they strengthen their safety net and support system.

Through political wisdom, hooks raises two questions that plague activists, advocates, and other agents of social change:

> How do you balance that commitment to social change where you don't just burn out and give yourself over to an almost negative ethic of sacrifice? How do you create inner harmony and balance that allows you to sacrifice when necessary and to withhold when necessary? (see Chua 1994, 27)

She implies that notions about the public and the private influence our capacity to achieve balance and remain effective agents of change, and emphasizes that the public/private dichotomy is "deeply connected . . . to ongoing practices of domination." In our "private" spaces, she says, "we are often most wounded, hurt, dehumanized; there . . . our selves are most taken away, terrorized, and broken" (hooks 1989, 2). If good manners, proper femininity, discretion, or propriety mandate silence about what is "private," we are left to grapple with the structures of domination individualistically and, therefore, ineffectually. Thus, hooks insists that "much that is private . . . must be openly shared, if we are to heal our wounds (hurts caused by domination and exploitation and oppression), if we are to recover and realize ourselves" (1989, 3).

Yet we need not become soul-baring, confession-ridden individuals. We need only to utter the once unutterable that, left unsaid, chains consciousness and undermines community. The choice to share is often the optimal one. Openness can lay bare the dense connections between the personal and the political. Yet the culture insistent on our substantial, systematic silencing is the same culture that often mandates lying rather than honesty for women. As Adrienne Rich observes, women are often taught that our "own truths are not good enough" (1980, 191).

Besides talking back, feminist methods often include outrageous acts that test the limits of our personal courage and creativity while challenging oppressive practices. As Steinem (1984) describes them, outrageous acts entail border crossing or boundary breaking, small or large scale. Observably, they challenge restrictions on our behavior, protest oppressive practices, or burst limits on our agency and growth. Such acts might include telling a male classmate—twice, if necessary—"I am not finished yet; don't interrupt me." They might include initiating a date with a person who is attractive to you, refusing to be informed about the sex of the baby you are going to have in five months, or talking with your parents about how they unduly feminize your daughter. Subjectively, what makes a given act outrageous is its agent's experience of it as a bold, risky, path-breaking, or liberating thing to do. Thus, what might be outrageous for me to do might be mild-mannered or even routine for you and vice versa.

Steinem advocates some outrageous acts as part of every feminist's regimen. Among them are writing five letters a week to protest or to praise; devoting 10 percent of our incomes to social-justice causes; demonstrating once a month or going to a consciousness-raising group weekly to reenergize ourselves; and putting our beliefs into daily practice. Steinem also emphasizes the need for outrageous group actions. She says that outrageous acts of all kinds are crucial to our well-being insofar as "We are in [feminism] for life—and for our lives" (Steinem 1993).

More recently, Anndee Hochman has written *Everyday Acts and Small Subversions: Women Reinventing Family, Community and Home.* Treating family as a "subversive refuge" not unlike Rich's "safe" place, Hochman (1994, v, vi) looks at women "trying to fashion lives of integrity and joy" not only by changing "their own relationships, the contours of their days," but also by "revising a centuries-old conversation about family." In such women's lives one finds "quiet experiments, each discovery in a separate room, each setback and triumph unknown by the experimenters next door." But, says Hochman, "Silence murders possibilities." Sooner or later and always in community, the experimenters—bold, outrageous, unafraid—share their stories. In the telling they gain strength; in the telling the world gets reshaped, however slightly, in the image of feminist visions. As Hochman tells her own story, feminist visions take palpable, potent form:

> My life descends not only from Ethel, Rose, Sarah, and Gloria but from Ruth and Naomi, Charlotte Perkins Gilman and Harriet Tubman, Frieda Kahlo and Emma Goldman, Zora Neale Hurston, Virginia Woolf and thousands of unknown others. As I listen to the stories of women's small subversions, everyday acts, I can hear these ancestors whispering encouragement. I take a breath and add my voice to the ongoing collection. (242–43)

5

Differences

We live in an age when group differences, both supposed and actual, figure prominently in politics, culture, education, and the workplace. However we come to terms with them, we need to keep in mind that *socially and politically consequential differences* revolve around characteristics Others presumably fail to have in common with elite males. We who are "different" are not the primary promulgators of difference. Our "differences" have been foisted upon us and then used to justify our subordination with a rhetoric emphasizing those "differences." Thus, it nearly always makes sense to ask, Different from whom or what? For whom is this difference pertinent or beneficial?

In a fair and reasonable world "difference" presupposes sameness, similarity, or common ground. To say F differs from G is to imply meaningful grounds for contrasting them. Once one knows those grounds, one knows some commonality between F and G. Grasping that commonality is usually as important to understanding F, G, and their relationship as is grasping their dissimilarity. Among human beings, grasping both similarities and differences across groups is essential to ethical maturity. Consciousness of both convergences and divergences requires resisting either/or categories that exaggerate group differences. Such resistance often evolves out of *postmodernism* (see chapter 2). Postmodernists point to the falsification inherent in either/or thinking, which overemphasizes the stability and homogeneity of social realities and cultural categories. As Seyla Benhabib illustrates, a postmodernist sensibility stamped the 1990s:

> If *fragmentation* was the code word of the 80s, *hybridity* is the code word of the 90s; if *incommensurability* was a master term for the 80s, *interstitiality* is one for the 90s; if the *clash of cultures* was the horizon

of the 80s, *multiculturalism* and *polyglotism* are the frameworks of the 90s. (1999, 336)

Without a postmodernist sensibility we are hard pressed to undo either/or formulations. Difference, in other terms, cannot be put in its place without the sort of consciousness associated with postmodernism.

Among feminists, "difference" has to do with the diversity among us, on the one hand, and with how we are contrasted with men, on the other hand. In practical terms these two measures of difference translate into issues of inclusiveness and identity. Our diversity raises questions about how inclusive our theories and politics are; our dissimilarities to men raise questions about whether our gender rests on innate or cultural grounds (cf. DiQuinzio 1993, 1).

In *Black Feminist Thought*, Patricia Hill Collins illustrates these matters. Collins acknowledges that in her book, she "deliberately decided to minimize the obvious heterogeneity among African-American women created by differences in experience because [she] had to attend to the political context in which [she] was writing" (1992, 518). Her decision exudes postmodernist irony. Women of color have often and justifiably complained about white women's monopoly of academic feminist theory and their disposition to extrapolate from their own experiences to other women's experiences (Collins 1991; hooks 1984; Lorde 1984). Such critiques commonly call for affirmative attention to diversity. For a prominent African American feminist like Collins to "minimize the obvious heterogeneity" among African American women, then, is both ironic and understandable.

More straightforwardly than most scholars, Collins explains that "The choice of whether to stress a unitary standpoint or to examine heterogeneity within that standpoint hinges less on the relative truth of each approach and more on the goals and political position of the scholar advancing the argument." She intended her book "to push the diversity/difference debate in the direction of taking difference seriously." Yet presenting black feminist thought "as a legitimate discourse" distinct from white feminist thought meant portraying African American feminists as more homogeneous than they are. In the aftermath of her authorship Collins sees "the difficulty we all face in investigating alternative worldviews in the intellectual and political context created by the dominant discourse" (1991, 518, 519).

Yet as we broach the matter of diversity among us, we must also remember that

> Too relentless a focus on historical heterogeneity . . . can obscure the transhistorical hierarchical patterns of white, male privilege that have informed the development of Western intellectual, legal, and political traditions. . . . Contemporary feminism, like many other social movements arising in the 1960s, developed out of the recognition that to live in our culture is not . . . to participate equally in some free play of individual diversity. (Bordo 1993, 234)

To repeat, our differences are socially constructed and maintained to a substantial degree. They are the sites of division among us, not because of their inherent meanings. Instead, our differences divide us foremost because of their supreme utility to those who would keep us from rebelling together against our subordination.

Multipolarity and Common Ground

Mere tolerance of diversity is insufficient among people aiming to change the world together. Making common cause with one another demands making spacious room for our different experiences, perspectives, and priorities. Overcoming institutionalized beliefs about race, sexual orientation, ethnicity, age, social class, and other circumstances that differentiate us is, to say the least, a mammoth challenge. Going against the grain of our culture is, though, what feminisms are all about. Feminists see that sexism, classism, racism, and other varieties of elitism cost high-status white males little, while costing the rest of us a great deal indeed. Looked at through the lens of elitism, our differences begin to look like a measure of our false consciousness—a measure of how much heteropatriarchal culture still grips our consciousness.

Much of our diversity comes down to one or several socially constructed ways we have been differentiated from one another *as subordinate members of society*. Most of us are subordinated in multiple ways. Few of us are high-earning, heterosexual, white, able-bodied, relatively young women who by mainstream standards "have it all" or "are going places." Thus, when someone contrasts white with black feminists or lesbian with heterosexual feminists, we should bristle with anxiety or dismay. Are trade-union white feminists being contrasted with academic black feminists? Are professional, midlife, white feminists who participated in the black civil rights movement being contrasted with professional, young-adult, black feminists who have no firsthand memories of

Martin Luther King Jr.'s murder, let alone of sit-ins, marches, and holding cells in county jails? Just who is being contrasted with whom when
either/or boundaries are drawn among us? In what ways are members
of the two groupings similar, and whose interests get served by obfus-
cating those similarities with either/or notions? Usually, a totalizing (see
chapter 3) notion of one grouping of women is being pitted against a totalizing notion of another grouping of women. With such constructions
"all of them" get rendered "all the same" so that a single social identity
serves as the summation of the individual's significant traits. False consciousness surfaces. By *false consciousness* Karl Marx meant an alienated
consciousness more or less incapable of letting the individual experience
self in community with others. It is a misguided consciousness. It buys
into the ideologies and value systems that keep individuals from recognizing the elite enemy by setting up diversionary false enemies like the
"opposite" sex or "people on welfare." We begin to grasp our diversity,
then, when we refuse to exaggerate it along the lines historically carved
out for our consciousness.

We also begin to grasp our diversity when we get honest about the
anxieties it evokes in us, if only because no one among us has emptied
her consciousness of elitism. "Fear of the Other . . . could be seen as a
central constituent of a politics of difference" (Walkerdine 1990, 208) or
an identity politics. Fear of the Other can lead us to join hands more
and more tightly until we have, by design or default, excluded those
whom we experience as different. Thereafter we are positioned to further fear the Other, for we have widened the distance that feeds the
anxieties bred by racism, misogyny, ageism, homophobia, and other
elitist stances. The Other is, after all, the Unknown. Overcoming our
anxiety about human beings unknown to us requires the same measures that any fear of the unknown requires. We need to experience it
judiciously. We need to lay hold of the "political potential of anxiety"
(Butler 2001, 421). We need to reach out a hand, make eye contact, open
our ears, and make as many receptive, responsive gestures as we are
capable of sincerely making. We need, too, to see that,

> as Maria Lugones says, a crucial aspect of respectful engagement is re-
> garding the other as a faithful mirror of the self—as giving back an
> image of oneself one has to take seriously—but also as someone with
> projects and engagements of her own. (Social Justice Group 2000, 1)

We also need to slough off whatever comfort we find in feeling that
"difference can be contained and kept at bay by the construction of a

single, powerful identity" (Michie 1992, 4) such as "women," "feminists," or "lesbians." As Helena Michie says, "It is tempting to treat these words as talismans against difference, these identities as sanctuaries of sameness" (1992, 5). We do ourselves as well as our Others a disservice with such totalizing tactics. We do better by treating these words as broad umbrellas that provide diverse females some shelter from the indignities and intolerance they face in mainstream society or mixed company. While one can hear homophobic remarks among lesbians, misogynistic comments among feminists, and other ironic speech rooted in false consciousness, one hears dramatically less of it within communities of women sharing this or that umbrella. One finds what Adrienne Rich (1986) calls a "safe place" (see chapter 4).

Safe places are where we go for respite *after* "learning how to stand alone, unpopular and sometimes reviled, and how to make common cause with those others identified as outside [mainstream] structures." They are where we go for renewal once we "recognize difference as a crucial strength" and thus "reach beyond the first patriarchal lesson. In our world, divide and conquer must become define and empower" (Lorde 1984, 112). Safe places are, to be sure, sometimes identifiable by the umbrellas their participants share. That circumstance fades, however, as we move past the false consciousness that makes differences scary or insurmountable. Safe places evolve into social spaces where we find other selves in community unafraid of dense, trying connections with one another. Safe places include women's studies classrooms, feminist therapists' offices, the kitchen table in a loving home or the back stoop in a closely knit neighborhood, women's bookstores, the folds of friendship, and potluck suppers with old friends and new allies.

Both within and beyond our safe places, we need to forswear identifying ourselves in sharp contrast with "them." We need to craft identities that reflect what we are doing and what we have done, not what "they" are like or how "they" behave. As Elizabeth Kamarck Minnich observes, "It is only when our self-definition is built on exclusions and devaluations of others that those others threaten" or frighten us (1990, 173). Groups that we do not prejudge, let alone exclude or devalue, cannot evoke our anxieties or fears. By creating identities focused more on ourselves as individuals and less on other people as group members, we can cultivate our consciousness of diversity as the "crucial strength" Audre Lorde knew it could be.

Thus, we should say "we" carefully. "We" does have a place in feminist rhetoric, as Judith Butler (1990, 142) points out. That place needs to be consciously hemmed in by "the internal complexity and indeterminacy of the term," however. Daring to use the word, "we" need to keep at the forefront of consciousness the startling diversity glossed over by that one consonant joined with that one vowel. At the same time we should curtail our "need to find that we are all . . . really in some fundamental way the same." Typically, that need is "a lingering and hard-to-shake form of racism" (Scheman 1993, 107) or ethnocentrism of some other sort.

What, then, in practical terms do our "differences" amount to? What do they mean in the workplace, classroom, church or synagogue, or neighborhood? What do they mean at the gym or in the voting booth? What do they mean for our social-change work together? Above all, they mean feminist methods have to come into play—methods smacking of postmodernist sensibilities and transformational actions.

As defamiliarizing, debunking strategies, feminist methods equip us to see our differences from many angles and in many lights. They let us see that the differences among women put us into various oppressed *and* oppressing groups (Grant 1993, 29). Yet membership in the latter groupings need not entail willingness to oppress any more than it entails acceptance of oppression. Just as we can resist oppression, we can forswear oppressive practices by becoming aware of and curtailing them at every opportunity. None of us can readily change her skin color, sexual identity, or ethnicity, yet we can commit to minimizing the advantages deriving from our membership in privileged—and thus to some extent oppressing—groupings in society. We can support restaurants and other businesses that have a good mix of racial and ethnic groups among their clienteles; we can speak out against homophobic remarks and antigay jokes told within (presumably) heterosexual groupings; with our money and energies we can support civil rights organizations dedicated to ensuring that citizens enjoy their full rights regardless of sexual orientation, race, marital status, and so forth. Although we cannot erase our privilege, we can do a great deal to counterbalance the unfair advantages it gives us.

Our social class is a singular exception to the rule about erasing privilege. We can give away the inflated portion of our paychecks; we can forswear using "Dr." socially because we happen to have a doctoral or medical degree; we can disavow ourselves of the status-enhancing privileges that come with being the boss or supervisor or professor but that have nothing to do with being an effective, inspiring incumbent of such positions. While we cannot erase the advantages of our schooling and the "developed insides" it gave us (Sennett and Cobb 1973), we can commit ourselves to never using those advantages to intimidate or otherwise lord it over people who lack those advantages. Our schooling requires of our best selves that we give a great deal back—to family, friends, community, and society—and that we refuse to use our diplomas or degrees as means of putting or keeping other people "in their places."

Thus, in many respects social class is the litmus test of feminist consciousness. Since it is more in our control than skin color or sexual orientation or ablebodiedness, social class often indicates where we stand *in the most practical, everyday ways* on the elitism/non-elitism continuum. Those who speak out against oppression, exploitation, and social injustice and then spend substantial discretionary income consuming the services of minimum-wage workers are suspect; those who say they abjure privilege and never pay serious attention to their own class privileges are suspect; those who get fired up about racism and sexism but seem to forget about classism are suspect; and on and on. The differences among us that weigh heavily at times routinely make their appearance within a class-skewed context such as academic conferences, university classrooms, and state-capitol protests. We are, in short, quick to see the racial and other differences among us while taking for granted the class privileges that let most of us work together at such sites. Such taken-for-grantedness is anachronistic. Airing our class privilege holds the promise of establishing a context wherein our other differences seem less overwhelming, though no less worthy of attention.

Diversity of all sorts does demand our attention, both individually and collectively. As Reina Lewis (1992, 20) observes, the very emergence of "diversity as a buzz-word in identity politics signals" progress of the sorts advocated above. She says that we need to see how "the determining factors of race, nationality, class, gender and sexuality are locked together in a shifting relationship in which different terms, or combinations of terms, will have precedence at different times." Thus, neither our race nor our social class nor our sexual orientation nor our gender nor any other part of our identity consistently seals our experiences and outcomes. No aspect of our identity can serve as its constant center. In that existential circumstance lies the grounds for seeing that our differences from other women are far from absolute or constant.

We need to see our diversity "as richness and opportunity for cultural enhancement and understanding" (Harding 1991, 89). We need to see it as multiplicity and variety capable of teaching us about ourselves as well as other women and capable of keeping us on the path of cultural transformation. After all, how well we work together without dodging or stifling our diversity demonstrates the viability of alternatives to institutionalized hierarchies based on all our "differences." Our work together also illustrates "divergence, breakage, splinter, and fragmentation as part of the often torturous process of democratization" (Butler 1990, 14–15). If we prove ourselves incapable of moving beyond mere tolerance of our diversity, we not only make status-quo supporters look reasonable but also undermine the feasibility of our social-justice goals.

In practical terms, as we have implied, our diversity demands that we see notions like "women's standpoint" or "*the* feminist movement" as totalizing fictions (cf. Di Stefano 1990, 74) masking our multipolarity. Our diversity also demands that we press forward with theorizing fresh connections between "equality" and "difference." Minnich offers superb grounds for launching that effort:

> Women of all sorts, Black men, and others excluded from the American promise have always had first to struggle to prove that we are "as good as"—that is, the same as—those who excluded us in order to gain any hearing or achieve any recognition from the dominant few. . . . That political as well as intellectual fact is one of the most glaring instances we have of the basic conceptual error of taking the few to be the inclusive term, the norm, and the ideal for all. It is that error that forces the absurd apparent . . . choice between being the same as those who have excluded us or being different from them—in a tradition in which difference is recognized primarily as deviance or deficiency. (1990, 106–7)

To be equal need not mean to be the same. Rather, says Minnich, "equality protects our right to be different" (70). It "give[s] us common ground" where "all that marks us as the same or different can be held irrelevant for some purpose." Thus, equality "challenge[s] us to make distinctions that are relevant and appropriate to a particular situation or set of considerations or principles" (107).

Every time, then, that "difference" asserts itself in ways irrelevant to the tasks at hand it announces inequality. To say, for instance, that white women monopolized second-wave feminism is to distort the social and cultural realities of feminism from the 1960s onward. As Cynthia Fuchs Epstein points out, among the "most serious myths" about the women's movement is the idea that it originated with and was led by "white, middle-class women" who aimed "to defend the interests of white, middle-class women" (1999, 84, 85). As a corrective to that widespread misperception, Epstein emphasizes the "heterogeneity of

[Betty] Friedan's allies and comrades." Josephine Donovan, who got active in New Left politics and the women's liberation movement early in the 1970s, observes that "People now ask if we thought about race and class in those days. That's *all* we thought about. . . . Feminism added gender to the mix" (2000, 94).

Even to say that bourgeois white women monopolized feminist theory during the 1970s and 1980s among North American academicians is to make a claim that may be credible but not necessarily meaningful. Most theorizing is academically sponsored, and most academicians are bourgeois creatures by virtue of their education and cultural authority, if not their paychecks and lifestyles. Thus, most feminist theorists of color would likely also be bourgeois. Also, unless white feminists in the past several decades ignored or excluded the contributions of colleagues of color, their race says nothing about the quality of their theorizing. Either their work effectively addresses the centrality of race in women's lives, as Margaret Andersen's (1987) and Carol Stack's (1975) does, or it does not. Characterizing them as "white," in other terms, says little about their work even while it does say a lot about the racist structure of the higher-education system.

When we swallow charges that divide us and them—heterosexual feminist theorists and lesbian feminist theorists, academic feminists and other feminists, feminists of color and white feminists—we accept dichotomies inimical to our interests. Yes, we need to examine our continuing participation in all the varieties of elitism that separate us from one another and let us injure one another. We need to talk openly about privilege and disprivilege, pleasure and pain, oppression and oppressing. We dare not think, though, that dichotomizing will make such talk dialogical, let alone fruitful. At every turn we need to resist totalizing conceptions; we need to demand more than two categories of people; we need to highlight the socially constructed, historical character of the names we call ourselves and others; we need to explore how those names serve elite interests at the expense of our own. We need, says Minnich, "to learn to particularize whatever and whomever we study, and then to contextualize, to historicize—to hold whatever abstractions we draw from the material of our study close to that material" (1990, 71) so as to avoid the snare of elitist thinking that rides roughshod over people's lived experiences.

Overall, "the new politics forged by feminists and others in liberation movements has led to the same conclusion: not what we have in common, but how our lives and choices affect each other, is what ties us together and makes coalitions possible" (Scheman 1993, 211). We need not share more than high-priority goals to be effective political allies. All the while it does help, though, to see

> how our very different ways of being constructed as women have implicated each other, how we have been used against each other, threatened by each other, and learned to see each other as an enemy, a rival, or a dreaded alter ego. To look for commonalities necessarily simplifies all our lives; when we look instead at webs of interconnection, we can do justices to the complexities of those lives. (Scheman 1993, 216)

Our diversity thus entails multiple bases for building coalitions. Take, for instance, maternal rights. They concern women of every hue, every sexual orientation, every social class, every religion, and so forth. Our maternal concerns do vary in specific shape, but—once taken into account—that variance enhances our collective stance by making it more comprehensive and inclusive.

We need no shared, totalizing identity to make common cause with one another. Instead, we need to understand that the very need "to be *different* or the *same as* [are] both impediments to *becoming ourselves*" (Steinem 1993). We both strengthen ourselves and expand our horizons by seeing our plural identities as points of convergence as well as divergence. We need, in short,

> to rethink alterity and otherness. What is at stake here is how to restore intersubjectivity so as to allow differences to create a bond, i.e., a political contract among women, so as to effect lasting political changes. It is the affirmation of a new kind of bond, a collectivity resting on the recognition of differences, in an inclusive . . . manner. (Braidotti 1993, 10–11)

Diversity among us is a given, and inclusiveness is essential to our anti-elitism. We can draw inspiration from our diversity even as we continue the struggle to empty our consciousnesses of the differences culturally and oppressively inscribed there. We can, in sum, affirm our multiple subject positions by "nurturing and acknowledging alliances with a lively array of others" (Haraway 1997, 269).

Only one variety of feminism impedes such progress. Judith Grant (1993, 188) calls it "corporate feminism"; Janice Raymond (1987, 169) talks about it in terms of assimilation, which we favor. *Assimilationist feminism* focuses on achieving the rights and rewards of men in one's own social class. As we will see in the next chapter, some high-status women favor such a feminism. Assimilationists have little interest in challenging the social structure giving them comfortable, privileged positions relative to other Americans but not equal to those of their male peers. When they stack their situations against those of their male counterparts, assimilationists feel the sting of relative deprivation and virtual subordination despite their high positioning in the class structure and, often enough, all the other major hierarchies except gender. These feminists are disinclined to talk about their class privileges. They look not to challenge heteropatriarchal institutions but to gain access to their higher reaches. These feminists say they support women's rights, but their work exhibits little interest in the welfare of women outside their circles of privilege. Kate Nash, among many others, insists that that's not good enough: "The explicit aim of the feminist project should be the equality of *all* women if some are not to gain ground at the expense of others" (1998, 146).

Assimilationists come in all shapes, sizes, colors, and orientations, but they are disproportionately the daughters and wives of privileged men whose "successes" they aim to emulate in some fashion. Assimilationists say little about the class structure, race relations in our society, hate crimes against lesbians and other women, or homeless women. They ignore, then, how "Gender reaches into disability; disability wraps around class; class strains against abuse; abuse snarls into sexuality; sexuality falls on top of race . . . [*sic*] everything finally piling into a single human body" (Clare 1999, 123). Assimilationist feminism is, in Grant's words, "a tepid feminism indeed" (1993, 188). It is a narrowly self-interested feminism that downplays diversity in favor of the sameness of considerable privilege, especially class privilege. Eve Kosofsky Sedgwick offers a practical antidote to such narrowness. Based on a Buddhist meditation, Sedgwick's practice centers on her consciousness of other people in public places. She says that "the substantance of it is to recognize that every other person there, one by one, male and female and young and old, has been, in some earlier life, your mother" (1999, 216).

Instincts and Institutions

In many respects "essentialism" and "constructionism" are like "creationism" and "evolution." Between the two perspectives stands a sharp divide, with people shouting at each other across the widening gap. "Essentialism" and "constructionism" constitute a kind of continental divide wherein European (especially French) feminists such as Hélène Cixous and Luce Irigaray often presuppose some essential differences between women and men, while North American feminists such as Judith Butler and Patricia Hill Collins are likelier to presuppose that such differences are socially constructed and maintained. To these two theoretical stances we can add little. Instead, we aim to undermine the either/or thinking this dichotomy breeds and look at the hum and buzz lying between these two theoretical poles.

To a large degree "constructionism" derives from the contemporary classic *The Social Construction of Reality: A Treatise on the Sociology of Knowledge*, coauthored by Peter L. Berger and Thomas Luckmann in 1967. Drawing from Karl Marx, Max Weber, and Émile Durkheim as well as phenomenologists Edmund Husserl and Alfred Schutz, Berger and Luckmann emphasized the role of habit, history, language, stratified knowledge, and everyday pragmatics in securing an abiding faith in the world "just there" as we pursue our daily routines. Central to their perspective is the notion of *typification*, the application of linguistic types to the objects of our experiences, whether those objects are people, places, or things. By naming, we familiarize the objects of our awareness in largely taken-for-granted, unthinking ways as long as no problem is at hand. When a problem presents itself, the same processes involve heightened awareness.

From Berger and Luckmann's perspective our shared realities are all socially constructed. They originate in interactional processes that form the basis of institutions as historical, transgenerational ways of doing certain types of things in society. Theirs is a kind of *culturalism*, a stance emphasizing the environment over heredity, nurture over nature, and culture over biology. Significantly, though, Berger and Luckmann reject those dichotomies. They leave lots of theoretical room for biological and other "natural" sources of variation. For starters, then, we emphasize that its original formulation made constructionism a both/and perspective wherein sociocultural processes are constrained by the supposed givens of the physical environment, human body, and all else lumped together as Nature.

But are social processes not "natural"? What shape does the precultural body, female or male, have? How "natural" is Nature these days when the ozone layer is punctured by a big hole and continues thinning at an alarming rate? Berger and Luckmann's treatise holds the advantage of crediting both nature and nurture while seeing that social interactions and cultural understandings determine what counts as "nature" and what counts as "nurture" and why the difference between the two even matters. Theirs is, to repeat, a both/and perspective emphasizing social processes over other "natural" processes.

Among feminist theorists, constructionism and essentialism fuel a debate that participants take very much to heart. For the time being, on this side of the Atlantic Ocean the debate favors constructionists. As Bonnie Zimmerman observes, the "unified, essentialist, ontological being" has disappeared; she has been replaced by "metaphor and/or subject position" (1992, 8, 3). Carole-Anne Tyler sizes matters up more colorfully:

> Their now radical chic has made the likes of Dolly Parton and Madonna (and their satin queen or Wanna-Be parodies or imitations) more than chicks with cheek; they have become draped crusaders for the social constructionist cause, catching gender in the act—as an act—so as to demonstrate there is no natural, essential, biological basis to gender identity or sexual orientation. (1991, 32)

Given neither to political correctness nor intellectual fashions, we hesitate to board the anti-essentialist bandwagon. Instead, we ask, Why all the hubbub? Even if a difference between the sexes proves to be biologically rooted, culture may still reinforce that difference. Indeed, for differences widely considered "natural" or "essential" divergences between the sexes, culture often exhibits aggressive, intense efforts at reinforcement. The maternal instinct is illustrative.

People widely assume that women have a keen propensity to bear and nurture children. While feminist and other scholars often reject any notion of a "maternal instinct," it holds a lot of popular appeal and some scholarly support. Even those who think the evidence supports the hypothesis of a maternal instinct, however, have to concede that cultures like ours do a great deal to promote females' maternal interests. From the dolls thrust into our arms during early childhood to gifts of homemaker-oriented toys, from queries into our parental plans and prospects to queries about our parental status, from limited access to safe, effective contraceptives to limited access to safe, affordable abortions, we get the message that motherhood centers our destiny more surely than work, wifehood, or anything else. Time and again we come up against what feels less like maternal affirmations and more like a maternal mandate. Ask nonmothers about the pitying looks they get from some people, the freedom some people feel to inquire into the reasons for their nonmaternal state, or the lack of feminine credibility they feel in certain circles, and you get a tangy taste of maternal-instinct thinking.

Are women essentially destined to mother? Given the terrorists, murderers, abusers, and unhappy mothers among us, the answer must be negative. Moreover, the desperation often felt by infertile couples sometimes speaks less to parenting instincts than to frustration at being unable to get (as many seem used to getting) what they want even after spending considerable money and energy. Given the happy non-mothers among us, too, the answer must be negative. Yet most women do mother, and most seem to do so with satisfaction and many with great satisfaction. What does that circumstance imply?

For one thing, it implies that many (if not most) other women's undertakings are relatively unsatisfying or limited. Their paid work is often unrewarding and monotonous; their friendships, while gratifying, can usually be only part time; their marriages, while more or less satisfying, are in the end also only part time until the retirement years; and so forth. What, in the end, is to center a woman's life? For some women, activism or career or civic involvements may—alone or together—constitute a meaningful, fulfilling center. For most women, though, circumstances make such a center unattainable. A daughter or son, felt in one's womb as a precious unknown, known from the very first moment of her or his conscious life, hugged, guided, seen and heard for year after year can surely center a human life in human terms on a human scale. Yet far from every woman will find that center appealing enough to devote herself to mothering. Neither physical nor cultural anomalies are necessary to account for such women; our diversity alone—the startling range of talents and dispositions among us—is sufficient explanation.

About essentialism we can now venture several preliminary observations. First, what seems an "essential" difference between women and men often gets massive cultural reinforcement. We think that whenever a behavior or trait exhibits strong cultural roots, that circumstance should get the bulk of our attention instead of the question of whether that matter essentially differentiates one from the other sex. Cultural conditioning, channeling, and constraining are open to countervailing cultural processes. They raise choice-making and public-policy issues that need airing in society as well as in our everyday lives.

Second, what seems an "essential" difference between women and men rarely includes all women or all men. Small as the overlap between the sexes may be—think of breast cancer, for instance—or small as the exceptional minority of women or men may be, few differences between the sexes are absolute or universal. Moreover, none of the differences dramatic enough to warrant the label "essential" seem to derive from or presuppose any maternal instinct. *Mothering theory*, which has a sizable feminist as well as nonfeminist following, suggests that maternal experiences may give rise to what look like essential differences between women and men. Mothering theory centers on the "claim that women have learned certain values from their practice as mothers that can be used to understand gender, and even to build alternative social theories centered around the 'female values,' like altruism and care" (Grant 1993, 59). While motherhood is often a patriarchal institution, as Adrienne Rich (1986) poignantly showed, it may involve some "universal experience[s]" capable of inculcating a distinctive array of values and sentiments in most women who mother (cf. Grant 1993, 59). If so, we need not invoke any instinct to account for such an array.

Pregnancy in and of itself *typically* lays the grounds for a singularly strong bond between nonadoptive mother and daughter or son—a bond stronger than that initially joining father with daughter or son (Chase and Rogers 2001). Moreover, in heteropatriarchal society most mothers do more than their fair share of nurturing their children, and this pattern intensifies when divorce rates are considerable and teenage motherhood is far from rare. Those who bathe a child day after day, prepare her meals, see her first steps and scratches, hear her first swear words, and struggle to see her safely into adulthood can scarcely help but be deeply affected by those experiences, especially if they have chosen these experiences and also enjoy relatively safe, secure circumstances. For many, many mothers, to think of that child being drafted into war, sexually abused, raped on a date or in a parking garage, pressured into having a child she does not want, or otherwise tripped up by mean individuals or a cruel system is to think the unthinkable. That their daily nurturance, year after year, would shape most mothers' consciousnesses along broadly similar lines should come as no surprise to anyone who has been blessed with a good mother, grandmother, aunt, or other caretaker or who has herself seen a child to adulthood. Still, not all mothers share the values such nurturing seems to foster. Despite the dramatic difference mothering may typically create between mothers and fathers—and thus, to a large extent, between women and men—that difference is far from universal, though probably noteworthy.

Judith Kay raises another point pertinent to essentialism. She indicates that "when human characteristics . . . are not evident, it should be assumed not that some people are 'just constituted differently' and should be abandoned to their habits" but that circumstances are such "as to prevent developing these capacities" (1994, 43–44). Kay implies how society and culture might systematically prevent most men from developing the values and behaviors widely associated with mothering. Do we seriously expect that tolerating boys' hitting and punching, putting toy guns and other mock weapons in their hands, having them sport football helmets as soon as they are big enough, and insisting that they not cry even with good reason will produce involved, loving fathers? Will such training make men feel deeply responsible for the long-term nurture of their children? Will it encourage a paternal instinct? Again, essentialism or constructionism seems a secondary issue. Whether or not any differences between the sexes derive substantially from the inherent nature of maternity and paternity, culture says a great deal about which differences are likely to manifest themselves. The more culture says, the more we doubt that an essential difference is at hand.

With the increasing use of human growth hormones, hormone replacement therapy, reconstructive surgery, and other biomedical interventions, for example, "nature" finds only ambiguous expression in and through our bodies. As we have seen, the same principle applies to the material environment that faces pillage or palliation as human beings continue making the planet a series of construction sites and tourist destinations. Jane Flax (see chapter 4) implies that the essentialism/constructionism debate ultimately lacks the clear-cut dichotomies it presupposes. Similarly, Judith Butler points to the difficulty of distinguishing reliably "between what is 'before' and what is 'during' culture" (1990, 78). Eva Lundgren emphasizes the connection between biology and culture "as an osmotic relationship, with fluid, ambiguous transitions, or as a pair of reciprocally dialectical terms which cannot logically be thought without one another" (1995, 394).

We call for a letup in the essentialist/constructionist debate. The more pressing debates have to do with cruelties and injustices known to derive from abuses of power, contempt for human rights, and gross elitism. Besides, in practice most of us land on the essentialist or constructionist side of the debate because of our politics and values rather than vice versa. A "politics of difference" and a "politics of equality" may divide us more than essentialism or constructionism. Specifically,

> Those who believe that gender differences are significantly basic . . . are more likely to pursue a politics of difference which can speak to women's alienated (with respect to dominant, male-stream culture) but also potentially critical identity and be employed on behalf of a reconstituted, nonmasculinist social order. Those who do not see gender

as basic in this deep and constitutive sense are more likely to argue for a politics of equality based on some presumption of eventual, attainable, and desirable androgyny; that is, on the basis of an identity which transcends gender difference. (Di Stefano 1990, 65)

Similarly, those who believe that "knowledge about women is simply additive to, or a subset of, or a complement to, knowledge about men" (Minnich 1990, 13) would seem to favor a politics of equality that treats gender as something other than a "deep, constitutive" reality. While we mean not to introduce a dichotomy into our discussion, we do find Di Stefano's stance useful inasmuch as it suggests how, at the broadest level, some of us find our way to essentialist or constructionist stances.

Tania Modleski suggests related grounds for our stances. She "worr[ies] that the position of female anti-essentialism as it is being theorized by some feminists today is a luxury open only to the most privileged women" (1991, 22). Indeed, a politics of equality may commonly coalesce with constructionism and privilege among some individuals, while a politics of difference may coalesce with essentialism and relative disprivilege among others. Whether or not such connections occur is beyond our purview. Reminding ourselves about the connections among our intellectual positions, politics, and relative privilege is not, however. We need awareness of those connections so that we can be clear about the corners we might be backing ourselves into or the hierarchies of privilege and disprivilege we may be taking for granted. In the end both/and thinking allows for a larger corner as well as more entries and exits than either/or thinking provides.

We return, then, to the inclusive promise built into Berger and Luckmann's constructionism. Feminists bent on undercutting dichotomous thinking can do a great deal with that perspective. If, for example, we want to see how "elaborate fears and desires construct" supposed truths about women (Walkerdine 1990, 61), we might turn to Berger and Luckmann for reminders that our fears, like our desires, are socially constructed. Tracing the ins and outs of such constructions is instructive and liberating. So might be the project of tracing the ins and outs of what are socially constructed as safe places or nonrisky behaviors. For example, the myth of a provocatively dressed female in the "wrong" part of town or in the "wrong" sort of bar "flaunting" her sexuality makes many women feel unreasonably secure against sexual assault.

We dare, then, consider ourselves essentialist in some of our thinking and constructionist in most of it. Whichever way we lean on this matter or that matter, however, we try to keep a close eye on both "nature" and "culture" as slippery complexities capable of muddying the waters as we seek clarity. We end our both/and discussion with two insights. First, all of us assessing essentialism and constructionism occupy specific social positions and have been culturally conditioned in more ways than we can grasp. Our positioning and conditioning may find expression in our thinking more than we are aware. Second, gender has discernible significance for virtually everyone and dramatic significance for many, many people. As Minnich, invoking Gerda Lerner, reminds us, it is

> necessary to take seriously the fact that . . . even when we look at brothers and sisters of the same family, of the same race, of the same class, the relation of the siblings to the power hierarchy is *not* the same. Gender constructs them differently and keeps them different in important ways. (1990, 60)

Essential or constructed or both, the consequential differences between women and men must focus our attention even as we continue looking into their multiple origins. At the same time we must look at how "differences" get exaggerated even within the social sciences that often ignore the enormous similarities and convergences between female people and male people (cf. Brekhus 1998; Epstein 1988).

What about Men?

From the beginning we meant our book to be about women, partly in connection with but mostly distinct from men. Our focus has been women's consciousnesses, our own included. We have tried to map out some key words and ideas capable of sharpening our awareness of ourselves, other people, and the world we make together. By "sharpening" we mean making our consciousness more incisive, inclusive, and flexible; making it less prone to either/or dead ends and elitist copouts; making it more attuned to honesty and compassion.

All the while that we have been focusing on our own and other women's consciousness, we have remained aware that some of you are men. We also know that women as well as men are often interested in how most feminists think about men, make homes and families with men, collaborate with men in trade unions and research projects, make lifetime friendships with men, and myriad other cross-gender achievements.

We have also been aware that criticizing patriarchy, some men's brutality and violence, and other men's silent witnessing of women's burdens are often heard as "male bashing." Such perceptions typically imply a double standard. When women are put down for crying too readily, being too sensitive, being dependent and codependent, or being too demanding and pushy, we seldom hear about "female bashing." Let one serious criticism be made about men who batter their wives, rape their dates, or fail to express outrage over such travesties, though, and the response is often a heated charge of male bashing. An interesting example emerged when one of us was using Wilkinson and Kitzinger's *Heterosexuality: A Feminism & Psychology Reader* (1993) as one of the texts in a social psychology course she was teaching. The readings in that volume, some of which we cite in chapter 3, comprise some intense critiques of heterosexuality as an institution. Almost to a person, the female students who found the volume emotionally challenging felt some of the authors were bashing heterosexuals; their male counterparts felt those same authors were bashing men. There was no discernible overlap between the two groups of students. We all do need to temper our generalizations so that they never smack of "all men" or "all" people in any other diverse grouping. We bow down to heteropatriarchy yet one more time, though, if we take the zing out of our generalizations so as to avoid the double-standard charge, "male bashing."

The alternative we favor avoids "a reverse-discourse that uncritically mimics the strategy of the oppressor instead of offering a different set of terms" (Butler 1990, 13). One of our standing interests is precisely those different terms, especially the ones focusing on history, social structure, cultural conditioning, and people's everyday experiences. Thus, terms like heteropatriarchy, institution, agency, and elitism center our discourse.

Neither at nor beneath its surface do we mean to demonize men and leave them without a feminist place to stand. All the while, we hold men to the same standards as women because we do not think of women and men as "fundamentally different *kinds* of human beings." Men as well as women, for instance, must be reproductively responsible. Yet little practical attention is given to how "male reproductive exposures" may cause "not only fertility problems but also miscarriages, low birth weight, congenital abnormalities, cancer, neurological problems, and other childhood health problems" (Daniels 1997, 594). Further, we reject stances that involve "essentializing gender or glossing over the roles of race, class, sexual identity, and so on in people's lives"

(Scheman 1993, 217). Above all, we reject the prospect of any human trait being *the* definitive, core trait of an individual or group. No characteristic any of us bears, whether essentially or culturally or both, defines us comprehensively enough that little more need be said to typify us even anonymously and broadly. To say, for instance, that I am a woman of color—whether yellow, red, black, brown, or some glorious combination—is only the beginning of the tale one might tell about people like me. A great deal depends on whether I am wealthy, affluent, getting by or falling behind; whether my sexual attractions are to women, men, or both; whether I am pagan, Muslim, Hindu, Greek Orthodox, atheist, Methodist, Southern Baptist, Conservative Jewish, or a witch; whether I am a mother or not; whether I am married or not; whether I am thirty-five or seventy-four years old; whether my health is excellent or poor; whether I live in rural Nebraska or the Atlanta suburbs.

To say of a human being, then, that he is a man is to say very little in and of itself. It is of course to say that he has a greater share of social entitlements than his female counterparts, but that is to say extremely little about his overall experiences and prospects in society. To claim, for example, that homeless men are more privileged than homeless women is a claim empty of ethical import in a society where privilege begins accruing long after people have a roof over their heads. As we saw, "privilege" involves excess, and we are hard pressed to say that a destitute, homeless person of either sex has an excess of anything generally found valuable or meaningful.

First, then, we hold men to the same standards as women. Second, we disavow efforts to "find what women have done that is as close as possible to what men have done" (Minnich 1990, 88). We reject androcentric standards in favor of less quantitative, less rigid measures of what counts as worthy and valuable. We seek standards tied neither to women nor to men but to people's lived situations independent of their sex or gender—standards of "good enough" parenting, a "good day's work," neighborliness, citizenship, friendship, and so forth that take into account the standing differences in people's everyday circumstances. We support standards that recognize diverse ways of doing society's important work such as raising children, producing goods and services, and making neighborhoods. We support standards, then, that valorize neither a feminine nor a masculine mode but a set of desirable ways whereby people know themselves and are recognized by others as contributing by honoring their responsibilities for themselves and to others.

So, what about men? Their experiences, prospects, and emotions warrant a good deal of airing in our society now that gender lies at the heart of substantial cultural changes. Men's studies has emerged, albeit fitfully. Men's movements have also taken shape around feminist, antifeminist, and nonfeminist agendas. Overall, though, outside elite circles men stand at the sidelines of gender shifts in our society. Profeminist men, countercultural men, and other nonelitist groupings are helping to shape gender dynamics in everyday life, but most men in our society are little more than spectators of the ongoing transformations of gender. Their agency falters when it comes to gender, suggesting how much masculinity takes its shape from femininity. In addition, masculinity and manhood historically presupposed women's exclusion or marginalization. As the sexes more and more become coparticipants in various institutions, masculinity becomes more vague and uncertain.

Big practical problems arise when people believe that their value, purposes, and contributions derive from their gender, even as it is changing shape. Apparently, many males feel that their worthwhileness hinges on being men.

> Being a man is exciting and attractive, but extremely vague and scary. About the only clear thing he knows about it is that it is *not* being a woman, and the importance of this fact is underscored by the social devaluation of women. (Scheman 1993, 48)

Not surprisingly,

> where women are not to be found, prohibitions against women *are*, revealing that the exclusive group, the "masculine" activity, depends on the *absence* of women for its own meaning—while making use of appropriated imagery of the female. (Minnich 1990, 120)

Under such circumstances misogyny to some degree contributes to males' development of a sustainable identity. In fact, misogyny is the "unavoidable obverse" of the "romanticized heterosexual love" (Minnich 1990, 123) routinely involving females in the project of subordinating themselves to their lovers.

Men who have come of age need positive, wider grounds for carving out their identities. The pro-feminists among them must begin their transformational labors that close to home: Their feminist practice first focuses on how they think of and feel about themselves. As Patricia Hill Collins implies, such men can, like "white 'race traitors,' . . . move into outsider-within spaces" (1998, 234) where they come to understand others' oppression as well as their own gender privilege. Peter Kwong illustrates:

> I feel that my knowledge should be gained from being part of the struggle . . . but not as a member of the leadership. Rather, my job is to listen to what people are telling me and to try to understand the issues from the point of view of the participants in the nitty-gritty conflict. (1998, 59)

Men need not concern themselves foremost with where women are picketing in protest, what kind of women's studies program they are fashioning, or where they are lobbying for a comparable-worth bill. Above all and long term, men need to look at the grounds of their identities and clear those grounds of culturally rooted beliefs, values, and norms devaluing women as well as women's commonplace situations and characteristic activities. Typically, men need to contextualize their universalistic standards so as to see how particularistic and androcentric they actually are. They need to see themselves as whole people unlikely to find long-term satisfaction if they narrowly center their identities on their paid work. The data on job satisfaction and wage stagnation alone suggest the misguidedness of a job-centered identity for most people. In this postmodernist age men of all social classes, races, and ethnic groups need as best they can to establish diverse bases for feeling their worthwhileness, assessing their contributions, and shaping enviable futures for themselves. They need to make themselves people that women and other men "will be pleased to live among" (Lorde 1984, 73).

Mothers and fathers, educators, religious leaders, the purveyors of popular culture, therapists, social workers, childcare workers, and many others can do a lot to shape boys' identities and behaviors. All should contribute to that effort whenever possible. We believe, though, that adult men seeking more affirmative, inclusive identities for themselves represent our single brightest hope for a more ambitious, complex masculinity—if masculinity, like femininity, is to remain a feature of the cultural landscape. Such a masculinity has little to do with what women are or are not doing and how women are or are not (seen as) being. Instead, it has to do with other men. Men need to raise their awareness of the many masculinities—the diverse, credible ways of being a man—currently available. Instead of looking to women as a foil, they better serve themselves by opening their eyes to the diverse life ways among contemporary North American men. They better serve themselves by looking at who among them is satisfied and moving forward (though not necessarily upward) than by casting women as "different" and therefore definitive of their masculinity. The time has come, in short, for men to stop looking to women, however inadvertently, to define their manhood and stamp it with the feminine seal of ego-enhancing approval. Men, like women, need to seize the improvisational, innovative possibilities available to those among them who are not destitute or otherwise impaired.

Some would say that "gender" as such must disappear before women and men can improvise and innovate along the lines we envision. Such a stance exaggerates current differences between the sexes, however. It overlooks the stunning similarities between women and men and between girls and boys. In her ethnography of elementary-school life Barrie Thorne found all sorts of occasions that "evoke stereotyped images of gender relations" (1993, 86). She says, though, that

> much of what has been observed about girls and boys, especially in the relationships they create apart from the surveillance of adults, can be fitted into the model of "different worlds or cultures." But as I've tried to line up that model with my own empirical observations and with the research literature, I have found so many exceptions and qualifications, so many incidents that spill beyond and fuzzy up the edges, and so many conceptual ambiguities, that I have come to question the model's basic assumptions. (90)

Thorne concludes, "The separate-and-different-cultures model has clearly outlived its usefulness," (107) if it ever was meaningful at all. Look at the women and men in your life, past and present. Do you not see the overlap between them and the diversity of styles within each grouping? The similarities between credibly feminine and credibly masculine people are palpable, amounting to diverse femininities and masculinities. The time has come to lay conscious hold of these actualities to benefit our selves in community.

For most of us most of the time, that community includes men as well as women. For extremely practical as well as eminently ethical reasons, then, we dare not exaggerate the differences between women and men any more than we dare exaggerate the differences among women as intractable or divisive. We need to treat differences between the sexes with the same care and circumspection that we treat differences within one or the other sex. How we acknowledge our similarities to and differences from one another as selves in community says, in the end, just how far we have come on the road to social justice and sustainable self-fulfillment. Men (as well as women) need to scrutinize their situations with all the imagination and energy they can muster. They need to do so, just as women do, with an open invitation to join hands with other gender-focused, transformation-minded people, namely, feminists.

That invitation is to help create a world without "gender bullies" (Bordo 1997, 168), a world where we might together value "quality of life over the material greed and status that seem to dictate all social relations today" (Friedan 1998, 51). The invitation might read something like this:

> Feminism has fought no wars. It has killed no opponents. It has set up no concentration camps, starved no enemies, practiced no cruelties. Its battles have been for education, for the vote, for better working conditions for women and children; for property rights for women, for divorce, for custody rights, for the right to safety on the streets. Feminists have fought for child care, for social welfare, for greater visibility for people with disabilities. And feminists have had to fight for rape crisis centers, women's refuges, reforms in the law. (Spender 1993, 45)

The invitation is nothing less than a call to "an honorable way to live their lives" (45). Part of that call must be the message, too, that "laughter in the face of serious categories is indispensable for feminism" (Butler 1990, viii).

6

Backlash

Susan Faludi's *Backlash: The Undeclared War against American Women* (1991) scarcely dealt with a new phenomenon. During the first wave of American feminism, from mid-nineteenth century until after the ratification of the Nineteenth Amendment (1920) entitling women to vote, backlash ebbed and flowed.

Henry James's *The Bostonians*, perhaps the first American novel with a lesbian feminist protagonist, is illustrative. The novel pits Olive Chancellor, a Boston bluestocking, against her cousin Basil Ransome, a Mississippi gentleman. In its first chapter Olive's sister says the participants in a "female convention" are "all witches and wizards, mediums, and spirit-rappers, and roaring radicals." Such "weird meetings" attract Olive, whom Basil sees as "unmarried by every implication of her being" (James 1986, 37, 47).

Olive has a "limited sense of humour" and little "feminine desire to please." Even though "manly things were, perhaps . . . what she understood best," Olive regards men themselves with a "kind of cold scorn"; she sees most of them as "palterers and bullies" (134, 136–37, 154). Olive is "fastidious, exclusive, uncompromising" (157). She is, like other targets of backlash, the inverse of what a proper woman should be.

Basil, who sees feminists as "mediums, communists, vegetarians," resists "inanities" about "the equality of the sexes" (59, 85). He wants women "not to think too much" or "feel any responsibility for the government of the world." Such activities belong to the "sex of tougher hide!" (41–42). Olive and Basil compete for the love of Verena Tarrant. In a diatribe to Verena, Basil insists that

> The whole generation is womanized; the masculine tone is passing out of the world; it's a feminine, a nervous, hysterical, chattering, canting

age, an age of hollow phrases and false delicacy and exaggerated solic-
itudes and coddled sensibilities. . . . The masculine character, the ability
to dare and endure, to know and yet not fear reality, to look the world
in the face and take it for what it is—a very queer and partly very base
mixture—that is what I want to preserve or rather . . . recover. (327)

Today Basil Ransome's counterparts speak in the pulpit, on the
Senate and House floors, at the lecterns of college classrooms; they ter-
rorize the clients of women's clinics; they write books about the horrors
of feminism; they are on talk radio and the op/ed pages of newspa-
pers. Anita Haya Patterson takes particular note of antifeminist backlash among the corporate media:

> Complaints, sometimes virulent, against feminism are now common-
> place in the mass media. We are told that feminist are immersed in ob-
> scure academic theory; they are out of touch with most women's con-
> cerns; their stridency has alienated a younger generation of would-be
> feminists; they are obsessed with male-bashing; they are neo-Puritans
> who deny the possibility of consensual [heterosexual] sex; they pro-
> mote reactionary stereotypes of women as victims; and so on. (2001,
> 254)

This chapter explores the rhetoric and motives associated with such
media-promulgated misconceptions.

Second-Wave Backlash

The *second wave* of American feminism took shape from women's participation in the Civil Rights movement during the 1950s and 1960s and
the antiwar movement during the 1960s. The corporate media dubbed
its participants "women's libbers" and "bra burners." Today the same
media promulgate such labels as "feminazi." Over the short span of
feminism's second wave the "women's movement" has served as a
scapegoat for nearly every prickly problem in our society.

Second-wave backlash is rooted in the late 1970s and early 1980s,
as Faludi shows. In 1984, for instance, the *National Review* published
"The Feminist Mistake." Its author was syndicated columnist Mona
Charen, then a second-year law student, whose title alludes to Betty
Friedan's second-wave classic *The Feminine Mystique* (1963). Charen
wrote,

In dispensing its spoils, the women's liberation movement has given my generation high incomes, our own cigarette, the option of single parenthood, rape crisis centers, personal lines of credit, free love and female gynecologists. In return, it has robbed us of one thing upon which the happiness of most women depends—men. (1984)

Misrepresenting feminists as victorious warmakers (whose booty is trivial), Charen ignores the question of how many women earn the "high incomes" she mentions.

Charen's reference to "our own cigarette" implies feminists somehow colluded with tobacco companies. Similarly, the "option of single parenthood" distorts feminists' stances, since feminists have never valorized single parenthood. Next comes Charen's reference to rape crisis centers, trauma centers for sexually assaulted women. Feminists did give such centers a name and these supportive places that now number 1,200 in American society (P. Martin 2001). As for personal lines of credit, Charen may be right. Feminists did fight for women's right to control their own financial lives. Wives should no more be financial hostages to their husbands than they should be cultural hostages to the 1960s ideology of "free love," which emerged out of male-dominated social movements and was mostly a guy, not a feminist, thing. Female gynecologists, like other female physicians, scarcely emerged out of second-wave feminism either. Feminists did formulate powerful critiques of the medical establishment and advocated medical self-help and health collectives among women, yet no feminist agenda made female gynecologists a top priority.

In the end Charen shifts metaphors and makes members of the "women's liberation movement" people who "have robbed" us of men. (If they are not warmongers, they are at least thieves.) By misnaming, distorting, and trivializing, Charen bypasses the hard-core data on how few women enjoy high salaries, how many women get sexually assaulted, how complex an "option" single parenthood is, and how neglected women's health needs are. She implies feminists have won a war but claims women are its losers. Her core message underlies most backlash rhetoric: Feminism hurts women.

Eight years later, more extreme backlash surfaced when Pat Robertson, religious entrepreneur and political aspirant, spoke at the 1992 Republican Convention. According to this son of a U.S. senator, "Feminists encourage women to leave their husbands, kill their children, practice witchcraft, become lesbians, and destroy capitalism." As Jennifer Baumgardner and Amy Richards go on to note, "To a fundamentalist, that's just a description of no-fault divorce laws, abortion rights, rejection of god as the Father, acceptance of female sexuality, and a commitment to workers" (2000, 61). Hysterical hype such as Robertson's closed a decade of backlash that made feminist baiting commonplace by the early 1990s. Robertson's litany of feminist offenses would be laughable, were it not for the credibility he and his ilk have with millions of Americans. Like Charen, Robertson illustrates Nett Hart's observation that "Tools of oppression are foremostly those that name reality falsely" (1989, 49).

As the 1990s began, the stage was set for a study like *Backlash*. Faludi documents how the corporate media send the message that women have made dramatic progress but now face personal misery. She looks at backlash in popular culture, including the fashion industry. She probes "intellectual" backlash as well as "reproductive rights backlash" where an "antiabortion iconography . . . feature[s] the fetus but never the mother" (414, 421).

Much to her credit, Faludi notes that backlash even includes women "claim[ing] to be feminists" (282). Such women get widespread media attention. Chris Atmore (1999, 183) dubs them "media feminists," who "claim a kind of dissident status for themselves" as critics of "contemporary feminism, or 'victim feminism' as they tend to rename it." Topping her list of these women with a "reactionary agenda" is Christina Hoff Sommers. Atmore says Sommers is "most clearly tied to a broad, right-wing, anti-PC [political correctness] response [to feminism], for which 'backlash' does seem apt" (187). Currently associated with the conservative American Enterprise Institute, Sommers wrote *Who Stole Feminism? How Women Have Betrayed Women* (1994). Here is a small sample of her ideas from a one-page piece she wrote for the *American Enterprise*:

> Theorists like Carol Gilligan and activists like Gloria Steinem are not about to promote policies that sustain marriage, help keep families intact, or restore fathers to the home. For Steinem, a major source of girls' trouble is their alienation from ancient goddess-worshipping cultures. If I may borrow an image from Camille Paglia, putting your girl in the hands of contemporary feminist leaders is like sending your dog to vacation at the taxidermist. (1998, 57)

In this chapter we look at such "media feminists" or what Lynne Segal calls "celebrity feminists/antifeminists like Camille Paglia" (1999, 2). Through their activities, Segal says, "women's political differences can be made to service antithetical desires: serious interest in gender issues *and* the satisfaction of misogynist expectation," such as cat fighting among women or "nice" feminism that doesn't make anyone uncomfortable. Here we discuss Paglia's ideas alongside those of Katie Roiphe, Daphne Patai, Noretta Koertge, and Elizabeth Fox-Genovese. Instead of focusing on their individual works, we look at what they have in common rhetorically.

Initially, we were tempted to discuss Rene Denfeld's *The New Victorians* (1995) as well as Karen Lehrman's *The Lipstick Proviso: Women, Sex & Power in the Real World* (1997) as instances of backlash. Denfeld's *is*, like Lehrman's, a harsh and sweeping criticism of contemporary feminism, and these authors *do* identify themselves as feminists. In the end, though, *The New Victorians* and *The Lipstick Proviso* stand as diatribes against specific strands of feminism by young women who explicitly assert feminist values. The shortcomings of both works are substantial and serious, but these volumes do not exhibit the rhetorical characteristics of what we call "insider backlash." (See Oakley [1997] for the opposite judgment.) We think Denfeld's and Lehrman's books lie somewhere between critiques of feminism and backlash against it. Both illustrate that "there is no *abrupt rupture* between feminist and 'antifeminist' women but rather a continuum of points of view" (Delphy 1984, 119; emphasis added).

In the end *The New Victorians* and, to a considerably lesser extent, *The Lipstick Proviso* fail as critiques of contemporary feminism. What most weakens these works are sweeping, insupportable claims (not unlike those that pervade backlash rhetoric alongside other antifeminist practices). Such claims are especially problematic in Denfeld's case. Denfeld begins, for instance, by citing a "new crop of feminist leaders" who "blame male sexuality for the world's woes" and see in heterosexual intercourse the "root cause of all oppression" (1995, 8–9). Because of these feminists' stranglehold on contemporary feminism and women's studies, such extreme ideas get "taught to women's studies students and promoted in organizations such as local chapters of NOW [National Organization for Women]" (11). This last assertion is typical of Denfield's sweeping, undocumented claims. In addition, it illustrates the leap she repeatedly makes from what women's studies students are exposed to and what they are "taught" or expected to endorse.

With scanty or no support Denfeld also says that

• today's feminists have changed the focus from political reform to that of advocating an entirely passive means of enacting change [15];

- women joining feminist organizations often find more energy is directed toward sensitivity training, consciousness-raising, and group prayers than to pursuing specific goals [15];
- a young woman encountering organized feminism will find [Andrea Dworkin] revered as a leader [33];
- many feminist leaders . . . advocate abolishing heterosexual sex [36];
- from the mid-seventies onward, many college students were told that they must be lesbians in order to call themselves feminists [44];
- *Ms.* is chock-full of articles denouncing sexual freedoms [54]; and
- some feminist leaders have even begun to question abortion rights because they are said to lead to increased heterosexual sex. [55]

Such unsubstantiated assertions make for distortions considerable enough to raise questions about editors' responsibilities and publishers' motives. Nevertheless Denfeld's diatribe does fall short of insider backlash. To repeat, she does explicitly assert feminist values and often cites *specific* strands of feminist thinking that she rejects. Lehrman's work also has these characteristics that pull it back from the ideological terrain of insider backlash. Writing as a liberal feminist who rejects other strands of feminism, Lehrman insists that feminism is "critical to women's lives," and she even recommends the "renewal of consciousness-raising groups" (1997, 192, 194).

The other works we are about to look at tilt more heavily toward harsh, unforgiving antifeminist stances. These works illustrate insider backlash. In the remainder of the chapter we discuss the rhetorical characteristics of this type of backlash and explore the circumstances giving rise to it.

The works that focus our attention include Katie Roiphe's *The Morning After: Sex, Fear, and Feminism on Campus*, which got a prepublication boost when the *New York Times Magazine* (June 13, 1993) excerpted a cover story from it. Later that year, the *Times* (November 29, 1993) also helped Roiphe become a media presence when it published her opinions about Lorena and John Bobbitt. Self-identified feminist Roiphe, whose bachelor's degree is from Harvard, was a doctoral student in English at Princeton University when *The Morning After* appeared. Roiphe claims only to "have written [her] impressions" (1993b, 6, 7).

We also include Camille Paglia's *Vamps & Tramps: New Essays* (1994) as an instance of insider backlash. Like Roiphe, Paglia is a media creation. In fact, a sixty-page appendix to her book consists of "Selected articles regarding Camille Paglia." She has been interviewed by Larry

King and Charlie Rose; she is a regular (though not weekly) columnist for *The Advocate*, the largest gay magazine in the country; *Esquire* (February 1995) published her interview of comedian Tim Allen. Paglia's Ph.D. in English is from Yale University. She teaches at the University of the Arts in Philadelphia.

Paglia scorns women's studies as "a corrupt autocracy . . . without regard for scholarly standards or objective criteria of professional credentialing" (1994, xxii–xxiii). She says "imposters and double-dealers . . . run women's studies" (354). Paglia's stance is not far afield from that of other self-identified feminists who have lambasted women's studies, including Denfeld and Lehrman. Ellen R. Klein's *Feminism Under Fire* (1996) and Sommers's *Who Stole Feminism?* (1994) also inveigh against women's studies, but we focus on Daphne Patai and Noretta Koertge's *Professing Feminism* (1994). Its very subtitle smacks of backlash: *Cautionary Tales from the Strange World of Women's Studies*. Both Patai and Koertge have taught women's studies as well as literature at the University of Massachusetts–Amherst and philosophy at Indiana University, respectively.

Our fourth instance of insider backlash puts us back near the ideological terrain Denfeld and Lehrman occupy. Ultimately, though, Elizabeth Fox-Genovese's recent work augments backlash. Fox-Genovese has long identified herself as a feminist and has had a substantially feminist career, including the directorship of the women's studies program at Emory University. Here *"Feminism Is Not the Story of My Life"* (1996) focuses our attention. In important respects it contrasts with her 1991 work, *Feminism Without Illusions: A Critique of Individualism*. Fox-Genovese presented this earlier book as a "critique of feminism's complicity in and acceptance of individualism" (7), yet in that work she refused to "blame" feminism for shortcomings in the larger society. Instead, she argued that "to lay the blame on women, or feminism, is to fail to understand that feminism itself is symptom rather than cause of the larger changes that are transforming our society" (66). Fox-Genovese also acknowledged anger's centrality to feminist consciousness (226). She cautioned, though, that "when this anger crystallizes in separatist tendencies, it easily slips into indiscriminate attacks on 'male knowledge' and 'male values'" (227). That mild-mannered caution finds fuller expression in Fox-Genovese's 1996 book, specifically in its concern with making comfortable room for men in her no-risk feminism.

One wonders what audience Fox-Genovese is addressing. As with Roiphe, Paglia, and Patai and Koertge, there is no reason to suppose that she is expecting feminists to read her work. Instead, these works seem mostly to address those with antifeminist inclinations. At best, they address those who support "equal rights [but] cannot go for the notion of opposing patriarchy, because that means a fundamental opposition to the culture as a whole" (hooks in "Let's Get Real" 1993, 35). These works thus contribute to an antifeminist backlash, that is, a countermovement to feminist movements.

So, too, may Susan Gubar's recent work. In *Critical Condition: Feminism at the Turn of the Century* (2000), this well-known coauthor of *Madwoman in the Attic*, finds herself "poised between causes for regret and for celebration" as she surveys the feminist terrain. Gubar is impatient with multiculturalist developments among feminists (not unlike Patai, as we will see). She decries "obeisance to the necessity of considering (without subordinating) race, class, gender, sexuality, and nation in routinized litanies that often translate into depressingly knee-jerk essays" (2000, 122). She also decries the posturing associated with "critical election," which rests on an "assumption of moral superiority on the part of scholars convinced of their ability to speak for those despised and rejected by everybody else" (124). Then, too, Gubar laments the "brouhaha over Katie Roiphe's book" (154). In the end we position her work alongside Denfield's and Lehrman's. All three books strike us as unfairly antifeminist at more than a few junctures, even though none goes as far in that direction as the backlash volumes focusing our attention in the remainder of the chapter.

Us/Them Polemics

One of the striking characteristics of insider backlash is references to feminists entirely (or nearly so) in the third person (they, them, their). A predominance of third-person usages suggests that "we" feminists are being talked about to "them," those intent on holding us back. Insider backlash thus involves Us/Them rhetoric where the narrator claims to be one of Us but sounds like one of Them. In Roiphe's volume, for instance, we find not a single use of the first-person plural with reference to feminists. Yet from the outset Roiphe does identify herself as a feminist.

Paglia's is, like Roiphe's, a third-person feminism. Paglia is an I-am-a-feminist-but writer intent on "liberating current feminism from these *false* feminists who have a death grip on it right now, who are anti-porn and so on" (1994, 247; emphasis added). Yet she issues no invitation for feminist debate and dialogue. Commenting on academic members of the "American feminist establishment" such as literary critic Elaine Showalter, Paglia announces,

> I'm afraid it's too late, ladies. You have abundantly shown your true character, in all its vicious, Kremlin-walled Stalinism. The reform movement that I helped launch is at your gates. Your desire for debate is touching, even pathetic. But *the time for negotiations is long past.* (433; emphasis added)

Like Roiphe's and Paglia's, Patai and Koertge's style distances them from (other) feminists. They decry, for example,

> feminists' repudiation of the sciences, especially their refusal to grant any explanatory power to biology. This is a posture we call BIODE-NIAL. Its obverse, social constructionism, is currently the leading contender in the search for an all-encompassing concept capable of sustaining *the* feminist worldview. (1994, 135, emphasis added)

Again, an Us/Them mentality predominates, yet the authors claim to be "feminists" and "friends of feminism" (218).

Like the preceding works, *"Feminism Is Not the Story of My Life"* refers to feminists in the third person. Yet unlike Roiphe, Paglia, and Patai and Koertge, Fox-Genovese engages in virtually no mean-spirited name calling. Like Paglia, however, she does refer to a "feminist elite" (1996, 19, 29, 96, 133), "official feminism" (2, 13, 127), and "upscale feminism" (14, 21, 59, 93, 235). Fox-Genovese thus implies that feminism has become a higher-class monolith, but she steers clear of the name calling generally associated with insider (as well as other forms of) backlash.

Such name calling typically targets both individuals and groups. Feminist theorist and antiporn activist Catharine MacKinnon is often targeted. Roiphe includes a chapter about her—"Catharine MacKinnon, the Antiporn Star." It portrays MacKinnon as "outspoken" and "uncompromising"; as "tall" and "elegant" enough to "slip past every stereotype of the radical feminist"; as having a "fierce gaze"; as a person who "despises" sex; as "Andrea Dworkin's presentable other half"; as "the embodiment of an unholy alliance between the right wing and feminists" (1993b, 140, 144, 151, 154, 156). Roiphe's Catharine MacKinnon sounds a lot like James's Olive Chancellor. (See Linda LeMoncheck [1997] for a feminist critique of MacKinnon's ideas.)

Like Roiphe, Paglia scorns MacKinnon, a "totalitarian" with "witchy tumbleweed hair" (1994, 108, 109–10). Paglia has other individual targets, too. She calls Anita Hill a "priggish, self-interested yuppie" (64); Patricia Schroeder, "one of the beaming Betty Crockers" (54); and Susan Faludi, "the Mary Tyler Moore of feminism" (55). Paglia says that Naomi Wolf has an "airhead, totally parent-pleasing way of talking and writing" (504); that Martina Navratilova's "hyperdeveloped masculine musculature is overcompensation for her creampuff interior" (81); and that Andrea Dworkin, "like Kate Millett, . . . has turned a garish history of mental instability into feminist grand opera" (109). In Paglia's book these instances have no male counterparts. Indeed, Paglia finds in Rush Limbaugh "courageous anti-establishment stands and defense of free speech" (502).

Like Fox-Genovese, Patai and Koertge engage in no mean-spirited name calling that targets specific individuals. They do tend, though, toward some name calling of feminists as a group. They describe, for example, "games" that academic feminists play, which they admittedly "treat . . . in a deprecating manner" (1994, 49). Like other backlash participants, Patai and Koertge sometimes invoke war metaphors. They refer to women's studies programs as a "combat zone" and to the "bunker mentality" of people in those programs (2, 196). Inconsistently, they also refer to the "happy-go-lucky," "accommodating" world of women's studies (189, 196) that nonetheless sets down "know-it-all strictures" (211). These collective characterizations are mild-mannered compared with those that Roiphe and Paglia favor.

Roiphe refers, for example, to "guerrilla feminists," the "zookeeper school of feminism," and the "radical cover-girl chic feminist" (1994, 10, 99, 126). Paglia favors such collective name calling, too. Apparently, she takes pride in having coined the phrases "establishment feminism" and "feminist establishment" (1994, 460). At least a dozen times in *Vamps & Tramps* Paglia mentions the latter, but she never delineates its members or the issues where it has held sway. Paglia also refers to "yuppie feminism" and "bourgeois feminism" (xii, 131, 281, 505; xiii, 281) as well as "Betty Crocker feminism" and "granola feminists" (26, 67), as if home-and-hearth metaphors were somehow damning. More cruelly, Paglia mentions "Infirmary Feminism, with its bedlam of bellyachers, anorexics, bulimics, depressives, rape victims, and incest survivors" (111). She also sees fit to label the so-called feminist establishment "Stalinist" (189).

Their Us/Them rhetoric and mean-spirited name calling suggest that backlash texts are polemical works rather than systematic, balanced reports or studies. In fact, backlash texts conform to neither the professional codes of investigative journalism nor the methodological strictures of the social sciences. Instead, they rest on personal opinions and anecdotal data selectively used to illustrate the author's judgments about feminism, gender, and social change.

As we have seen, Roiphe makes no claims about presenting an objective, comprehensive portrait of contemporary feminism. Using her "impressions" (1994, 7) as her guide, she offers a polemical, not a methodically empirical, work. Her book contains few systematic data.

Paglia's *Vamps & Tramps* is also foremost polemical. Paglia regards "abuse," for instance, as the "feminist stock response to anything ambiguous in human behavior" (134). Such fare is a Paglia trademark. Usually, her assertions are empirically testable, and pertinent data are available. Nearly always, Paglia ignores them. Like Roiphe's, her claims typically build up around the authority of her own impressions. Paglia says, for example, that

- By midlife and early old age . . . women are in total, despotic control of their marriages [46];
- the overwhelming majority of contemporary women continue to avoid hazardous, dirty, low-prestige jobs that men take in order to earn a higher income for their families [393];
- *women* are as aggressive in sexual relationships and as vengeful as *men*! [420]

Unlike *The Morning After* and *Vamps & Tramps*, *Professing Feminism* presents itself as an empirical study. In a three-paragraph "Note on Method," Patai and Koertge say that thirty women participated in "lengthy and detailed taped interviews." They report that "Most . . . are or have been faculty members; some are or were students and staff members in Women's Studies programs." Patai and Koertge supplemented their interview data with "correspondence, memos, and journal entries, as well as communications from the International Electronic Forum for Women's Studies." They offer no details about these additional sources before claiming that "the voices heard in this book, and the problems discussed, *are characteristic*" (xviii, emphasis added).

Patai and Koertge's work is no less polemical but a lot more misleading than Roiphe's or Paglia's. We focus on ninety-six interview excerpts long enough to be indented passages in their book. (The only excerpts that we excluded were the few from Marilyn, the only respondent with whom the authors take issue.) Among these ninety-six passages four professors' voices predominate. Identified as Margaret

(N = 14), Angela (N = 14), Anna (N = 11), and Jeanne (N = 9), these four account for fully half (50 percent; N = 48) of the indented excerpts. The addition of three more professors (Alice Rossi, "Linda," and one of the authors) accounts for three-fifths (60.4 percent; N = 58) of the indented passages. Students and alumni account for a mere thirteen passages, representing only four people. We cannot find the staff members in Patai and Koertge's sample. The eight remaining passages derive from Silvia, a biologist (N = 4), three e-mailers, and one person identified only as "one of the women we interviewed."

Clearly, this "study" rests on a nonrandom sample that is unacceptably small. To repeat, half of the data most emphasized in Patai and Koertge's work comes from only four professors. Moreover, the authors cite no studies about the dynamics and consequences of women's studies programs. As we will see, that circumstance does not prevent them from making gross generalizations about women's studies.

Like Patai and Koertge's subtitle, the subtitle of *"Feminism Is Not the Story of My Life"* implies a polemical stance: *How Today's Feminist Elite Has Lost Touch with the Real Concerns of Women.* Also similar to Patai and Koertge's stance is Fox-Genovese's claim to have gathered data for her book by "taping interviews, studying polling data, and doing systematic research." Although she makes no claim to a "scientific sample," Fox-Genovese does claim to "have made every effort to include women of different backgrounds, generations, and parts of the country" (1996, 2, 3). By our count, she includes thoughts from one hundred different individuals. Sixteen (16 percent) were personal acquaintances, including graduate and undergraduate students, colleagues, a "college classmate," a "manicurist friend," an "old friend" of her mother, professional friends in publishing and in psychology, and even "fellow passengers" on a plane (one white, one black) as well as her Italian American sister-in-law. The other participants in her study include five people (5 percent) quoted in *USA Today* (two men, three women; four white, one black). The remaining seventy-nine people comprise eleven men and sixty-eight women; eighteen African Americans and four Latina/o Americans. Fox-Genovese's sample is, then, small (though far bigger than Patai and Koertge's) as well as nonrepresentative.

Lamentations and Scapegoat

Another characteristic of insider backlash is to lament how feminists have made life harder—whether the author's own life, women's lives in general, or both. In her introduction, for example, Roiphe says that entering Harvard in 1986, she "found something called feminism that was unfamiliar to [her]." Among other things it not only "meant being angry about men looking at you in the street" but also entailed a "rigid orthodoxy." During a date-rape workshop, first-year student Roiphe found herself thinking that "*this has nothing to do with me*" (1993b, emphasis added). Eventually, she concluded, "It was feminists against the backlash, us against them, and increasingly I was 'them.'" So Roiphe's book grew "out of frustration, out of anger, out of the names [she's] been called, out of all the times [she] didn't say something [she] was thinking because it might offend the current feminist sensibility." In large measure her polemical book is about having felt silenced and *victimized*. Yet Roiphe expresses disgust at such characterizations of women. Ironically, she attributes such thinking to the kinds of feminism she rejects.

Jennifer Baumgardner and Amy Richards point out that Roiphe "is just a critic, not an assassin, which she makes clear when speaking on panels with the real conservative women who are working to undermine feminism" (2000, 247). These two feminists conclude that Roiphe's work "expanded feminism because [she] spoke up instead of censoring herself" (251). They go on to draw the same conclusion about Camille Paglia's work. On that point we entirely part company with Baumgardner and Richards.

Unlike Roiphe, Paglia does not much decry how (other) feminists have excluded or silenced her, but she does say that "The refusal or inability of the academic feminists to engage my work has eloquently demonstrated their insularity and hypocrisy" (1994, 64). In Patai and Koertge's work, by contrast, we found the voice of the victim time and again. Anna describes a senior seminar in women's studies as "a ghastly experience, one of the worst I've ever had in my life" (1994, 14). Margaret reports being "constantly terrified" that her gay and straight students "would attack each other physically, hate each other, hate me"(15). Angela reports a "kind of devastating character assassination and posturing that [she] can't stand anymore" (205). Silvia reports, "Basically, people don't talk to me" (156). Boredom, fatigue, and being "made to feel like shit" (21) also show up in these accounts.

We need not doubt the veracity of these respondents to find their stories palpably incredible. The authors have pared them down to accounts that involve scapegoating more than analyzing; too few voices are heard to conclude much of anything. All things considered, we believe the excerpts reveal more about Patai and Koertge's perceptions than about what is typical in women's studies.

Fox-Genovese's work expresses no discernible concern with how (other) feminists have treated her or how women's studies sometimes cast her in the role of victim. Yet Fox-Genovese's recent work exemplifies the tendency to blame feminism for shortchanging or even hurting many women. Here we focus on assertions about how feminists have been unfair to mothers and children as well as to men. Especially in the latter half of her book, Fox-Genovese argues that feminism has been patently biased against, if not hostile to, mothers. She insists "it is difficult to find much feminist support for women who decide that their commitment to family must, at least for a while, take precedence over their commitment to work" (1996, 118). That feminist organizations strongly supported the federal Family Leave Act and have a consistent record of supporting other measures that widen mothers' options goes unacknowledged. That absence seems predictable in view of Fox-Genovese's rhetorical stance. She assumes that "it is reasonable to conclude that feminists intend to free women from motherhood" (188). Indeed, according to her, they "expect children to fit into the nooks and crannies of women's lives, the way women have traditionally fit into the nooks and crannies of men's" (216). Fox-Genovese claims that a *"covert* determination to free women from children shapes much feminist thought and most feminist policies" (228; emphasis added). Her stance follows a pattern that Ann Oakley observes in backlash texts, namely, "an emotional appeal to a higher good—usually that of 'society' or children" (1997, 35).

According to Fox-Genovese, feminists' disregard for children shows up less covertly in their support for women's access to abortion. Early in her book she draws a shocking picture based on a single item in a 1995 issue of the *Wall Street Journal*:

> official feminism insists that a woman's right to choose means that it is wrong to save the life of a child who survives the abortion, for saving that life impinges on the mother's "rights." The defense of women's independence requires that a twenty-day-old child be killed—or allowed to die from lack of medical attention. (1996, 13)

Similarly, Fox-Genovese later argues,

> To the extent that the pro-choice forces acknowledge the claims of babies, they insist, with astonishing presumption and no less astonishing absurdity, that no self-respecting baby would want to be born deformed or poor, and some might not even want to be born in the sex that its mother did not choose. (74)

Fox-Genovese does make comparable assertions about the "pro-life forces" (74). All the while, she uncritically supports the latter's characteristic insistence that human life begins at conception. Without a single footnote Fox-Genovese insists there is "evidence" that "from the moment of conception, the fetus is a form of human life, albeit a very primitive one" (230). Consistently enough, Fox-Genovese concludes that "The disposition of abortion relates directly to our other policies (or lack thereof) for women *and children*" (231; emphasis added).

In her concern for men Fox-Genovese tilts toward Paglia, as we will see. Like Denfeld, she refers to "feminist stories of heterosexuality as a male conspiracy to keep women in their place." Fox-Genovese immediately observes that women in general, however, "do not see men as The Enemy" (1996, 21). That is a feminist hang-up, she implies. She herself overrides that hang-up with recurrent expressions of concern for men's feelings and acknowledgment of their difficulties. She says, for example, that "as important as work is to growing numbers of women, it may be even more important to those men who have the greatest difficulty in finding jobs" (122). Here Fox-Genovese alludes to black and Latino men, as if black and Latino women have much less difficulty finding paid work. Another example of male-oriented posturing that fails to stand up empirically is Fox-Genovese's observation that "the corporate world that still treats women shabbily is beginning to treat many men *even worse*" (133). As her single statistic supporting that generalization Fox-Genovese compares a decade-long net loss of management jobs among men with a huge increase in management jobs among women. She ignores the dramatically diverse responsibilities, salaries, and benefits associated with "management," where women continue to predominate in the lower reaches.

Similarly, without any earnings data, Fox-Genovese is sure that "The pay gap between women and men is on the verge of extinction. The one exception is the most important case of all, namely, mothers. But their needs do not rank at the top of anyone's agenda" (1996, 134). More alarming is Fox-Genovese's generalization about domestic violence: "Scholars claim that women and men now engage in domestic violence in about equal numbers, although women may be less likely to initiate physical confrontations." That generalization is not documented. On the basis of an article in a 1994 *New Republic*, Fox-Genovese immediately goes on to say that "although men are more likely than women to molest children, women commit more than half of all child murders."

Fox-Genovese also derides feminists for putting down men. Without documentation she claims that

> Some feminists . . . have turned a worthy campaign for equity, justice, and common decency into an assault on all manifestations of masculinity. Believe it or not, there are feminist theorists . . . who denounce an erection as "an act of aggression." (1996, 145)

Fox-Genovese later observes that given feminists' "intensified . . . claims that men are inherently dangerous" and daily news stories about violence against women, it is sometimes "hard not to believe that our society has collapsed into an all-out war between the sexes" (163). Feminists are mostly to blame. They often misuse statistics so as "to promote a perception of women as the bloodied victims of men's war of conquest against them." Fox-Genovese concedes that the claims do "apply to some situations" but "have been wildly exaggerated." In the end, Fox-Genovese concludes, "the real struggle is not between women and men, but between children and work" (186).

Paglia's rhetoric about gender expresses more concern about men. She implies that feminist stances oversimplify the dynamics of gender. Paglia exudes sympathy toward men whom she sees as "*tormented* by women's flirtatiousness and hemming and hawing, their manipulations and changeableness, their humiliating rejections" (1994, 35; emphasis added). She sees rape as "an act of desperation, a confession of envy and exclusion" (32). She also sees it as "'unbridled lust,' like gluttony a sin of insufficient self restraint," an idea that "seems to be beyond feminist ken" (41). Paglia "see[s] not a world of male oppression and female victimization but an international conspiracy by women to keep from men the knowledge of men's own frailty" (47). Thus, her "motto for men is . . . 'Get it up!'" For women: "'Deal with it'" (251). Before long, Paglia not only says, "When I'm in the presence of real male dominance, I can feel it" but also claims, "I enjoy it" (256). Hers is no woman-centered feminism; it may well be what Teresa Ebert calls "patriarchal feminism" (1996, 257). Paglia insists that "Women will never know who they are until they let men be men" (1994, 111).

The Illogic of Backlash Rhetoric

A fifth characteristic of backlash rhetoric is its faulty logic, which typically entails recurrent inconsistencies as well as dubious assumptions.

Inconsistencies pervade Paglia's *Vamps & Tramps*, for example. One is particularly glaring. Paglia claims that "feminism has to . . . realize that it's not made a *dent* in anything outside a small group of white, upper-middle-class men" (1994, 248). Yet she refers to the "academic and feminist establishment" and claims that "contemporary feminism" has "*silenced* dissenting women and men" (xv, 249). Feminism also accounts for how the media have "indulged in [what Warren Farrell calls] 'a quarter century of male bashing'" (392). Paglia says feminism is "totally out of sync with what is *needed* now" but has apparently convinced more than a few people that Paglia is wrongheaded when she exclaims, "We want *more* pornography, *better* pornography. Pornography everywhere!" (259). Here Paglia is far from being sarcastic. Her feminism—her "Neo-Sexism" or "New Sexism"—"celebrates all historical depictions of women" (115).

Interwoven with such inconsistencies are Paglia's often untenable assumptions. She observes, for instance, that "Modern middle-class women cannot bear the thought that their hard-won professional achievements can be outweighed in an instant by a young hussy flashing a little tits and ass" (1994, 67). Paglia's dual assumptions here—that a little flesh can outweigh professional achievements and that middle-class women are not up to dealing with that alleged circumstance—are dubious, even silly. Similarly, she says that "Any woman . . . who cannot respond to penises or who finds them hideous or laughable . . . is neither complete as a woman nor healthy as a person" (83). Also problematic are Paglia's assertions such as:

> Equal opportunity feminism, which I espouse, demands the removal of all barriers to woman's advance in the political and professional world—but not at the price of special protections for women, which are infantilizing and anti-democratic. (x)

Assumed here is that *other* feminists espouse "special protections," when in fact second-wave feminists have struggled against such biased mechanisms.

What kind of feminism is this? Paglia (1998, 13) herself claims to be "a comedian, essentially"! Whatever this feminism is, its rhetoric generally entails two more characteristics worth mentioning. Its sixth characteristic is that unlike feminisms challenging gender hierarchies, this sort ultimately reassures readers (cf. Chisholm 1993, 56). It is what Faludi calls a "no-risk feminism for a fearful age" (1995, 33), which demands neither social transformation nor personal struggle. This is the assimilationist feminism (see chapter 5) of privileged women who conveniently ignore women's diversity. It may also be what bell hooks (2000a, 10, 11) calls "career feminism" or "lifestyle-based feminism"—a feminism based on opportunism and adaptable to any lifestyle.

Seventh, this rhetoric comprises disclaimers about contributing to a backlash. Roiphe vaguely implies that considering her as part of a backlash is wrong: "As I see it, there are more than two sides to any issue, and feminists are closer to their backlash than they'd like to think" (6). Paglia's disclaimer is more straightforward. She says that feminism "goes into the outside world and says, 'What, what? You don't agree with us? Then you must be a *backlash* to *us*! Yes, you must be having a backlash to us because of our *success*'" (249). Paglia dismisses backlash as a myth promulgated by the "feminist establishment," it seems.

Like Roiphe and Paglia, Patai and Koertge deny they are participating in a backlash. Their formulaic disclaimer denies backlash even exists. Instead, the term represents "a pejorative that is today slapped onto any and every criticism of feminism and whose main function seems to be to shut down discussion" (1994, xv).

In this (and other) connections Patai's more recent contributions to backlash merit passing mention. Although multiculturalism is also a target of Patai's (1998–99) scorn, she continues to reserve most of it for women's studies and feminism. Her 1998 book, for instance, is titled *Heterophobia: Sexual Harassment and the Future of Feminism*. There she claims that "'harassment' threatens to become the predominant word associated with 'sexual,'" in part because of "the MacKinnonite orthodoxy" (1998, 3, 5). Patai also claims that "heterophobic discourse" is "prevalent in feminism" and that "the entire English-speaking world [seems] in thrall to feminist ideology" (11, 99). Toward the end of her book Patai writes, "To those predisposed to dismiss my arguments as reactionary or as an example of 'backlash,' I respond: Unassailable ideas create totalitarian policies" (212). This book's closing sentence is at least as ironic:

> A feminism deeply compromised by hatred and scorn, pious and narrow, scurrilous and smug, dismissive of those it injures and derisive to those who dare to disagree—this is not a feminism with a future. (212)

Also, Fox-Genovese follows these other authors by implying that her work has nothing to do with backlash. She says, for instance, that feminists "explain" the "attitudes, which they reject as outright bigotry, backlash, or mere stupidity" (1996, 29). All the while, the more important similarity to the other works is Fox-Genovese's tendency to make sweeping assertions whose validity is questionable or problematic, especially her claims about how feminists have shortchanged mothers and children.

Before looking at historical patterns of backlash in the next section, a brief look at the New Right proves illuminating. It comprises two distinct strands of thought pertinent to feminism and backlash. As Rebecca Klatch (1987) found in studying New Right women, *social conservatives* see feminism as antifamily and self-centered. Often basing their stance on religious grounds, they regard feminism as symptomatic of a decadent or deteriorating society. By contrast, *laissez-faire conservatives* largely support feminist goals but reject collective or governmental means of achieving those goals, mostly because they emphasize the efficacy of rational, self-interested individuals while ignoring institutional grounds for social inequalities. Laissez-faire conservative feminists thus represent the possibility of backlash *within* feminism alongside the backlash *against* feminism that often comes from social conservatives (cf. Stacey 1996; Oakley and Mitchell 1997; Walters 1997; Yuval-Davis 1997). Paglia's work illustrates laissez-faire conservativism, while Roiphe leans in that direction. Fox-Genovese, however, leans toward social conservatism, while Patai and Koertge's narrow focus on women's studies makes it hazardous to infer their broader stance. Noteworthy are Denfeld's and Lehrman's departures from the ideas of both laissez-faire and social conservatives.

Backlash and Its Genesis

Seymour Martin Lipset cites "'backlash' politics" as "a recurrent phenomenon in American politics" (1970, 305). He and Earl Raab define such politics

> as the reaction by groups which are declining in a *felt sense* of importance, influence, and power, as a result of secular endemic change in society, to seek to reverse or stem the direction of change through political means. (1970, 29, emphasis added)

Backlash rhetoric conveys the subjective sense Lipset and Raab describe. Roiphe seems to feel, for instance, that her feminism counted for less than it should have on the campuses where she studied; Paglia seems to think her ideas would be more influential were it not for the substantial power feminists wield; Patai and Koertge imply that in the earlier days of women's studies people like them and their respondents had greater credibility and authority; Fox-Genovese blames feminism for turning against and diminishing the influence of relatively conservative feminists such as herself. These authors lament loss.

Lipset calls backlash "a politics of alienation" (1970, 311), and backlash rhetoric appears foremost in what can be read as narratives of alienation. These narratives express the (relative) powerlessness associated with alienation; they concern shifting norms that leave narrators at a loss as to how to cope and get along; they describe how absurdity infiltrated experiences that the narrators had expected to yield reliable meaning. Lipset goes on to identify backlash as a politics of "nostalgia." Lipset and Raab observe that participants in backlash feel their "way of life" is "at stake," that it is "losing its dominance" (1970, 114). "Reasonable" feminists, this rhetoric implies, no longer control women's movements and women's studies. Instead, extremists (called all sorts of names) have taken over.

Lipset and Raab mention two broad groupings inclined toward such feelings. Some feel "'dispossessed' . . . as a result of the rise of other types of communities, occupations, or ethnic groups"(1970, 306). For example, Roiphe resents feminists who focus undue attention on sexual assault and closely related issues, while Patai and Koertge (1994, 14–15, 20, 24–25, 27, 32, 62, 67–71) seem to resent the issues that women of color and white lesbians, in particular, tend to raise. These individuals imply a nostalgia for a time when feminism provided them a less challenging political home. Paglia, on the other hand, seems to represent a grouping whose members "have recently risen, but find themselves barred from being able to claim the concomitants of success" (1994, 306). She insists she was "the only openly gay person at the Yale Graduate School (1968–72), a candor that was professionally costly" (73). She also says she comes from an immigrant family (209) and has "working-class roots" (Carey 1995, H4). Conceivably, with those identifications Paglia feels that her Ivy League degree represents a dramatic rise in society's status hierarchy. Yet she has had to deal with "job problems, poverty, and the rejection of *Sexual Personae* [her first book] by seven major publishers" (1994, xiv). Thus, she may feel that until recently she could not "claim the concomitants of success" that Lipset and Raab mention.

The latter scholars indicate that backlash attracts "those whose privileges, status, and opportunities do not correspond to their expectations" (307). Thus, the voices of backlash are often voices of privilege. Moreover, backlash involves "see[ing] limitations on their position as a result of the planned actions of those who now control the polity or other parts of the power structure" (Lipset and Raab 1970, 307). Backlash rhetoric involves blaming certain kinds of feminists for anxiety and discomfort, loss of status or privilege, and uncertain credibility. At least implicitly, it concerns "the changing times: a disappearing way of life, a vanishing power, a diminishing group prestige, a heart-sinking change of social scenery, a lost sense of comfort and belongingness" (429). Those who use backlash rhetoric seem to feel that their status— or that of the group(s) they identify with—has deteriorated, which gets interpreted "as a general social deterioration" (429). Roiphe bemoans the blue-light fears and irrational feminist rhetoric on American campuses, for example; Paglia laments the misguided posturing of the "feminist establishment" supposedly aimed at protecting, not liberating, women; Patai and Koertge tie women's studies to lack of professionalism, second-rate scholarship, and politicized education; Fox-Genovese links feminism with the neglect of children and exacerbated relationships between the sexes.

Lipset and Raab indicate that backlash involves more "symbolic investment in the past than in the future" (1970, 504). It glorifies the past as less complex than the present. At the same time it inclines toward "the repression of difference and dissent, the closing down of the market place of ideas," with "cleavage and ambivalence [seen] as *illegitimate*" (6). Here lies the most poignant irony underlying backlash rhetoric. While it commonly alleges silencing and orthodoxy among feminists, it revolves itself around explicit, sometimes mean-spirited, intolerance of certain attitudes, values, or practices among feminists (cf. Minnich 1990).

Lipset and Raab remind us that backlash by and large involves "ordinary people caught in certain kinds of stress" (1970, 484). We dare not demonize or otherwise dehumanize them. Yet like many an insider peddling backlash, some of its participants are people of significant privilege taking potshots at a grouping that has long been an easy target in American life, as James's novel implies. Since feminisms challenge the very "foundations of the existing order" (Freeman 1994, 173) and thus evoke anxieties among people benefiting from or comfortable with the status quo, feminists serve as a ready scapegoat for people frustrated by the felt diminution of their status, security, or authority. We return briefly to these notions in our afterword where we focus on the question, Who's afraid of women's studies?

In the meantime we look briefly to other feminists for a few more insights into insider backlash. Teresa Ebert sees, as we do, that what she calls "Retrofeminism is largely the province of the privileged who—in their localized experience—indeed find little oppression" (1996, 267). Barbara Smith insists, though, that feminism "struggles to free *all* women. . . . Anything less than this vision . . . is not feminism but merely female self-aggrandizement" (1998, 96). As we have seen, some visions of feminism are in fact about a good deal less than freeing women of color, low-income women, queer women, women with disabilities, immigrant women, and other women whose oppression rests on more than gender alone. Such limited visions are not only more modest but also less uncomfortable for many women. Thus, "antifeminist seduction" (Zahra 1999) often works.

This seduction works by trying to convince women that feminism denies them "their 'essential' womanhood, along with all the institutions, practices, and prerogatives attached to it" (Moody-Adams 1997, 77). It works, too, by dodging the tough questions of how to acknowledge both women's victimization and their agency and how to affirm women's strengths while acknowledging their pain (Lamb 1999, 11). The antifeminist seduction also works by "refusing to acknowledge that we live in a patriarchal culture" (Bulbeck 1997, 222). To that extent this seduction is largely drained of anything likely to threaten most men (and the women who want to keep peace with them). As bell hooks has noted,

> Any profound critique of patriarchal masculinity that touches the minds and hearts of men of all ages in our culture threatens patriarchy in such a way that it engenders fierce backlash. It is no accident that the arenas where we have most worked to raise male consciousness— around domestic violence, reproductive rights for women, sexual harassment—have been the space of patriarchal, antifeminist backlash. (1998, 49)

In sum, insider backlash is an expression of a narrow, relatively privileged feminism. Mostly rooted in academe, insider backlash is a far cry from what the "founding mothers" of women's studies had in mind. As one of them observes,

> We did not support women's studies as a way of advancing ourselves within the university. On the contrary. We identified with the oppositional stance of those who had been and were still making trouble for the university by insisting that it become more humane and diverse. (Sklar 2000, 140)

We favor an ambitious, embracing feminism—a feminism based on "remember[ing] that the word 'feminist' has a history" (Segal 1999, 35). We believe that girls' and women's progress is sure to continue if we keep "sexual freedom, pleasure, choice, personal growth, and creativity . . . among our most cherished values, no matter what the political climate" (Rapping 1994, 18).

Afterword

Who's Afraid
of Women's Studies?

The emergence of women's studies has been fraught with conflict. On a campus where one of us teaches, for instance, establishing a mere minor in women's studies was challenging. Several committee members insisted that women's studies would be divisive, as if the faculty were united across gender and other social lines. No member spoke on behalf of women's studies. The university curriculum committee, all male and nearly all white, repeatedly charged "separatism," a code word used much as antigay ideologues use "family values." (Annette Kolodny [2000, 284], among others, tells a similar story. In her experience, a senior colleague went so far as to liken women's studies to Nazism.) The vote was ultimately in support of the minor, but the committee added one restriction: No directed (independent) studies could count among the elective credits for the fifteen-hour minor. What did the committee members fear?

On that same campus at least one faculty member has asked a student whether or not one of us has gotten over our "social disease," meaning our feminism. The student, a white male, was outraged not only by the question but also by the professor's presumption that guys stick together in such matters. Another faculty member has repeatedly told students that one of us does not really know anything reliable about all that "gender stuff" she teaches. What are these professors afraid of?

In an introductory women's studies course one of us taught, the required books included Maxine Baca Zinn and Bonnie Thornton Dill's anthology *Women of Color in U.S. Society* (1994). Several white female students implied the instructor was racist because of the book's focus on women (apparently) unlike themselves. Like some of the white professors quoted in Patai and Koertge's book, these students resisted

131

learning about American women who happened not to be white. What were they afraid of?

Beyond campuses little is known about women's studies (Luebke and Reilly 1995). By contrast, a lot of people have opinions about feminism and feminists. Painted by Roiphe or Paglia, Robertson or Charen, feminists are unreasonable, unpleasant individuals who vent their frustrations on as many people as possible. Backlash rhetoric paints them as miserable failures trying to project their unhappiness onto other people or trying to impose their distorted sense of justice on society. What are these media-sponsored backlashers afraid of?

In everyday life resistance comes in the form of taunts, "jokes," refusals to cooperate or change, and other mundane protests that make feminist life all the more challenging. Young feminists often report, for instance, that they dislike labeling themselves "feminists" because of the negative reactions that word evokes (Glickman 1993). What are their peers afraid of?

As research on backlash suggests, fear often grows out of a sense of loss—imminent or otherwise. We fear losing credibility or popularity; we fear losing power and control; we fear losing privilege; we fear losing the uneven playing field where we have routinely won; we fear losing the people who "need" us or love us. Thus, when feminists talk about transformation and social justice and equalizing opportunities, many people hear not prospects of a better world but threats to their advantages and social status.

The hyperprivileged among us have reason to be resistant and fearful. In principle, they *will* lose those privileges that rest not on meaningful merit, hard work, resourcefulness, and demonstrable achievements but on inherited advantages, dominant-group memberships, and artificially restricted competition. As feminists and kindred agents of change continue attacking the matrix of domination, the hyperprivileged have increasing cause for alarm. Their wealth, lack of accountability and self-serving stances will meet with more and more challenges, as will their media-based demagoguery and institutionalized opportunism. Their grossly unfair share of power, wealth, and prerogatives will come to seem increasingly outrageous and, therefore, unjustifiable.

Most people, however, are far from hyperprivileged. As we have seen, most of us are privileged in some respects and disprivileged in others. Thus, on some counts most of us are vulnerable to fears that change evokes. We have seen, for instance, that white-skin privilege evokes anxiety and tension about race among some white women.

Perhaps more common are fears about loss of class privilege as social-justice concerns take hold of people's consciousness. Many professional women like Charen or Patai and Koertge, many upper-middle-class daughters like Roiphe, many media favorites like Paglia, and many wives of privilege like Fox-Genovese seem to fear the material and social losses they stand to incur if we begin taking seriously the inhumane situations low-income and many working-class women chronically face. Many men who are not hyperprivileged also feel the prospect of loss—loss of nurturance that flows mostly in their direction, loss of their predominance as breadwinners, loss of their female partners' disproportionate domestic labor, loss of their right to expect the women in their lives to honor their priorities and preferences, loss of the right to dominate women sexually, loss of the deference that has long assured them they are *real men*.

Most of the losses we are talking about are likely to eventuate as feminism succeeds. Thus, we need a counterbalancing focus, especially for those who resist and fear feminist transformations, on the gains people stand to make outside society's hyperprivileged sectors. Together, we stand to gain a profoundly better world—a world that emanates from understanding that "it is not enough to patch up [our] faulty institutions and hope that they will be strong and flexible enough to bear the weight of genuine social justice" (Social Justice Group 2000, 3). A world based on feminist transformation also builds up from understanding that

> concern with either gender justice or the fate of women overall must also engage us in social struggle for economic redistribution, alongside (and inevitably enmeshed with) issues of identity involving cultural recognition and respect. (Segal 1999, 34)

For starters, a world based on feminist understandings will be a world with a larger, sturdier safety net. When we lose our jobs, have special-needs children, become disabled, seek an abortion, look for high-quality childcare or elder care, want to return to school, or face a life-threatening disease, we will be dramatically less likely to fall through the cracks of a system that insists on individualistic solutions to social problems and life's biggest challenges. We will find that previously unemployed or underemployed people have been trained as childcare workers, health-care technicians, preschool educators, assistants for those wanting to continue living as independently as possible in their own homes. We will find that the taxes we have paid and the hard work we have done mean something when our needs outpace our resources. We will find that "health" means physical and emotional *well-being*, not just the absence of illness.

Second, we will find that our world is a more civil, tolerant one. The fulfillment of feminism ensures, in a word, dignity centering on the right of each human being to live the life she chooses for herself as long as her choices do not injure other people or curtail their choices. In such a world ambiguity is no justification for cultural repression or social rejection; fluid identities are commonplace; group boundaries are permeable; the common good entails both self-cultivation and community development. In a world where feminist values prevail, self and other meet as prospective collaborators; friends and strangers refuse to pigeonhole one another; younger and older sense that they need one another to be fully in touch with the human world; color loses its stranglehold on people's life chances; sexuality is pleasure-oriented and passionately mutual; gender bends in as many directions as humanness itself. People approach and deal with one another using rituals that affirm their kindredness. Civility prevails, and open censures of people who violate it are widely accepted as necessary means of maintaining a worthy collective life.

Finally, we land in a world that is less unfair. In the world driven by feminist values people's prospects are unrelated to their gender, sexual orientation, class of origin, skin color, age, ethnicity, ablebodiedness, or any other circumstance beyond their control. What opportunities they have and what rewards they get depend, rather, on what lies firmly within their control—how hard and long they work, how many skills they command, how much they cooperate with their coworkers and neighbors and family members, and how much they devote themselves to community and self-cultivation. With the demise of today's privileges comes a self in community.

To illustrate the spirit and the substance of what is to come, we turn to statements from two students who recently completed an introductory women's studies course. These are excerpts from an essay written in class about how they could recognize a feminist individual. They had one week to consider the question. Their thoughts reveal a lot about what students gain from women's studies and thus serve as an antidote to the nonsensical impressions left by Patai and Koertge's *Professing Feminism*. At the same time these students' words imply why some individuals fear women's studies.

Before introducing you to these two extraordinary yet ordinary women, let us tell you what they had read during the semester. Among the required books their favorite was Anndee Hochman's *Everyday Acts and Small Subversions* (1994). They had also read Michelle Fine's *Disruptive Voices: The Possibilities of Feminist Research* (1992a) and Sandra Lee Bartky's *Femininity and Domination: Studies in the Phenomenology of Oppression* (1990). The students had also read Paula Gunn Allen's *The Sacred Hoop: Recovering the Feminine in American Indian Traditions* (1992) as well as Zinn and Dill's *Women of Color in U.S. Society* (1994).

The first voice belongs to Mimi, who is a wife as well as mother of a son and daughter. Mimi is in her thirties, has completed her bachelor's degree, and is nearly finished with a master's degree program. Mimi writes:

> At the heart of women's subordinate position in the hierarchy of gender is their perceived lack of value. This affects our educational and employment opportunities, our position in the home and family, our legal standing, and even the way we view ourselves. In many ways we are taught we are less important than men. Bartky's main theme in her essays is disempowerment—we are sexually objectified, culturally dominated, and stereotyped. By the time we reach adulthood we are so trained in the ways of pleading and pleasing that we have developed our own body language and body rituals that attest to and perpetuate our powerlessness. As a feminist, Bartky recognized our devaluing and says we need to inspect the things we do to our bodies and understand that even when we master the disciplinary practices necessary to make us "beautiful women," we are still "only" women. . . .
>
> If devaluing is at the heart of women's subordination, then it would seem that a feminist would recognize . . . the true value of all [females]: disabled women, women of color, lesbians, female children, and elderly women. . . . While valuing all women is key to being a feminist, that alone would not be enough to make up a feminist. . . . What our authors share as well is a commitment to change. Feminists recognize the value of women, and they seek, tell, resist, and act in the hopes of making women's lives better. To me, the authors we read this semester are very clearly feminists. By examining them I have a better idea of what a feminist is. Feminists, like women, come in various strengths and varieties. . . . Some are loud activists, and some protest personally and quietly. Some feminists are men. Feminists, those who see the value in women and make a commitment to making women's lives better, look at women and see possibilities.

The second voice is that of Afa, then a first-year undergraduate who was born in Nicaragua. Like Mimi, Afa has now completed her bachelor's degree and is pondering her prospects before beginning graduate studies. Afa is neither married nor a mother. She writes:

A feminist individual is a person committed to defending and promoting the right of women to be autonomous and complete persons—to be more than a set of roles that suit the expectations of a . . . patriarchal society. Coming across a feminist individual, or being able to designate a person as such, does not depend on that person's fulfillment of a particular set of requirements. A dedication to upholding the claim of women to personhood can be manifested in a number of ways—"feminist" is not a stamp designating one common way of thinking and acting. Rather, it is a way to identify the numerous ways in which people think, interact, behave, and work in order to uphold the basic truth that women are not a strange variation from the rational human being, "man," but are whole human persons in their own right.

Bringing the concept "We are complete persons" to life involves a number of things. A feminist individual may be a woman who is just beginning to see how she is denied full personhood in her society and is willing to work on understanding and changing her personal condition. Or it might be a woman who, having realized this, organizes community groups in order to alleviate the consequences of this denial (e.g., working with women who have suffered rape). Feminism, in other words, may happen in different manners and levels—from the development of individual awareness to the undertaking of collective work. . . .

Feminism as personal is connected with feminism as communal and activist: the personal is political. Women may choose to "adopt" family members, live single, live with other women as lovers or partners or friends, gain ancestors—create and recreate their lives in ways that say "I am entitled to my life." All the ways in which people choose to interact [involve feminist] possibilities for breaking from the norms that say: A woman must be heterosexual, married, a mother, normal.

Global Feminisms in Everyday Life

Although spatial limitations have narrowed our attention to North American women, we want to include a global note that extends Mimi's and Afa's insights. The consciousness and the commitments they describe find expression in women's daily lives around the planet. Nowhere, perhaps, is that clearer than in women's worldwide efforts to stop environmental degradation, to gain equal access to natural resources, and to ensure sustainable communities through sustainable development. While many of these women do not identify themselves as feminists, their efforts characteristically reflect values and visions not unlike those associated with "ecofeminism."

In the northern rich countries feminism and environmentalism increasingly intersect as social movements. Feminist environmentalists and environmental feminists may or may not call themselves ecofeminists, however. Even though *ecofeminism* is at root the theory and practice of both ecological and feminist values, its emergence alongside the women's spirituality movement during the 1970s made it problematic for some women. Since the latter movement encompasses pagans and goddess worshipers as well as less radical challenges to mainstream religion, some feminist environmentalists abjure the label "ecofeminist." Still, as a generic name, "ecofeminist" does a good job of designating those who combine environmental and feminist priorities in their personal/political lives.

In any case such feminism is no longer a phenomenon mostly in northern countries. The late 1980s and early 1990s showed how ecofeminism could help to advance an "international feminist movement" (Sturgeon 1997, 146). Feminism around the globe began to influence policies of economic development during the very period when environmental concerns could not go unaddressed. Thus were laid substantial grounds for political alliances between southern and northern feminists (145).

Noel Sturgeon shows, in particular, how U.S. ecofeminism can help to promote such alliances. At its core, she says, it

> is a political theory that attempts to deploy at once a number of radical analyses of injustice and exploitation focused on racism, classism, sexism, heterosexism, imperialism, speciesism, and environmental degradation. (1997, 18)

Aiming to be radically inclusive, U.S. ecofeminism "aims to be a multi-issue, globally oriented movement with a more diverse constituency than either its environmentalist or feminist predecessors." As Sturgeon goes on to observe,

> A name that can usefully if partially describe the work of Donna Haraway and Mary Daly, Alice Walker and Rachel Carson, Starhawk and Vandana Shiva, ecofeminism is a shifting theoretical and political location that can be defined to serve various intentions. (24)

Ecofeminism can thus help to build common ground across national boundaries for women around the world whose commitments
are fundamentally feminist as well as environmentalist. It can support
and further mobilize all those women whose first activism often derives from "concern for human health and habitat, issues that the large
environmental groups have been slow to take on" (Seager 1993, 181).
Ecofeminism makes statistical as well as social sense:

> Women are the backbone of virtually every environmental group
> around the world. With few exceptions, women constitute approxi-
> mately 60 to 80 percent of the membership of most environmental
> organizations—averaging 60 percent of the membership of general-
> interest environmental groups, 80 percent or more of small grass-
> roots groups and animal-rights groups. (263–64)

Further, their typical familial responsibilities often make women the
first witnesses of environmental degradation. In that respect women's
experiences hold two ecofeminist lessons. First, the environment is part
and parcel of our everyday lives; it is not a "separate realm" lying beyond everyday life. Second, since "environmental destruction shows
up in small ways in ordinary lives, we need to change our perception
of who are reliable environmental narrators" or whose environmental
voices should be heard (Seager 1993, 271, 272, 282; cf. Rocheleau,
Thomas-Slayter, and Wangari 1996, 9).

Surely the voices of environmental activists such as Judi Bari, Pat
Costner, and Diane Wilson need to be heard a great deal more. All
North American environmental activists—a carpenter, a scientist, and
a shrimper, respectively—and all physically intimidated because of
their activism (Helvarg 1997, 330–51), women like these get far too little media attention. Even less attention goes to women elsewhere on
the planet whose environmental commitments and achievements are,
to say the least, newsworthy.

In their volume on feminist political ecology, which builds on feminist scholarship in ecology, economics, and geography, Dianne Rocheleau, Barbara Thomas-Slayter, and Esther Wangari (1996) bring together the stories of many such women. They include Brazilian women
living in the Amazonian rainforest whose grassroots work to save their
livelihood as rubber tappers led to a national organization for land reform; they include Spanish women, mostly mothers and homemakers,
holding the line on hazardous waste dumps in their communities with
marches, music, mutual aid, and nightly ruckus made by beating pots
and pans from their windows and rooftops; they include Kenyan

women forming self-help groups that plant trees, gather knowledge about medical uses of local vegetation, weed together for pay, build houses for one another, and eventually buy a goat for each member and open a cooperative together to market their produce (Campbell 1996; Bru-Bistuer 1996; Rocheleau, Thomas-Slayter, and Wangari 1996). Others resisting environmental degradation include women struggling for fair access to environmental resources in the Philippines and India, women institutionalizing a food-testing program in Poland, mothers available "to rally at a moment's notice" in Japan, and women joining efforts with men in the U.S. environmental justice movement aimed at reversing the environmental exploitation of minority and low-income communities and neighborhoods (Shields et al. 1996; Mehta 1996; Bellows 1996; Seager 1993; D. Taylor 1996).

Globally, then, women represent a powerful environmental force. While they do often join hands with men in these efforts, they frequently work in predominantly or exclusively women's groups. As individuals responsible for their families' health and safety, as individuals left behind when men move to cities in pursuit of waged labor, as individuals denied equal access to natural resources, women around the globe are working to clean up the planet and reverse the tide of environmental destruction. In that work they characteristically chart transnational courses capable of rallying the women of the world to a common cause. With their eyes on the prize of a sustainable planet where social justice prevails, all these women share a fundamentally ecofeminist vision. Their labors attest to women's practical power and feminism's enduring promise. Above all, their efforts illustrate that "feminism's distinct legacy still lies in its potential, however difficult and complex, to connect personal and cultural issues to economic and political affairs" (Segal 1999, 5).

Never Fear!

The "visionary feminism" (hooks 2000a) capable of keeping women's activism and women's studies lively and transformative remains under fire, even among self-identified feminists. The age of backlash is far from over, then. We end with one more example, noteworthy for its publication by a university press as well as its author's background of feminist activism, namely, Joan Mandle's *Can We Wear Our Pearls and Still Be Feminists? Memoirs of a Campus Struggle.*

Mandle is a sociologist who, like historian Elizabeth Fox-Genovese, has served as director of a women's studies program. In fact, in her preface Mandle (2000, x) thanks not only Fox-Genovese but also Daphne Patai. Claiming that her administrative "experience represents a case study" (ix) as well as a memoir, Mandle describes in great detail all the challenges she faced during her six-year administrative stint at Colgate University. Most of her challenges, it seems, came from women's studies faculty and students.

Although it engages in neither individual nor collective name calling, Mandle's book does exhibit the usual characteristics of backlash texts. She loathes "identity politics" (6), often another code word among critics of women's studies and other interdisciplinary studies focusing on specific sociocultural groups. In these circles "identity politics," as we have seen, means that race and sexuality (among other things) get attention alongside gender—attention that makes many white, heterosexual women anxious or resistant. Needless to say, such attention is capable of displacing these women from the center stage of women's studies. Serious, sustained attention to race and sexuality also means that those of us who are white, heterosexual, or both, need to interrogate our privilege and come to feminist terms with our racial and sexual identities.

Mandle's text implicitly denies the worthwhileness, not to mention the necessity, of such efforts. At Colgate, for instance, she insisted that "sexuality be given a less than dominant place" in feminist programming so as to "not privilege homosexuality and bisexuality" (107, 113). Mandle does not question whether such privileging is practically possible in a heterosexist society, nor does she acknowledge that such "privileging" could stimulate helpful explorations of their sexual identities among heterosexual students and colleagues.

In any case Mandle faults women's studies at her university for its "underlying antimale bias" (24). Then, too, she criticizes her women's studies colleagues for their "turf-fighting" and their "ill will" toward the "Greek system" on campus. (35–36, 124). She even bemoans how "Most of the women's studies faculty vehemently opposed" Mandle's decision to let an anti-abortion organization schedule a program at Colgate's Center for Women's Studies. Like other backlash texts, Mandle's insists that reasonable feminists like herself need to combat the powerful "feminist orthodoxy" (47, 76) that has overtaken women's studies programs. She even criticizes women's studies students for their "disingenuous invocation of orthodoxy" (87). At times, then, Mandle's text illustrates how "Yesterday's visionaries are today's scapegoats, when not newly tamed and domesticated" (Segal 1999, 1).

But this is all old hat to analysts of backlash narratives. What makes Mandle's text eminently worthy of attention is her straightforwardness about her own priorities and administrative style as Colgate's director of women's studies. Her honesty, it seems to us, implies what sorts of politics undergird backlash within women's studies programs—insider backlash of the face-to-face, anticollegial sort.

Mandle's report revolves around woeful paradoxes. She describes an autocratic mode of administering yet cannot seem to conjure up any good reasons for resistance from women's studies colleagues. At the same time Mandle uses exclusionary methods, she claims to move toward an inclusive program. In our judgment her behavior seems patently inflammatory. For anyone aiming to instigate resistance, Mandle's administrative style is exemplary. Worse yet, her credentials for directing a women's studies program as recently as the 1990s were dubious. Mandle herself admits, "Before becoming director of women's studies at Colgate, I had never participated in a formal women's studies program. Indeed, I was somewhat skeptical of the effectiveness of such programs" (2000, 3). So why did she seek the position? Why was she chosen? Perhaps her administrative priorities and style go a long way toward answering these questions.

From the beginning Mandle's priorities are clear. She aimed "to reach beyond those already committed" to women's studies (2000, 5). She also hoped to "overcome feminism's negative stereotype on campus" (6). Her goals, then, involved "outreach" and inclusiveness (8, 9). Mandle believed, in short, that "Women's studies was for everyone." Thus, for example, "all faculty members were potential contributors to women's studies" (24). The sole criterion would be whether a faculty member's work "address[es] in a scholarly way issues of gender and women's role [sic] in society" (26–27). Apparently, a feminist approach is optional.

Not surprisingly, Mandle reports that some faculty members "continued to flatly reject [her] effort to expand and reinvigorate feminist education on the campus" (37). "Seen by some as insufficiently feminist" (210), Mandle says that "Faculty who complained about being silenced . . . were simply those who disagreed with the direction [she] had taken women's studies" (205). Yet her own text depicts an anticollegial stance that in our judgment would alienate and outrage faculty members committed to and invested in the program that Mandle first entered as its director.

Instead of treading lightly as a newcomer, Mandle took charge in no uncertain terms. She refers to "taking over as director" (1). Her first-person narrative offers insistently singular, pronominal evidence of her style:

> Soon after my appointment as director, I proposed to the administration that we replace the [Women's Resource Center] with . . . a center totally housed within women's studies. It would be my vehicle for outreach. When it came to naming the new center, I rejected the obvious title. . . . One of the first decisions I made . . . was to avoid discussing my planned changes in the program with women's studies faculty and students. I chose this path because I was sure that if I did otherwise I would fail to win approval for an inclusive and outward-looking center. Instead of consultation, what I planned to do was . . . put my ideas into motion and simply hand the women's studies faculty and students a fait accompli. (8, 9, 14)

Mandle goes on to say that she "would not have been able to achieve [her] objectives if [she] had attempted . . . any other way" (15). So she "sent [her] proposal to the provost without showing it to anyone" (16). Mandle's use of the first-person singular continues to be instructive:

> To inaugurate the Center for Women's Studies, *I* planned a grand opening. . . . *I* invited the entire campus. Jamaica Kincaid . . . was *our* guest of honor. *I* saw this opening celebration as my opportunity to reach everyone with the message that changes were being made in the women's studies program. (17, emphasis added)

In the end Mandle advocates gender studies but insists on calling it "women's studies." She says that "as a field, women's studies had to study men as well as women" and "pursue an uncensored exploration of gender" (181, 210). However it is named, the study of gender cannot be both narrowly focused and widely effective. We agree with Biddy Martin that the concept of gender

> may have outlived its usefulness, requiring of us more substantive forms of reflection and change if interdisciplinary feminist studies are to contribute again to the changes that are occurring and need to occur in our modes of thinking and writing in higher education. (2001, 356)

Meanwhile within the field that Mandle advocates it seems that people *can* wear their pearls and still be feminists but *cannot* wear anything the least bit controversial and still be included in gender studies.

As Mandle herself concedes, "Conflicting views of feminism or of women's studies were seen as threatening rather than as a diversity to be welcomed" (2000, 25). What she does not acknowledge, though, is that she herself felt threatened by diversity of opinion, especially those stances that make some people uncomfortable or resistant. We endorse Mandle's goal of "nurturing and protecting multiple points of view" (25), including of course the very points of view she short-circuited or even excluded in her decision making.

In the end Mandle is not credible when she insists that "Women's studies [is] for everyone" (22). Neither, at first, is bell hooks. In *Feminism Is for Everybody: Passionate Politics* hooks belies her title early in her text. In her first chapter she declares that a person "cannot be anti-abortion and an advocate of feminism" (hooks 2000a, 6). Yet hooks, unlike Mandle, really does believe that feminism and women's studies are for everyone. They are for everyone as prospective beneficiaries of "feminist revolution," not as students enrolled in classes that hopefully add up to a degree. Feminism *is* for everybody, hooks argues, because feminist movement

> will make it possible for us to be fully self-actualized females and males able to create beloved community, to live together, realizing our dreams of freedom and justice, living the truth that we are all "created equal." Come closer. See how feminism can touch and change your life and all our lives. Come closer and know firsthand what feminist movement is all about. Come closer and you will see: feminism is for everybody. (hooks 2000a, 6)

References

Addelson, Kathryn Pyne, and Elizabeth Potter. 1991. "Making Knowledge." Pp. 259–77 in Joan E. Hartman and Ellen Messer-Davidow (eds.), *(En)Gendering Knowledge: Feminists in Academe*. Knoxville: University of Tennessee Press.

Allen, Amy. 1999. *The Power of Feminist Theory: Domination, Resistance, Solidarity*. Boulder, Colo.: Westview.

Allen, Paula Gunn. 1992 [1986]. *The Sacred Hoop: Recovering the Feminine in American Indian Traditions*. Boston: Beacon.

Andersen, Margaret. 1987. *Denying Difference: The Continuing Basis for the Exclusion of Race and Gender in the Curriculum*. Memphis, Tenn.: Memphis State University Center for Research on Women.

Arrington, Marie. 1987. "Under the Gun." Pp. 173–78 in Laurie Bell (ed.), *Good Girls/Bad Girls: Sex Trade Workers and Feminists Face to Face*. Toronto: Women's Press.

Atmore, Chris. 1999. "Victims, Backlash, and Radical Feminist Theory (or, The Morning After They Stole Feminism's Fire)." Pp. 183–201 in Sharon Lamb (ed.), *New Versions of Victims: Feminists Struggle with the Concept*. New York: New York University Press.

Auslander, Leora. 1997. "Do Women's + Feminist + Men's + Lesbian + Queer Studies = Gender Studies?" *differences: A Journal of Feminist Cultural Studies* 9, no. 3 (Fall 1997): 1–30.

Bailey, Peter. 1990. "Parasexuality and Glamour: The Victorian Barmaid as Cultural Prototype." *Gender & History* 2, no. 2 (Summer): 148–72.

Bal, Mieke. 2001. "Enfolding Feminism." Pp. 321–52 in Elisabeth Bronfen and Misha Kavka (eds.), *Feminist Consequences: Theory for the New Century*. New York: Columbia University Press.

Bammer, Angelika. 1991. "Mastery." Pp. 237–58 in Joan E. Hartman and Ellen Messer-Davidow (eds.), *(En)gendering Knowledge: Feminists in Academe*. Knoxville: University of Tennessee Press.

Banner, Lois W. 1983. *American Beauty*. Chicago: University of Chicago Press.

145

Bartky, Sandra Lee. 1990. *Femininity and Domination: Studies in the Phenomenol-
ogy of Oppression*. New York: Routledge.
Batt, Sharon. 1998. "'Perfect People': Cancer Charities." Pp. 137–46 in Rose
Weitz (ed.), *The Politics of Women's Bodies: Sexuality, Appearance and Behavior*.
New York: Oxford University Press.
Baumgardner, Jennifer, and Amy Richards. 2000. *Feminist Manifesta: Young
Women, Feminism, and the Future*. New York: Farrar, Straus, & Giroux.
Behar, Ruth. 1994. "Dare We Say 'I'? Bringing the Personal into Scholarship."
Chronicle of Higher Education (June 29): B1–B2.
Bellows, Anne C. 1996. "Where Kitchen and Laboratory Meet: The 'Tested Food
for Silesia' Program." Pp. 251–70 in Dianne Rocheleau, Barbara Thomas-
Slayter, and Esther Wangari (eds.), *Feminist Political Ecology: Global Issues and
Local Experiences*. New York: Routledge.
Beloff, Halla. 1993. "On Being Ordinary." Pp. 39–40 in Sue Wilkinson and Celia
Kitzinger (eds.), *Heterosexuality: A Feminism & Psychology Reader*. Newbury
Park, Calif.: Sage.
Benhabib, Seyla. 1999. "Sexual Difference and Collective Identities: The New
Global Constellation." *Signs: Journal of Women in Culture and Society* 24, no. 2
(Winter): 335–61.
Benjamin, Jessica. 1988. *The Bonds of Love: Psychoanalysis, Feminism, and the Prob-
lem of Domination*. New York: Pantheon.
Berger, Peter L. 1963. *Invitation to Sociology: A Humanistic Perspective*. New York:
Anchor Books.
Berger, Peter L., and Thomas Luckmann. 1967. *The Social Construction of Knowl-
edge: A Treatise on the Sociology of Knowledge*. New York: Anchor Books.
Blais, Madeleine. 1998. "Who's Got Time to Stay at Home?" *New York Times
Magazine* (April 5): 48–50.
Blumstein, Philip, and Pepper Schwartz. 1983. *American Couples: Money, Work,
Sex*. New York: William Morrow.
Bordo, Susan. 1990. "Feminism, Postmodernism, and Gender-Scepticism."
Pp. 133–56 in Linda J. Nicholson (ed.), *Feminism/Postmodernism*. New York:
Routledge.
———. 1993. *Unbearable Weight: Feminism, Western Culture, and the Body*. Berke-
ley: University of California Press.
———. 1997. *Twilight Zones: The Hidden Life of Images from Plato to O.J.* Berkeley:
University of California Press.
———. 1999. *The Male Body: A New Look at Men in Public and in Private*. New
York: Farrar, Straus, & Giroux.
Boyle, Mary. 1993. "Sexual Dysfunction or Heterosexual Dysfunction?"
Pp. 203–18 in Sue Wilkinson and Celia Kitzinger (eds.), *Heterosexuality: A
Feminism & Psychology Reader*. Newbury Park, Calif.: Sage.
Bradford, Judith, and Caitlin Ryan. 1991. "Who We Are: Health Concerns of
Middle-Aged Lesbians." Pp. 147–63 in Barbara Sang, Joyce Warshow, and
Adrienne J. Smith (eds.), *Lesbians at Midlife: The Creative Transition*. San Fran-
cisco: Spinsters Book.

Braidotti, Rosi. 1993. "Embodiment, Sexual Difference, and the Nomadic Subject." *Hypatia* 8 (Winter): 1–13.
———. 2001. "Becoming-Woman: Rethinking the Positivity of Difference." Pp. 381–413 in Elisabeth Bronfen and Misha Kavka (eds.), *Feminist Consequences: Theory for the New Century*. New York: Columbia University Press.
Brekhus, Wayne. 1998. "A Sociology of the Unmarked: Redirecting Our Focus." *Sociological Theory* 16, no. 1 (March): 34–51.
Bru-Bistuer, Josepa. 1996. "Spanish Women against Industrial Waste: A Gender Perspective on Environmental Grassroots Movements." Pp. 105–24 in Dianne Rocheleau, Barbara Thomas-Slayter, and Esther Wangari (eds.), *Feminist Political Ecology: Global Issues and Local Experiences*. New York: Routledge.
Brumberg, Joan. 1998. *The Body Project: An Intimate History of American Girls*. New York: Random House.
Buhle, Mari Jo. 2000. "Introduction." Pp. xv–xxvi in Florence Howe (ed.), *The Politics of Women's Studies: Testimony from Thirty Founding Mothers*. New York: Feminist Press.
Bulbeck, Chila. 1997. *Living Feminism: The Impact of the Women's Movement on Three Generations of Australian Women*. Cambridge: Cambridge University Press.
Burch, Beverly. 1993. *On Intimate Terms: The Psychology of Difference in Lesbian Relationships*. Urbana: University of Illinois Press.
Burd, Stephen. 1994. "Defiant Conservative Relishes the NEH Fights to Come." *Chronicle of Higher Education* (June 29): A25.
Butler, Judith. 1990. *Gender Trouble: Feminism and the Subversion of Identity*. New York: Routledge.
———. 2001. "The End of Sexual Difference?" Pp. 414–34 in Elisabeth Bronfen and Misha Kavka (eds.), *Feminist Consequences: Theory for the New Century*. New York: Columbia University Press.
Butler, Sandra, and Barbara Rosenblum. 1991. *Cancer in Two Voices*. San Francisco: Spinsters Book.
Cahn, Susan K. 1994. *Coming on Strong: Gender and Sexuality in Twentieth-Century Women's Sport*. New York: Free Press.
Campbell, Connie, in collaboration with The Women's Group of Xapuri. 1996. "Out on the Front Lines But Still Struggling for Voice: Women in the Rubber Tappers' Defense of the Forest in Xapuri, Acre, Brazil." Pp. 27–61 in Dianne Rocheleau, Barbara Thomas-Slayter, and Esther Wangari (eds.), *Feminist Political Ecology: Global Issues and Local Experiences*. New York: Routledge.
Carey, Art. 1995. "Firebrand in Academia." *Philadelphia Inquirer* (March 5): H1, H4.
Carbado, Devon W. (ed.). 1989. *Black Men on Race, Gender, and Sexuality: A Critical Reader*. New York: New York University Press.
Castro, Ginette. 1990 [1984]. *American Feminism: A Contemporary History*. Trans. by Elizabeth Loverde-Bagwell. New York: New York University Press.
———. 1992. "A Celebration of Butch-Femme Identities in the Lesbian Community." A panel of eight women—including Amber Hollibaugh and Joan

Nestle—plus a moderator. Pp. 454–63 in Joan Nestle (ed.), *The Persistent Desire: A Butch-Femme Reader*. Boston: Alyson Publications.

Charbonneau, Claudette, and Patricia Slade Lander. 1991. "Redefining Sexuality: Women Becoming Lesbian in Midlife." Pp. 35–43 in Barbara Sang, Joyce Warshow, and Adrienne J. Smith (eds.), *Lesbians at Midlife: The Creative Transition*. San Francisco: Spinsters Book.

Charen, Mona. 1984. "The Feminist Mistake." *National Review* (March 23).

Chase, Susan E., and Mary F. Rogers. 2001. *Mothers and Children: Feminist Analysis and Personal Narratives*. New Brunswick, N.J.: Rutgers University Press.

Chisolm, Dianne. 1993. "Violence against Violence Directed against Women: An Avant-Garde for the Times." Pp. 28–66 in Arthur Kroker and Marilouise Kroker (eds.), *The Last Sex: Feminism and Outlaw Bodies*. New York: St. Martin's.

Christian, Harry. 1994. *The Making of Anti-Sexist Men*. London: Routledge.

Christian-Smith, Linda K. 1990. *Becoming a Woman through Romance*. New York: Routledge.

Chua, Lawrence. 1994. "bell hooks." [An Interview]. *BOMB*. (Summer): 25–28.

Clare, Eli. 1999. *Exile and Pride: Disability, Queerness, and Liberation*. Cambridge, Mass.: South End Press.

Cole, Ellen, and Esther D. Rothblum. 1991. "Lesbian Sex at Menopause: As Good as Ever or Better than Ever." Pp. 184–93 in Barbara Sang, Joyce Warshow, and Adrienne J. Smith (eds.), *Lesbians at Midlife: The Creative Transition*. San Francisco: Spinsters Book.

Collins, Patricia Hill. 1986. "Learning from the Outsider Within: The Sociological Significance of Black Feminist Thought." *Social Problems* 33, no. 6: 14–32.

———. 1991. *Black Feminist Thought: Knowledge, Consciousness, and the Politics of Empowerment*. New York: Routledge.

———. 1992. "Reply." *Gender & Society* 6 (September): 517–19.

———. 1998. *Fighting Words: Black Women and the Search for Justice*. Minneapolis: University of Minnesota Press.

Combahee River Collective. 1998. "A Black Feminist Statement." Pp. 13–15 in Mary F. Rogers, *Contemporary Feminist Theory: A Text/Reader*. New York: McGraw-Hill.

Connell, R. W. 1987. *Gender and Power: Society, the Person and Sexual Politics*. Stanford, Calif.: Stanford University Press.

Cordova, Jeanne. 1992. "Butches, Lies, and Feminism." Pp. 272–92 in Joan Nestle (ed.), *The Persistent Desire: A Butch-Femme Reader*. Boston: Alyson Publications.

Counihan, Carole M. 1989. "An Anthropological View of Western Women's Prodigious Fasting: A Review Essay." *Food and Foodways* 3: 357–75.

Crawford, Mary. 1993. "Identity, 'Passing' and Subversion." Pp. 43–45 in Sue Wilkinson and Celia Kitzinger (eds.), *Heterosexuality: A Feminism & Psychology Reader*. Newbury Park, Calif.: Sage.

Crawley, Sara L. 2001. "Are Butch and Fem Working-Class and Antifeminist?" *Gender & Society* 15, no. 2 (April): 175–96.

Daniels, Cynthia R. 1997. "Between Fathers and Fetuses: The Social Construction of Male Reproduction and the Politics of Fetal Harm." *Signs* 22, no. 3 (Spring): 579–616.

Delphy, Christine. 1984. *Close to Home: A Materialist Analysis of Women's Oppression.* Trans. by Diana Leonard. Amherst: University of Massachusetts Press.

Denfeld, Rene. 1995. *The New Victorians: A Young Woman's Challenge to the Old Feminist Order.* New York: Warner.

DiQuinzio, Patrice. 1993. "Exclusion and Essentialism in Feminist Theory: The Problem of Mothering." *Hypatia: A Journal of Feminist Philosphy* 8, no. 3 (Summer): 1–20.

Di Stefano, Christine. 1990. "Dilemmas of Difference: Feminism, Modernity, and Postmodernism." Pp. 63–82 in Linda J. Nicholson (ed.), *Feminism/Postmodernism.* New York: Routledge.

Doherty, Sharon. 2000. "To Challenge Academic Individualism." Pp. 347–74 in Social Justice Group at the Center for Advanced Feminist Studies, University of Minnesota (ed.), *Is Academic Feminism Dead? Theory in Practice.* New York: New York University Press.

Donovan, Josephine. 2000. "A Cause of Our Own." Pp. 93–103 in Florence Howe (ed.), *The Politics of Women's Studies: Testimony from Thirty Founding Mothers.* New York: Feminist Press.

DuCille, Ann. 1993. *The Coupling Convention: Sex, Text, and Tradition in Black Women's Fiction.* New York: Oxford University Press.

Dunne, Gillian A. 1997. *Lesbian Lifestyles: Women's Work and the Politics of Sexuality.* Toronto: University of Toronto Press.

———. 2000. "Opting into Motherhood: Lesbians Blurring the Boundaries and Transforming the Meaning of Parenthood and Kinship." *Gender & Society* 14, no. 1 (February): 11–35.

Ebert, Teresa L. 1996. *Ludic Feminism and After: Postmodernism, Desire, and Labor in Late Capitalism.* Ann Arbor: University of Michigan Press.

Epstein, Cynthia Fuchs. 1988. *Deceptive Distinctions: Sex, Gender, and the Social Order.* New Haven, Conn.: Yale University Press.

———. 1999. "The Major Myth of the Women's Movement." *Dissent* (Fall): 83–86.

Faith, Karlene. 1993. *Unruly Women: The Politics of Confinement and Resistance.* Vancouver: Press Gang.

Faludi, Susan. 1992. *Backlash: The Undeclared War against American Women.* New York: Anchor Books.

———. 1995. "'I'm Not a Feminist But I Play One on TV.'" *Ms.* 5, no. 5 (March–April): 30–39.

———. 1999. *Stiffed: The Betrayal of the American Man.* New York: William Morrow.

Fine, Michelle. 1992a. *Disruptive Voices: The Possibilities of Feminist Research.* Ann Arbor: University of Michigan Press.

———. 1992b. "Sexuality, Schooling, and Adolescent Females: The Missing Discourse of Desire." Pp. 31–59 in Michelle Fine (ed.), *Disruptive Voices: The Possibilities of Feminist Research.* Ann Arbor: University of Michigan Press.

Fine, Michelle, and Susan Merle Gordon. 1992. "Feminist Transformations of/ despite Psychology." Pp. 1–25 in Michelle Fine (ed.), *Disruptive Voices: The Possibilities of Feminist Research.* Ann Arbor: University of Michigan Press.

Fine, Michelle, and Pat Macpherson. 1992. "Over Dinner: Feminism and Adolescent Female Bodies." Pp. 175–203 in Michelle Fine (ed.), *Disruptive Voices: The Possibilities of Feminist Research.* Ann Arbor: University of Michigan Press.

Finkelstein, Joanne. 1991. *The Fashioned Self.* Philadelphia: Temple University Press.

Flax, Jane. 1990. "Postmodernism and Gender Relations in Feminist Theory." Pp. 39–62 in Linda J. Nicholson (ed.), *Feminism/Postmodernism.* New York: Routledge.

Fox-Genovese, Elizabeth. 1991. *Feminism Without Illusions: A Critique of Individualism.* Chapel Hill: University of North Carolina Press.

———. 1996. *"Feminism Is Not the Story of My Life": How Today's Feminist Elite Has Lost Touch with the Real Concerns of Women.* New York: Doubleday.

Fraser, Nancy. 1998. "Heterosexism, Misrecognition and Capitalism: A Response to Judith Butler." *New Left Review* 228 (March–April): 140–49.

Frechet, Denise. 1991. "Toward a Post-Phallic Science." Pp. 205–21 in Joan E. Hartman and Ellen Messer-Davidow (eds.), *(En)Gendering Knowledge: Feminists in Academe.* Knoxville: University of Tennessee Press.

Freeman, Jo. 1994. "Feminism vs. Family Values: Women at the 1992 Democratic and Republican Conventions." Pp. 70–82 in Marianne Githens, Pippa Norris, and Joni Lovenduski (eds.), *Different Roles, Different Voices: Women and Politics in the United States and Europe.* New York: HarperCollins College.

Friedan, Betty. 1998. "The New Frontier of Feminism: Busting the Masculine Mystique." *New Perspectives Quarterly* 15, no. 1 (Winter): 50–52.

Frueh, Joanna. 1999. "Monster/Beauty: Midlife Bodybuilding as Aesthetic Discipline." Pp. 212–26 in Kathleen Woodward (ed.), *Figuring Age: Women, Bodies, Generations.* Bloomington: Indiana University Press.

Fuss, Diana. 1991. "Inside/Out." Pp. 1–10 in Diana Fuss (ed.), *Inside/Out: Lesbian Theories.* New York: Routledge.

Gagne, Patricia, and Richard Tewksbury. 1998. "Conformity Pressures and Gender Resistance among Transgendered Individuals." *Social Problems* 45, no. 1 (February): 81–102.

Garfinkel, Harold. 1967. *Studies in Ethnomethodology.* Englewood Cliffs, N.J.: Prentice-Hall.

Gavey, Nicola. 1993. "Technologies and Effects of Heterosexual Coercion." Pp. 93–119 in Sue Wilkinson and Celia Kitzinger (eds.), *Heterosexuality: A Feminism & Psychology Reader.* Newbury Park, Calif.: Sage.

Gillespie, Marcia Ann. 1994. "Family Values." *Ms.* (July/August): 1.

Glenn, Eveyln Nakano. 1986. *Issei, Nisei, War Bride: Three Generations of Japanese American Women in Domestic Service.* Philadelphia: Temple University Press.

Glickman, Rose L. 1993. *Daughters of Feminists.* New York: St. Martin's.

Goffman, Erving. 1959. *The Presentation of Self in Everyday Life.* New York: Anchor Books.

Gorn, Elliott J., and Michael Oriard. 1995. "Taking Sports Seriously." *Chronicle of Higher Education* (March 24): A52.

Gornick, Vivian. 1999. "The Second Sex at Fifty." *Dissent* (Fall): 69–72.

Govier, Trudy. 1993. "Self-Trust, Autonomy, and Self-Esteem." *Hypatia* 8 (Winter): 99–120.

Grahn, Judy. 1984. *Another Mother Tongue: Gay Words, Gay Worlds.* Updated and expanded ed. Boston: Beacon.

Grant, Judith. 1993. *Fundamental Feminism: Contesting the Core Concepts of Feminist Theory.* New York: Routledge.

Gubar, Susan. 2000. *Critical Condition: Feminism at the Turn of the Century.* New York: Columbia University Press.

Hanssen, Beatrice. 2001. "Whatever [sic] Happened to Feminist Theory?" Pp. 58–98 in Elisabeth Bronfen and Misha Kavka (eds.), *Feminist Consequences: Theory for the New Century.* New York: Columbia University Press.

Haraway, Donna. 1990 [1985]. "A Manifesto for Cyborgs: Science, Technology, and Socialist Feminism in the 1980s." Pp. 190–233 in Linda J. Nicholson (ed.), *Feminism/Postmodernism.* New York: Routledge.

———. 1997. *Modest_Witness@Second_Millennium.FemaleMan_Meets_OncoMouse: Feminism and Technoscience.* New York: Routledge.

Harding, Sandra. 1990. "Feminism, Science, and the Anti-Enlightenment Critiques." Pp. 83–106 in Linda J. Nicholson (ed.), *Feminism/Postmodernism.* New York: Routledge.

———. 1991. "Who Knows? Identities and Feminist Epistemology." Pp. 100–115 in Joan E. Hartman and Ellen Messer-Davidow (eds.), *(En)Gendering Knowledge: Feminists in Academe.* Knoxville: University of Tennessee Press.

Hargreaves, Jennifer. 1994. *Sporting Females: Critical Issues in the History and Sociology of Women's Sports.* New York: Routledge.

Hart, Lynda. 1998. *Between the Body and the Flesh: Performing Sadomasochism.* New York: Columbia University Press.

Hart, Nett. 1989. *Spirited Lesbians: Lesbian Desire as Social Action.* Minneapolis: Word Weavers.

Hartsock, Nancy. 1990. "Foucault on Power: A Theory for Women?" Pp. 157–75 in Linda J. Nicholson (ed.), *Feminism/Postmodernism.* New York: Routledge.

———. 1996. "Theoretical Bases for Coalition Building: An Assessment of Postmodernism." Pp. 256–74 in Heidi Gottfried (ed.), *Feminism and Social Change: Bridging Theory and Practice.* Urbana: University of Illinois Press.

———. 1998a. *The Feminist Standpoint Revisited and Other Essays.* Boulder, Colo.: Westview.

———. 1998b. "Marxist Feminist Dialectics for the 21st Century." *Science & Society* 62, no. 3 (Fall): 400–13.

Helvarg, David. 1997. *The War against the Greens: The "Wise Use" Movement, the New Right, and Anti-Environmental Violence.* San Francisco: Sierra Club Books.

Hennessy, Rosemary. 1993. "Women's Lives/Feminist Knowledge: Feminist Standpoint as Ideology Critique." *Hypatia* 8 (Winter): 14–34.

Heywood, Leslie. 1996. *Dedication to Hunger: The Anorexic Aesthetic in Modern Culture*. Berkeley: University of California Press.
Hoagland, Sarah Lucia. 1988. *Lesbian Ethics: Toward New Value*. Palo Alto, Calif.: Institute of Lesbian Studies.
Hochman, Anndee. 1994. *Everyday Acts and Small Subversions: Women Reinventing Family, Community and Home*. Portland, Oreg.: Eighth Mountain.
Hochschild, Arlie Russell. 1983. *The Managed Heart: Commercialization of Human Feeling*. Berkeley: University of California Press.
Hollibaugh, Amber, and Cherrie Moraga. 1992. "What We're Rolling around in Bed With: Sexual Silences in Feminism." Pp. 243–53 in Joan Nestle (ed.), *The Persistent Desire: A Butch-Femme Reader*. Boston: Alyson Publications.
hooks, bell. 1984. *Feminist Theory: From Margin to Center*. Boston: South End Press.
———. 1989. *Talking Back: Thinking Feminist, Thinking Black*. Boston: South End Press.
———. 1993. "Let's Get Real about Feminism: The Backlash, the Myths, the Movement." (A Discussion by bell hooks, Gloria Steinem, Urvashi Vaid, Naomi Wolf) Ms. (September/October): 34–43.
———. 1994. *Outlaw Culture: Resisting Representations*. New York: Routledge.
———. 1998. Pp. 39–52 in *Talking about a Revolution: Interviews*. Boston: South End Press.
———. 2000a. *Feminism Is for Everybody: Passionate Politics*. Boston: South End Press.
———. 2000b. *Where We Stand: Class Matters*. New York: Routledge.
Hunter, Allan. 1993. "Same Door, Different Closet: A Heterosexual Sissy's Coming-Out Party." Pp. 150–68 in Sue Wilkinson and Celia Kitzinger (eds.), *Heterosexuality: A Feminism Psychology Reader*. London: Sage.
Hurston, Zora Neale. 1978. *Their Eyes Were Watching God*. New York: Perennial Classics.
Irigaray, Luce. 1985 [1974]. *Speculum of the Other Woman*. Trans. by Gillian C. Gill. Ithaca, N.Y.: Cornell University Press.
Jackson, Stevi. 1995. "Gender and Heterosexuality: A Materialist Feminist Analysis." Pp. 11–26 in Mary Maynard and June Purvis (eds.), *(Hetero)Sexual Politics*. London: Taylor & Francis.
James, Henry. 1986 [orig. 1886]. *The Bostonians*. New York: Penguin Classics.
Johnson, Allan G. 2001. *Privilege, Power, and Difference*. Mountain View, Calif.: Mayfield.
Jonasdottir, Anna G. 1994. *Why Women Are Oppressed*. Philadelphia: Temple University Press.
Jordan, Judith V. 1991. "Empathy, Mutuality, and Therapeutic Change: Clinical Implications of a Relational Model." Pp. 283–89 in Judith V. Jordan, Alexandra G. Kaplan, Jean Baker Miller, Irene P. Stiver, and Janet L. Surrey, *Women's Growth in Connection: Writings from the Stone Center*. New York: Guilford.
Kaminer, Wendy. 1995. "Feminism's Third Wave: What Do Young Women Want?" *New York Times Book Review* (June 4): 3, 22–23.

Kaplan, Alexandra G. 1991. "The 'Self-In-Relation': Implications for Depression in Women." Pp. 206–22 in Judith V. Jordan, Alexandria G. Kaplan, Jean Baker Miller, Irene P. Stiver, and Janet L. Surrey, *Women's Growth in Connection: Writings from the Stone Center*. New York: Guilford.

Katz, Jonathan Ned. 1995. *The Invention of Heterosexuality*. New York: Dutton.

Kaw, Eugenia. 1998. "Medicalization of Racial Features: Asian-American Women and Cosmetic Surgery." Pp. 167–83 in Rose Weitz (ed.), *The Politics of Women's Bodies: Sexuality, Appearance, and Behavior*. New York: Oxford University Press.

Kay, Judith W. 1994. "Politics without Human Nature? Reconstructing a Common Humanity." *Hypatia* 9 (Winter): 21–52.

Keller, Evelyn Fox. 1985. *Reflections on Gender and Science*. New Haven, Conn.: Yale University Press.

Kennedy, Elizabeth Lapovsky, and Madeline Davis. 1992. "'They Was No One to Mess With': The Construction of the Butch Role in the Lesbian Community of the 1940s and 1950s." Pp. 62–79 in Joan Nestle (ed.), *The Persistent Desire: A Femme-Butch Reader*. Boston: Alyson Publications.

Kimmel, Michael S. 1989. *Men's Lives*. New York: Macmillan.

Kimmel, Michael S., and Thomas E. Mosmller (eds.). 1992. *Against the Tide: Pro-Feminist Men in the United States, 1776–1990*. Boston: Beacon.

Klatch, Rebecca. 1987. *Women of the New Right*. Philadelphia: Temple University Press.

Klein, Ellen R. 1996. *Feminism Under Fire*. Amherst, N.Y.: Prometheus Books.

Kolodny, Annette. 2000. "A Sense of Discovery, Mixed with a Sense of Justice." Pp. 276–90 in Florence Howe (ed.), *The Politics of Women's Studies: Testimony from Thirty Founding Mothers*. New York: Feminist Press.

Krieger, Susan. 1996. *The Family Silver: Essays on Relationships among Women*. Berkeley: University of California Press.

Kwong, Peter. 1998. Interviewed in South End Press Collective, *Talking about a Revolution: Interviews with* [Nine Individuals]. Boston: South End Press.

Lamb, Sharon. 1999. "Introduction." Pp. 1–12 in Sharon Lamb (ed.), *New Versions of Victims: Feminists Struggle with the Concept*. New York: New York University Press.

LaPorte, Rita. 1992. "The Butch-Femme Question." Pp. 208–19 in Joan Nestle (ed.), *The Persistent Desire: A Femme-Butch Reader*. Boston: Alyson Publications.

Lehrman, Karen. 1997. *The Lipstick Proviso: Women, Sex & Power in the Real World*. New York: Doubleday.

LeMoncheck, Linda. 1997. *Loose Women, Lecherous Men: A Feminist Philosophy of Sex*. New York: Oxford University Press.

Lewis, Reina. 1992. "The Death of the Author and the Resurrection of the Dyke." Pp. 17–32 in Sally Munt (ed.), *New Lesbian Criticism: Literary and Cultural Readings*. New York: Columbia University Press.

Lips, Hilary, and Susan Alexandra Freedman. 1993. "Heterosexual Feminist Identities: Private Boundaries and Shifting Centers." Pp. 56–58 in Sue

Wilkinson and Celia Kitzinger (eds.), *Heterosexuality: A Feminism & Psychology Reader*. Newbury Park, Calif.: Sage.

Lipset, Seymour Martin. 1970. *Revolution and Counterrevolution: Change and Persistence in Social Structures*. New York: Basic.

Lipset, Seymour Martin, and Earl Raab. 1970. *The Politics of Unreason: Right-Wing Extremism in America, 1790–1970*. New York: Harper & Row.

Little, Margaret Olivia. 1995. "Seeing and Caring: The Role of Affect in Feminist Moral Epistemology." *Hypatia* 10, no. 3 (Summer): 117–37.

Lorber, Judith. 1993. "Believing Is Seeing: Biology as Ideology." *Gender & Society* 7, no. 4 (December): 568–81.

Lorde, Audre. 1980. *The Cancer Journals*. San Francisco: Spinsters Ink.

———. 1984. *Sister Outsider: Essays and Speeches*. Freedom, Calif.: Crossing Press.

———. 1991. "Two Excerpts from *A Bust of Light: Living with Cancer*." Pp. 265–68 in Barbara Sang, Joyce Warshow, and Adrienne J. Smith (eds.), *Lesbians at Midlife: The Creative Transition*. San Francisco: Spinsters Book.

Lovejoy, Meg. 2001. "Disturbances in the Social Body: Differences in Body Image and Eating Problems among African American and White Women." *Gender & Society* 15, no. 2 (April): 239–61.

Luebke, Barbara F., and Mary Ellen Reilly. 1995. *Women's Studies Graduates: The First Generation*. New York: Teachers College Press, Columbia University Press.

Lundgren, Eva. 1995. *Feminist Theory and Violent Empiricism*. Aldershot: Avebury.

Luttrell, Wendy. 1993. "'The Teachers, They All Had Their Pets': Concepts of Gender, Knowledge, and Power." *Signs* 18 (Spring): 505–46.

MacCowan, Lyndall. 1992. "Re-Collecting History, Renaming Lives: Femme Stigma and the Feminist Seventies and Eighties." Pp. 299–328 in Joan Nestle (ed.), *The Persistent Desire: A Butch-Femme Reader*. Boston: Alyson Publications.

MacKinnon, Catharine A. 1987. *Feminism Unmodified: Discourses on Life and Law*. Cambridge, Mass.: Harvard University Press.

Mandle, Joan D. 2000. *Can We Wear Our Pearls and Still Be Feminists? Memoirs of a Campus Struggle*. Columbia: University of Missouri Press.

Mansbridge, Jane J. 1986. *Why We Lost the ERA*. Chicago: University of Chicago Press.

Martin, Biddy. 2001. "Success and Its Failures." Pp. 353–80 in Elisabeth Bronfen and Misha Kavka (eds.), *Feminist Consequences: Theory for the New Century*. New York: Columbia University Press.

Martin, Patricia Yancey. 2001. "Rape Crisis Centers: A Summary of Remarks." *SWS Network News* 18, no. 1 (Spring): 5.

McDermott, Patrice. 1998. "The Meaning and Uses of Feminism in Introductory Women's Studies Textbooks." *Feminist Studies* 24, no. 2 (Summer): 403–27.

McKinley, Nita Mary, and Janet Shibley Hyde. 1996. "The Objectified Body Consciousness Scale: Development and Validation." *Psychology of Women* 20, 2 (June): 181–215.

Meese, Elizabeth A. 1992. *(Sem)Erotics: Theorizing Lesbian Writing*. New York: New York University Press.

Mehta, Manjari. 1996. "'Our Lives Are No Different from That of Our Buffaloes': Agricultural Change and Gendered Spaces in a Central Himalayan Valley." Pp. 180–208 in Dianne Rocheleau, Barbara Thomas-Slayter, and Esther Wangari (eds.), *Feminist Political Ecology: Global Issues and Local Experiences*. New York: Routledge.

Michie, Helena. 1992. *Sororophobia: Differences among Women in Literature and Culture*. New York: Oxford University Press.

Miller, Jean Baker. 1991a. "The Construction of Anger in Women and Men." Pp. 181–96 in Judith V. Jordan, Alexandra G. Kaplan, Jean Baker Miller, Irene P. Stiver, and Janet L. Surrey, *Women's Growth in Connection: Writings from the Stone Center*. New York: Guilford.

———. 1991b. "The Development of Women's Sense of Self." Pp. 11–26 in Judith V. Jordan, Alexandra G. Kaplan, Jean Baker Miller, Irene P. Stiver, and Janet L. Surrey, *Women's Growth in Connection: Writings from the Stone Center*. New York: Guilford.

Minnich, Elizabeth Kamarck. 1990. *Transforming Knowledge*. Philadelphia: Temple University Press.

Mirowsky, John, and Catherine E. Ross. 1995. "Sex Differences in Distress: Real or Artifact?" *American Sociological Review* 60 (June): 449–68.

Modleski, Tania. 1991. *Feminism Without Women: Culture and Criticism in a "Postfeminist" Age*. New York: Routledge.

Moody-Adams, Michelle M. 1997. "Feminism by Any Other Name." Pp. 76–89 in Hilde Lindemann Nelson (ed.), *Feminism and Families*. New York: Routledge.

Morris, Debra. 1997. "The Feminist-Postmodernist Debate over a Revitalized Public Policy." *Social Theory and Practice* 23, no. 3 (Fall): 479–506.

Naples, Nancy, with Emily Clark. 1996. "Feminist Participatory Research and Empowerment: Going Public as Survivors of Childhood Sexual Abuse." Pp. 160–83 in Heidi Gottfried (ed.), *Feminism and Social Change: Bridging Theory and Practice*. Urbana: University of Illinois Press.

Nash, Kate. 1998. *Universal Difference Feminism and the Liberal Undecidability of "Women."* London: Macmillan.

National Lesbian and Gay Survey. 1992. *What a Lesbian Looks Like: Writings by Lesbians on Their Lives and Lifestyles*. New York: Routledge.

Nelson, Mariah Burton. 1994. *The Stronger Women Get, the More Men Love Football: Sexism and the American Culture of Sports*. New York: Harcourt Brace.

Nestle, Joan, Madeline Davis, and Amber Hollibaugh. "The Femme Tapes." Pp. 254–67 in Joan Nestle (ed.), *The Persistent Desire: The Butch-Femme Reader*. Boston: Alyson Publications.

———. 1991. "Desire Perfected: Sex After Forty." Pp. 180–83 in Barbara Sang, Joyce Washow, and Adrienne J. Smith (eds.), *Lesbians at Midlife: The Creative Transition*. San Francisco: Spinsters Book.

Oakley, Ann. 1997. "A Brief History of Gender." Pp. 29–55 in Ann Oakley and Juliet Mitchell (eds.), *Who's Afraid of Feminism? Seeing Through the Backlash.* New York: New Press.

Oakley, Ann, and Juliet Mitchell. 1997. "Introduction to the American Edition." Pp. xix–xxxvii in Ann Oakley and Juliet Mitchell (eds.), *Who's Afraid of Feminism? Seeing Through the Backlash.* New York: New Press.

O'Neil, C. 1992. "'The Famine Within' Probes Women's Pursuit of Thinness." *Christian Science Monitor* (August 31).

Orbach, Susie. 1993. "Heterosexuality and Parenting." Pp. 50–51 in Sue Wilkinson and Celia Kitzinger (eds.), *Heterosexuality: A Feminism & Psychology Reader.* Newbury Park, Calif.: Sage.

Paglia, Camille. 1991. *Sexual Personae: Art and Decadence from Nefertiti to Emily Dickinson.* New York: Vintage.

———. 1994. *Vamps & Tramps: New Essays.* New York: Vintage.

———. 1998. "I Am a Celebrator of Decadence." Interview by Michael Hattersley. *Harvard Gay & Lesbian Review* 5, no. 2 (Spring): 11–14.

Parrenas, Rhacel Salazar. 2000. "Migrant Filipina Domestic Workers and the International Division of Reproductive Labor." *Gender & Society* 14, no. 4 (August): 560–80.

Patai, Daphne. 1996. "Heterophobia: The Feminist Turn Against Men." *Partisan Review* 63, no. 3: 580–94.

———. 1998. *Heterophobia: Sexual Harassment and the Future of Feminism.* Lanham, Md.: Rowman & Littlefield.

———. 1998–99. "The Vaguest Measure of Faculty Merit." *Academic Questions* 12, no. 1 (Winter): 35–42.

Patai, Daphne, and Noretta Koertge. 1994. *Professing Feminism: Cautionary Tales from the Strange World of Women's Studies.* New York: Basic.

Patterson, Anita Haya. 2001. "Contingencies of Pleasure and Shame: Jamaican Women's Poetry." Pp. 254–82 in Elisabeth Bronfen and Misha Kavka (eds.), *Feminist Consequences: Theory for the New Century.* New York: Columbia University Press.

Penelope, Julia. 1992. *Call Me Lesbian: Lesbian Lives, Lesbian Theory.* Freedom, Calif.: Crossing Press.

Phelan, Shane. 1989. *Identity Politics: Lesbian Feminism and the Limits of Community.* Philadelphia: Temple University Press.

Rafkin, Lousie. 1998. *Other People's Dirt: A Housecleaner's Curious Adventures.* Chapel Hill, N.C.: Algonquin Books.

Ramazanoglu, Caroline. 1993. "Love and the Politics of Heterosexuality." Pp. 59–61 in Sue Wilkinson and Celia Kitzinger (eds.), *Heterosexuality: A Feminism & Psychology Reader.* Newbury Park, Calif.: Sage.

Randall, Vicky. 1994. "Feminist and Political Analysis." Pp. 4–16 in Marianne Githens, Pippa Norris, and Joni Lovenduski (eds.), *Different Roles, Different Voices: Women and Politics in the United States and Europe.* New York: HarperCollins College.

Rapping, Elayne. 1994. *Media-tions: Forays into the Culture and Gender Wars.* Boston: South End Press.

Raymond, Janice. 1987. "Female Friendship and Feminist Ethics." Pp. 161–74 in Barbara Hilkert Andolsen, Christine E. Gudorf, and Mary D. Pellauer (eds.), *Women's Consciousness, Women's Conscience: A Reader in Feminist Ethics*. San Francisco: Harper & Row.

Razack, Sherene H. 1998. *Looking White People in the Eye: Gender, Race, and Culture in Courtrooms and Classrooms*. Toronto: University of Toronto Press.

Reinharz, Shulamit. 1992. *Feminist Methods in Social Research*. New York: Oxford University Press.

——. 1993. "How My Heterosexuality Contributes to My Feminism and Vice Versa." Pp. 65–67 in Sue Wilkinson and Celia Kitzinger (eds.), *Heterosexuality: A Feminism and Psychology Reader*. Newbury Park, Calif.: Sage.

——. 1994. "Report Cites Heavy Toll of Rapes on Young." *New York Times* (June 23): A12.

Reskin, Barbara, and Irene Padavic. 1994. *Women and Men at Work*. Thousand Oaks, Calif.: Pine Forge.

Rich, Adrienne. 1976. *Of Woman Born: Motherhood as Experience and Institution*. New York: Norton.

——. 1980. *On Lies, Secrets, and Silence: Selected Prose 1966–1978*. New York: Norton.

——. 1986. *Blood, Bread, and Poetry: Selected Prose 1979–1985*. New York: Norton.

Ridgeway, Cecilia L., and Shelley J. Correll. 2000. "Limiting Inequality through Interaction: The End(s) of Gender." *Contemporary Sociology* 29, no. 1 (January): 110–20.

Robinson, Victoria. 1993. "Heterosexuality: Beginnings and Connections." Pp. 80–82 in Sue Wilkinson and Celia Kitzinger (eds.), *Heterosexuality: A Feminism & Psychology Reader*. London: Sage.

Rocheleau, Dianne, Barbara Thomas-Slayter, and Esther Wangari. 1996. "Gender and Environment: A Feminist Political Ecology Perspective." Pp. 3–23 in Dianne Rocheleau, Barbara Thomas-Slayter, and Esther Wangari (eds.), *Feminist Political Ecology: Global Issues and Local Experiences*. New York: Routledge.

Roiphe, Katie. 1993a. "Date Rape's Other Victim." *New York Times Magazine* (June 13): 26–28, 30, 40, 68.

——. 1993b. *The Morning After: Sex, Fear, and Feminism on Campus*. Boston: Little, Brown.

Rollins, Judith. 1985. *Between Women: Domestics and Their Employees*. Philadelphia: Temple University Press.

Romero, Mary. 1992. *Maid in the U.S.A.* New York: Routledge.

Roof, Judith. 1991. *A Lure of Knowledge: Lesbian Sexuality and Theory*. New York: Columbia University Press.

Rubin, Gayle. 1975. "The Traffic in Women: Notes on the 'Political Economy' of Sex." Pp. 157–210 in Rayna R. Reiter (ed.), *Toward an Anthropology of Women*. New York: Monthly Review Press.

——. 1992. "Of Catamites and Kings: Reflections on Butch, Gender, and Boundaries." Pp. 466–82 in Joan Nestle (ed.), *The Persistent Desire: A Butch-Femme Reader*. Boston: Alyson Publications.

Sabo, Donald, and Michael A. Messner. 1993. "Whose Body Is This? Women's Sports and Sexual Politics." Pp. 15–24 in Greta L. Cohen (ed.), *Women in Sport: Issues and Controversies*. Newbury Park, Calif.: Sage.

Salvaggio, Ruth. 1999. *The Sounds of Feminist Theory*. Albany: State University of New York Press.

Sang, Barbara E. 1991. "Moving toward Balance and Integration." Pp. 206–14 in Barbara Sang, Joyce Warshow, and Adrienne J. Smith (eds.), *Lesbians at Midlife: The Creative Transition*. San Francisco: Spinsters Book.

Sapiro, Virginia. 1994. *Women in American Society: An Introduction to Women's Studies*. 3rd ed. Mountain View, Calif.: Mayfield.

Schacht, S. F., and Patricia H. Atchison. 1993. "Heterosexual Instrumentalism: Past and Future Directions." Pp. 120–36 in Sue Wilkinson and Celia Kitzinger (eds.), *Heterosexuality: A Feminism & Psychology Reader*. Newbury Park, Calif.: Sage.

Scheman, Naomi. 1993. *Engenderings: Constructions of Knowledge, Authority, and Privilege*. New York: Routledge.

Schuman, David, and Dick Olufs. 1995. *Diversity on Campus*. Boston: Allyn & Bacon.

Schwartz, Pepper. 1994. *Peer Marriage: How Love between Equals Really Works*. New York: Free Press.

Schweickart, Patrocinio P. 1993. "In Defense of Femininity: Commentary on Sandra Bartky's *Femininity and Domination*." *Hypatia* 8 (Winter): 178–91.

Scott, James C. 1994. "Prestige as the Public Discourse of Domination." Pp. 473–86 in Peter Kollock and Jodi O'Brien (eds.), *The Production of Reality: Essays and Readings in Social Psychology*. Thousand Oaks, Calif.: Pine Forge Press.

Seager, Joni. 1993. *Earth Follies: Coming to Feminist Terms with the Global Environmental Crisis*. New York: Routledge.

Searles, Patricia, and Ronald J. Berger. 1987. "The Feminist Self-Defense Movement: A Case Study." *Gender & Society* 1, no. 1 (March): 61–84.

Sedgwick, Eve Kosofsky. 1990. *Epistemology of the Closet*. Berkeley: University of California Press.

———. 1999. *A Dialogue on Love*. Boston: Beacon.

Segal, Lynne. 1999. *Why Feminism? Gender, Psychology, Politics*. New York: Columbia University Press.

Sennett, Richard, and Jonathan Cobb. 1973. *The Hidden Injuries of Class*. New York: Vintage.

Shields, M. Dale, Cornelia Butler Flora, Barbara Thomas-Slayter, and Gladys Buenavista. 1996. "Developing and Dismantling Social Capital: Gender and Resource Management in the Philippines." Pp. 155–79 in Dianne Rocheleau, Barbara Thomas-Slayter, and Esther Wangara (eds.), *Feminist Political Ecology: Global Issues and Local Experiences*. New York: Routledge.

Skeggs, Beverley. 1997. *Formations of Class and Gender: Becoming Respectable*. London: Sage.

Sklar, Kathryn Kish. 2000. "The Women's Studies Moment: 1972." Pp. 130–41 in Florence Howe (ed.), *The Politics of Women's Studies: Testimony from Thirty Founding Mothers*. New York: Feminist Press.

Smith, Barbara. 1998. *The Truth That Never Hurts: Writings on Race, Gender, and Freedom*. New Brunswick, N.J.: Rutgers University Press.

Smith, Dorothy E. 1999. *Writing the Social: Critique, Theory, and Investigations*. Toronto: University of Toronto Press.

———. 1990. *Texts, Facts, and Femininity: Exploring the Relations of Ruling*. New York: Routledge.

Social Justice Group at the Center for Advanced Feminist Studies, University of Minnesota. 2000a. "Introduction." Pp. 1–3 in Social Justice Group at the Center for Advanced Feminist Studies, University of Minnesota (ed.), *Is Academic Feminism Dead? Theory in Practice*. New York: New York University Press.

Sommers, Christina Hoff. 1994. *Who Stole Feminism? How Women Have Betrayed Women*. New York: Touchstone.

———. 1998. "On the Other Hand." *American Enterprise* 9, no. 1 (January–February): 57.

South End Press Collective. 1998. *Talking about a Revolution: Interviews*. Boston: South End Press.

Spender, Dale. 1993. "An Alternative to Madonna: How to Deal with 'I'm Not a Feminist, But. . . .'" *Ms.* (July–August): 44–45.

Sprague, Joey. 1997. "Holy Men and Big Guns: The Can(n)on in Social Theory." *Gender & Society* 11, no. 1 (February): 88–107.

Stack, Carol. 1975. *All Our Kin*. New York: Harper Paperback.

Stack, Carol B. 1994. "Different Voices, Different Visions: Gender, Culture, and Moral Reasoning." Pp. 291–301 in Maxine Baca Zinn and Bonnie Thornton Dill (eds.), *Women of Color in U.S. Society*. Philadelphia: Temple University Press.

Stacey, Judith. 1996. *In the Name of the Family: Rethinking Family Values in the Postmodern Age*. Boston: Beacon.

Starhawk. 1990. *Truth or Dare: Encounters with Power, Authority, and Mystery*. San Francisco: HarperCollins.

Steinem, Gloria. 1993. "Changing: Reaching a Maturity As Well As a Majority." *Ms.* 4 (July–August): 3.

———. 1984. *Outrageous Acts and Everyday Rebellions*. New York: New American Library.

Stevens, Patricia E. 1996. "Lesbians and Doctors: Experiences of Solidarity and Domination in Health Care Settings." *Gender & Society* 10, no. 1 (February): 24–41.

Sturgeon, Noel. 1997. *Ecofeminist Natures: Race, Gender, Feminist Theory and Political Action*. New York: Routledge.

Suggs, Welch. 2001. "Lack of Resources Hampers Graduation Rates in Division II." *Chronicle of Higher Education* (January 5): A49–A51.

Surrey, Janet L. 1991. "Eating Patterns as a Reflection of Women's Development." Pp. 237–49 in Judith V. Jordan, Alexandra G. Kaplan, Jean Baker

Miller, Irene P. Stiver, and Janet L. Surrey (eds.), *Women's Growth in Connection: Writings from the Stone Center.* New York: Guilford.

Taylor, Dorceta E. 1996. "Environmentalism and the Politics of Inclusion." Pp. 373–80 in Mary F. Rogers (ed.), *Multicultural Experiences, Multicultural Theories.* New York: McGraw-Hill.

Taylor, Verta. 1996. *Rock-a-By Baby: Feminism, Self-Help, and Postpartum Depression.* New York: Routledge.

Thomas, Alison M. 1993. "The Heterosexual Feminist: A Paradoxical Identity?" Pp. 83–85 in Sue Wilkinson and Celia Kitzinger (eds.), *Heterosexuality: A Feminism & Psychology Reader.* Newbury Park, Calif.: Sage.

Thompson, Becky Wangsgaard. 1992. "'A Way Outa No Way': Eating Problems among African-American, Latina, and White Women." *Gender & Society* 6 (December): 546–61.

Thompson, Shona M. 1999. *Mother's Taxi: Sport and Women's Labor.* Albany: State University of New York Press.

Thorne, Barrie. 1993. *Gender Play: Girls and Boys in School.* New Brunswick, N.J.: Rutgers University Press.

Tyler, Carol-Anne. 1991. "Boys Will Be Girls: The Politics of Gay Drag." Pp. 32–70 in Diana Fuss (ed.), *Inside/Out.* New York: Routledge.

Wadler, Joyce. 1992. *My Breast: One Woman's Cancer Story.* Reading, Mass.: Addison Wesley.

Walkerdine, Valerie. 1990. *Schoolgirl Fictions.* London: Verso.

Wallace, Bill. 1995. "But the Rise of Women's Sports Should Be Encouraged." *Philadelphia Inquirer* (May 27): A9.

Walters, Margaret. 1997. "American Gothic: Feminism, Melodrama and the Backlash." Pp. 56–76 in Ann Oakley and Juliet Mitchell (eds.), *Who's Afraid of Feminism? Seeing Through the Backlash.* New York: New Press.

Wearing, Betsy. 1998. *Leisure and Feminist Theory.* London: Sage.

Weiler, Kathleen. 1988. *Women Teaching for Change: Gender, Class, and Power.* South Hadley, Mass.: Bergin & Garvey.

Wilkinson, Sue, and Celia Kitzinger (eds.). 1993. *Heterosexuality: A Feminism & Psychology Reader.* Newbury Park, Calif.: Sage.

Wilton, Tamsin. 1993. "Sisterhood in the Service of Patriarchy: Heterosexual Women's Friendships and Male Power." Pp. 273–76 in Sue Wilkinson and Celia Kitzinger (eds.), *Heterosexuality: A Feminism & Psychology Reader.* Newbury Park, Calif.: Sage.

Witt, Doris. 1998. "What (N)ever Happened to Aunt Jemima: Eating Disorders, Fetal Rights, and Black Female Appetite in Contemporary American Culture." Pp. 408–22 in Mary F. Rogers, *Contemporary Feminist Theory: A Text/Reader.* New York: McGraw-Hill.

Wolf, Naomi. 1992. *The Beauty Myth: How Images of Beauty Are Used against Women.* New York: Anchor Books.

Young, Iris Marion. 1990. *Throwing Like a Girl and Other Essays in Feminist Philosophy and Social Theory.* Bloomington: Indiana University Press.

Yuval-Davis, Nira. 1993. "The (Dis)Comfort of Being 'Hetero.'" Pp. 52–53 in Sue Wilkinson and Celia Kitzinger (eds.), *Heterosexuality: A Feminism & Psychology Reader*. Newbury Park, Calif.: Sage.

———. 1997. "Women, Ethnicity and Empowerment." Pp. 77–98 in Ann Oakley and Juliet Mitchell (eds.), *Who's Afraid of Feminism? Seeing Through the Backlash*. New York: New Press.

Zahra, Tara. 1999. "The Antifeminist Seduction." *American Prospect* 45 (July–August): 84–89.

Zimmerman, Bonnie. 1992. "Lesbians Like This and That: Some Notes on Lesbian Criticism for the Nineties." Pp. 1–15 in Sally Munt (ed.), *New Lesbian Criticism: Literary and Cultural Readings*. New York: Columbia University Press.

Zinn, Maxine Baca, and Bonnie Thornton Dill (eds.). 1994. *Women of Color in U.S. Society*. Philadelphia: Temple University Press.

Index

163

About the Authors

Mary Rogers teaches sociology and diversity studies at the University of West Florida in Pensacola. She is the author of several books and is currently working to establish a sociology center in Pensacola that will promote community research, social justice, and social change.

C. D. Garrett is a community activist who has worked as an organizer and fundraiser around various issues of social and ecological justice. Her involvements include community gardening, urban land trusts, and the Philadelphia Neighborhood Murals Project. She is pursuing dual graduate degrees in Information Science and Technology at Drexel University and has also done graduate work in Clinical Psychology at the University of North Carolina, Chapel Hill.